THE
ISLAMIC WORLD IN
ASCENDANCY

THE
ISLAMIC WORLD IN
ASCENDANCY

From the Arab Conquests to the
Siege of Vienna

Martin Sicker

 PRAEGER

Westport, Connecticut
London

Library of Congress Cataloging-in-Publication Data

Sicker, Martin.
  The Islamic world in ascendancy : from the Arab conquests to the siege of Vienna /
  Martin Sicker.
      p.   cm.
  Includes bibliographical references and index.
  ISBN 0–275–96892–8 (alk. paper)
  1. Islamic Empire—History.   I. Title.
  DS38.2.S53   2000
  909'.097671—dc21   00–037326

British Library Cataloguing in Publication Data is available.

Library of Congress Catalog Card Number: 00–037326
ISBN: 0–275–96892–8

First published in 2000

Praeger Publishers, 88 Post Road West, Westport, CT 06881
An imprint of Greenwood Publishing Group, Inc.
www.praeger.com

Printed in the United States of America

The paper used in this book complies with the
Permanent Paper Standard issued by the National
Information Standards Organization (Z39.48–1984).

10 9 8 7 6 5 4 3 2 1

Contents

Introduction

In an earlier book, *The Pre-Islamic Middle East*, I pointed out that in addition to the critical geopolitical factors of geography and topography, religion also played a major political role in justifying, if not conditioning, the pattern of political decision-making in the region. The ancient Macedonians first introduced the politicization of religious belief in the form of pan-Hellenism, which essentially sought to impose Greek forms of popular religion and culture on the indigenous peoples of the Middle East as a means of solidifying Macedonian political control. This subsequently led to the institution of religious persecution as a state policy in the Seleucid Empire by Antiochus IV, in turn precipitating the first recorded war of national-religious liberation under the leadership of the Hasmoneans in Palestine. Subsequently, the Persian Sassanid Empire adopted Zoroastrianism as the state religion, making it an instrument of state policy intended to unify the diverse peoples that lived within the imperial frontiers. Later, when Armenia adopted Christianity as the state religion, followed shortly by the Roman Empire, religion became a fundamental ingredient in the politics of the Middle East and has remained such ever since. But it was with the emergence of Islam that the combination of geopolitics and religion, or theopolitics, reached its most volatile form and provided the ideological context for war and peace in the Middle East for more than a millennium.

The conflation of geopolitics and religion in Islam is predicated on the concept of *jihad* (struggle), which is a religious obligation imposed on all Muslims by the faith. The jihad may be understood as a *crescentade*, in the same sense as the later Christian *crusade*, which seeks to achieve a religious goal by militant means. The basis for the religious obligation of jihad is the professed universality of the Muslim revelation. As Bernard Lewis put it,

"God's word and God's message are for all mankind; it is the duty of those who have accepted them to strive (*jahada*) unceasingly to convert or at least to subjugate those who have not. This obligation is without limit of time or space. It must continue until the whole world has either accepted the Islamic faith or submitted to the power of the Islamic state."[1]

Until that universal conversion or submission to Islam takes place, the world is considered to be divided into two parts, the *dar al-Islam*, the territory or abode of Islam, and the *dar al-harb*, the territory or abode of war. Dar al-Islam refers to those lands in which the *Pax Islamica* prevails—that is, lands under the rule of a Muslim government in which the laws of Islam are the laws of the land. The dar al-harb is regarded as all territories outside the orbit of the *Pax Islamica*, the communities of which are considered to be in a state of nature, that is, uncivilized. This is because, as Majid Khadduri put it, according to Islamic law, "they lacked legal competence to enter into discourse with Islam on the basis of equality and reciprocity because they failed to conform with its ethical and legal standards."[2] There is therefore a state of obligatory war between the two abodes that must go on until the final victory of Islam. According to the authoritative jurists of Islam, this state of war might be interrupted, when expedient, by an armistice or truce of limited duration. However, it could not be terminated by a permanent peace treaty, but only by a final and decisive victory of Islam. The jihad is therefore the ultimate means, the instrument, for transforming the dar al-harb into the dar al-Islam.

Some modern Islamic scholars argue that there is no precedent for this extreme geopolitical-theopolitical doctrine of the two territories or abodes either in the Koran or in the accepted traditions. They insist that no one has been able to trace the doctrine to an original source. Moreover, some modern expositors of Islam argue that it cannot be true Muslim doctrine because it actually contradicts some fundamental tenets of the faith. Nonetheless, the fact is that it has been part of the Muslim worldview from the very outset. Even an apologist scholar such as Maulana M. Ali is compelled to admit as much. He reluctantly noted that Muslim "jurists apply the word [dar al-harb] to all states and countries which are not *dar al-Islam* or under Muslim rule, though they may not be at war with the Muslims, and thus look upon a Muslim state as being always in a state of war with the whole of the non-Muslim world."[3]

Clearly, the concept of being in a state of perpetual war with the non-Muslim world could prove counterproductive in some instances, precluding amicable relations with countries that could not readily be conquered. Moreover, as will be amply demonstrated, the concept often bore little relation to the political realities of the region that as often as not saw Muslims and non-Muslims aligned against and at war with other Muslims. Perhaps for these reasons, some jurists, especially those of the Shafi'i school, introduced a third category of territory or abode into the Muslim geopolitical constellation. They defined the *dar al-sulkh* (territory of peaceful arrangement) and *dar al-ahd* (territory of covenant) as arrangements under which non-Muslim rulers could continue to govern autonomously through their own agents while acknowledging the suzerainty of a Muslim state. Some also included in the definition of dar al-sulkh a country that has treaty relations with a Muslim state, and which thereby represented an intermediate stage between dar al-Islam and dar al-harb, preliminary to its ultimate incorporation into the abode of Islam.

These concepts underlay Muslim geopolitical thinking throughout the 1,000-year period covered in this book. They provided an extraordinary religious and ideological context for the naked imperialism that succeeded in creating an Islamic universe reaching, at its zenith, from Spain and North Africa to Southeast Asia, and from the Indian Ocean littoral to the steppes of Russia and the gates of Vienna. These geopolitical-theopolitical concepts have undergone a renaissance with the reappearance of militant Islam in various parts of the world in the latter part of the twentieth century. This is most especially the case in the Middle East, as that term may be understood in its broadest geopolitical connotation, which is the sense in which it is used in this work.

The term Middle East, which has come into near universal use, clearly reflects a fundamentally Eurocentric perspective. The region it describes is east of Europe, albeit not as distant as the Far East. The American naval historian Alfred T. Mahan coined the term at the beginning of the century to designate the region reaching from Arabia to India, with its center in the Persian Gulf region. The territories originally included in this designation did not constitute a natural geographic body. Mahan's application of the term merely reflected his particular strategic interest, a perspective that was not shared by other writers on the history and foreign affairs of that part of the world, who often assigned different geographical content to the designation. As a result, to this day there continues to be little consensus on the precise delimitation of the territories that are or should be included in the Middle East.

For the purposes of this book, the Middle East is considered to consist of a core area circumscribed by a peripheral region of intrinsic geopolitical and historical importance to the core. The core area is held to consist of Iran and the Persian Gulf littoral, and the Fertile Crescent. Historian James Breasted coined the latter term early in the twentieth century to describe the swath of territory that reaches from the Persian Gulf to Egypt in the shape of a relatively narrow crescent. The crescent arches northward from the gulf, encompasses the territory between the Tigris and Euphrates Rivers, circumscribes the perimeter of the northern Arabian Desert, and then descends to Egypt along the coastal region of the eastern Mediterranean. The Fertile Crescent thus includes the modern states of Iraq, Syria, Lebanon, Jordan, and Israel. East of the core area, the peripheral region includes

Afghanistan, Transcaspia, and the southern reaches of Central Asia. In the west, it includes the Aegean and Balkan regions. In the north, it includes Turkey, the southern, western, and eastern littorals of the Black Sea, and the Caucasus region; and in the south, the Arabian Peninsula and the Horn of Africa.

The story of the emergence and phenomenal ascendancy of the Islamic world from a relatively small tribe in sparsely populated Arabia is one that both stirs and taxes the imagination. What took place, however, becomes more comprehensible when viewed through a geopolitical prism. Notwithstanding the extent of its conquests and the establishment of its supremacy over vast areas, the Islamic world did not become transformed into an Islamic Empire, any more than the Christian world became transformed into a Christian Empire. As in the case of the latter, religion in the Islamic world was repeatedly and often shamelessly harnessed to geopolitical purpose, albeit with arguably greater success, and contributed mightily to the achievement of such purpose. However, Muslim unity of political purpose did not last for very long, and the professed universality of Islam was co-opted by a long roster of ambitious political leaders to serve diverse and more limited ethnic and tribal political interests. Nonetheless, the ideal of Pax Islamica remained an important theopolitical concept, particularly as it was applied to the non-Muslim world, although it had relatively little restraining effect on the incessant conflicts that raged within the Islamic world throughout most of the period considered in this book.

Islamic ascendancy began as an Arab project, initially focused on the Arabian Peninsula. For reasons to be discussed, it was soon transformed into an imperialist movement with expansive ambitions. As it grew, it quickly registered highly impressive gains, but soon lost much of its Arab content, with the notable exception of its central religious text, the Koran, and the cultural inroads made possible through the wide adoption of its language, Arabic. It ended a millennium later as a Turkish, more specifically an Ottoman, project with many intermediate transformations. The reverberations of the 1,000-year history of that ascendancy are still felt today in many parts of the greater Middle East. The emotive power of the idea of Pax Islamica in its more modern form of Pan-Islamic politics still inspires political and military attempts to alter the configuration of the region. From Bosnia to Afghanistan and the Caucasus to the Sudan, theopolitics and geopolitics have fused once more in numerous instances to ignite interminable conflict.

In dealing with the long period of history covered in this book, it has been necessary to introduce the names of a large number of political leaders, many of whom may not be familiar to the nonspecialist. Wherever possible, their dates of office have been provided to assist the reader in maintaining a grasp on the time frame in which the events that they are concerned with took place. It should be noted, however, that there is considerable disagreement among scholars regarding the specific dates of events in early medieval times, and there are, as well, numerous variations with regard to the names of persons and places. The literature on the region also reflects wide variances in the transliteration of Arabic, Persian, and Turkish names. As a result, some inconsistencies in the spelling of such names may be reflected in the pages that follow.

NOTES

1. Bernard Lewis, *The Political Language of Islam*, p. 73.
2. Majid Khadduri, *The Islamic Law of Nations*, p. 12.
3. Maulana M. Ali, *Religion of Islam*, p. 558.

1

Empire of the Quraish

For more than 600 years, since Pompeius had redrawn the political map of the Middle East in the first century B.C.E., the general frontier between the Roman (later Byzantine) and Parthian (later Persian) empires had been the Euphrates River. In the north, the frontier was guarded by a number of small buffer states, while in the south it was flanked by the virtually impassable Arabian or Syrian Desert that actually extended as far north as the approaches to Aleppo and as far west as the outskirts of Damascus. As a consequence, most of the contacts between the two empires, as well as the wars they fought, were along the northern reaches of the Euphrates and in Armenia, strategically vital regions that were studded with fortifications. By contrast, no comparable significance was attributed to the region of the southern Euphrates, Babylonia or Iraq. In general, the desert was considered too inhospitable an environment for effective military operations on a significant scale, and measures to defend against attack from that quarter were kept to a minimum. Moreover, although the sedentary Arab tribes that lived on the fringes of the desert were a constant irritant, they were not viewed as a potentially serious threat to the imperial armies of either Byzantium or Persia.

To protect against raiding from the desert by the Bedouin tribes that roamed the region, both empires maintained dynasties of Arab vassal princes along the fringes of their desert frontiers. On the western rim of the desert, the sedentary Arab tribes of Syria and Damascus came under the domination of the Christianized Ghassanids. Across the expanse, on the lower reaches of the Euphrates, the Lakhmids similarly served the Persian king by containing the Bedouin within the bounds of the desert. However, these two Arab houses were occupied in endless raiding and fighting with each other, keeping the desert frontiers aflame, particularly in the north where their spheres of control converged. These conflicts, however, did not normally affect the vital interests of either the Byzantines or the Persians. The balance of power along the common Arabian desert frontiers of the Byzantine and Persian empires had been preserved in this manner for generations. But, this situation was to change dramatically just at the point in time when both empires were on the verge of exhaustion from their virtually incessant wars.

In the west, the circumstance that precipitated the significant change in the political environment arose as a consequence of intercommunal religious intolerance. During the sixth century, the majority of the people of rural Syria, including the Ghassanids, became adherents of the Monophysite doctrine of the Christian faith. But this form of Christian belief, which contradicted the Diophysite views of the established Byzantine Orthodox Church, had recently been declared heretical. In 581, the leading prince of the Ghassanids, al-Mundhir, was arrested and taken to Constantinople. This act of intolerance irreparably damaged the long-established relationship of the Ghassanids as vassals of Byzantium, and had the immediate consequence of triggering rebellion and anarchy along the fringes of the desert. The conquest and temporary occupation of Antioch, Damascus, and Jerusalem by the Persian king Chosroes II (590–627) in 613–614 further exacerbated the already volatile situation.

In the east, the circumstance that precipitated a radical change in the prevailing political environment was different in origin but produced a similar outcome to that which occurred in the west. About 602, the king of the Lakhmids, Numan III (c. 580–602), who had been the only member of the Lakhmid house to adopt Nestorian Christianity, had a falling out with the Persian king. As a result, Chosroes abolished the privileged position that the Lakhmids enjoyed within the Sassanid Empire as defenders of the desert frontier, and imposed Persian governors over the region to which the Arab chieftains were made subordinate. This policy soon produced the revolt of the Arab tribes inhabiting the banks of the Euphrates, further destabilizing the desert frontier zone.

By the time of the decisive defeat of Chosroes at Nineveh in 627, and the re-conquest of Syria by the Byzantine emperor Heraclius (610–641) two years later, the desert flanks of both exhausted empires were left essentially unprotected and in a state of anarchy. This occurred in part because of Heraclius' failure to continue the payment of annual subsidies to the Arab tribes south of the Dead Sea and along the caravan route from Gaza to Medina. While these events were transpiring along the Byzantine and Persian frontiers, other portentous developments were taking place farther south in Arabia that would have extraordinary consequences for the history of the world in general, and the Middle East in particular.

The prophet Muhammad (570–632), the founder of Islam, was a member of the Banu Hashem, a clan of the Quraish, a tribe of the Hejaz whose center was located at the oasis town of Mecca. The Banu Hashem was one of the four clans that had a traditional claim to custodianship of the Kaabah at Mecca, a *haram* (prominent spiritual sanctuary) of western Arabia. From Mecca, the Quraish established a widespread commercial and diplomatic network—including commercial alliances with other tribes who controlled segments of the trade routes to the south—that permitted caravans organized under their aegis to travel to Syria, Iraq, and the Yemen in relative safety. Moreover, with the sudden decline of the Lakhmids in their traditional position of importance within the Sassanid Empire, some of the tribes of the northeastern region of Arabia such as the Tamim turned to the Quraish for assistance, further enhancing the latter's claim to paramount leadership in the vast peninsula.

After an initial period of rejection, the Quraish adopted the faith of Muhammad and, under his inspiration, began to impose its rule on the numerous independent tribes of the Arabian Peninsula in the name of the new religion. The wars of the Quraish and their vassals thus took on a religious dimension that both inspired and justified their expansionism. Because of the assertion that the Islam preached by Muhammad was the ordained and accepted religion of the Arabs, those who refused to adhere to the new faith were considered as rebels against legitimate authority who had to be suppressed. Nonetheless, the true extent of Muhammad's dominion in the Arabian Peninsula during his lifetime is quite uncertain and subject to widely differing opinions.

The primary allegiance of the Arab was to clan and tribe. There was no tradition in the Hejaz or elsewhere in central Arabia of anything resembling a super-tribal government, and it seems most unlikely that many of the tribes were prepared to voluntarily relinquish their autonomy and subordinate themselves to the Quraish. The view expressed by one historian would seem to reflect a realistic nonparochial assessment of the probable situation:

It may be said generally that Arabia, during all of its existence, never recognized a sole ruler for the entire land. In reality Muhammed dominated a territory which occupied perhaps less than a third of the peninsula. This area became strongly influenced by the new ideas of Islam, but the remaining part of Arabia persisted under a political and religious organization differing very little from that which had existed before the appearance of Muhammed. . . . Thus, at the time of his death Muhammed was neither the political ruler of all Arabia nor its religious leader.[1]

In any case, it was clear that neither Byzantium nor Persia could be very sanguine about the emergence of a dynamic expansionist power on their respective southern flanks, particularly at a time when both were preoccupied with events elsewhere. Another circumstance that was bound to result in an eventual collision of the Quraish with both Byzantium and Persia was the fact that neither the Arab tribes nor the desert over which they ranged were confined to the Arabian Peninsula. Indeed, the desert extended from the Yemen and Hadhramaut in the south as far as the approaches to Aleppo in the north. Because of this geopolitical reality, neither the Byzantines nor the Persians could be expected to look on passively as the Quraish attempted to impose their political will on the tribes located along their respective desert perimeters.

For Byzantium in particular, there were also very important commercial implications to Quraish expansionism. By their domination of the Hejaz, which included the towns of Medina and Mecca that became the political and religious centers respectively of their fledgling empire, the Quraish also took effective control of the important maritime trade route from India and Southeast Asia to Aden. In addition, they also controlled the caravan route from the transshipment point of Aden along the western coast of Arabia to Egypt, Palestine, and Syria.

With the passing of Muhammad, many of those tribes that had accepted the new faith, and with it the political leadership of the Muslim establishment in Medina, revolted against the hegemony of the Quraish. With the political achievements of Muhammad seemingly about to unravel, the Quraish were compelled to undertake a series of campaigns to forcibly reimpose their rule over the tribes of the peninsula, whose defection was characterized in the political lexicon of Islam as *Ridda* (apostasy). Under Abu Bakr (632–634), the father-in-law and a companion of Muhammad, who assumed the religious title of *caliph* (successor) and the secular title of "commander of the faithful," challenges to the rule of the Quraish were suppressed in Bahrain, Yemen, and Hadhramaut by the spring of 633.

As a result of these campaigns, for the first time in its known history a period of peace was experienced throughout the entire Arabian Peninsula. However, this quickly proved to be a mixed blessing from Abu Bakr's perspective. For thousands of years, the tribes of the peninsula had engaged in virtually perpetual warfare and raiding, the celebration of their feats of arms being an integral component of their traditional culture. But Muhammad had forbidden his followers, the Muslims, to wage war against each other. This created a problem that Abu Bakr had to resolve as a matter of urgency. The dilemma before him was how to maintain the peace between the Arabian tribes that were warlike by culture and tradition, and to whom raiding and fighting were as natural as eating. Indeed, for some, the tribal economy was heavily dependent on brigandage. As one recent author summarized the situation:

The Arab tribes . . . were, in Arabia as along the peripheries of Syria and Iraq, the chief source of the manpower which the Moslem *umma* needed to survive. Hence, as the *Ridda* wars neared their end in 634, the caliphs, supported by the Quraysh establishment in Medina and Mecca, began to pamper the tribes, giving them license to conduct raids wherever they pleased outside the realm of the *umma*. The peripheral garrison towns of Syria and Iraq were natural targets for such raids, and it was only as the first of these towns began to fall into the hands of the tribal raiders that the caliphs stepped in to organize the random process into a conquest.[2]

It cannot be known with any certainty if Abu Bakr had made a conscious and deliberate decision to launch the tribes on a career of territorial conquest, as a means of dealing with the problem of tribal troublemaking. It may also have come about as a result of unforeseen and uncontrollable circumstances that were especially conducive to such a policy. In either case, the Arab onslaught was soon to bring disaster to both Byzantines and Persians.

One of the consequences of the disenfranchisement of the Arab Lakhmids by Chosroes II was the revolt of the Beni Bakr ibn Wail, a large Bedouin tribe that occupied Bahrain and parts of Chaldea, the region west of the head of the Persian Gulf. Although the territory was still nominally under Sassanid suzerainty, it now became fair game for the Quraish and their allies, particularly after their pacification of Bahrain in 633. Muthanna ibn Haritha, a sheikh of the Bedouin Beni Shaiban that had played a major role in the military campaign, requested that Khalid ibn al-Walid, the pre-eminent Muslim commander, join forces with him for an expedition to northeastern Arabia to secure the region along the frontier of Chaldea. Although the Quraish, centered in the Hejaz, had little immediate interest in the Persian Empire, which lay across the desert, Abu Bakr gave his endorsement to the joint venture, possibly as a defensive measure against any attempt by the Sassanids to reassert their authority in the region.

The operational tactics adopted by the Arabs were designed to take into consideration that the Byzantines and Persians both had far more powerful regular armies, against which the Arabs would be seriously disadvantaged in conventional warfare. However, because of their expert use of camels, which gave them great mobility in the desert environment, the Arabs were able to raid with virtual impunity along the fringes of the desert. Then, if confronted by superior forces, they would quickly retreat into the desert that was effectively impenetrable by the regular armies of their opponents. Following this pattern of attack and withdrawal, the forces of Khalid and Muthanna fought their way northward along the Euphrates with great success, defeating and subjugating the local tribes they encountered. By the end of the year, they seized the Lakhmid capital at Hira on the fringe of the desert. The Persians, still wallowing in the chaos that followed the Byzantine defeat of Chosroes five years earlier, were unable to take any significant defensive measures against the raiders. Before long, the Persian forces were pushed across the Euphrates, and the Sassanid vassal state of Hira, peopled primarily by Nestorian Christian Arabs, was annexed and forced to pay tribute to the caliphate.

Initially, as already suggested, the Quraish, who at this time still constituted the principal leadership of the Arabian tribes, were far more interested in Syria and Palestine than Iraq. The former two countries lay directly to the north, and were linked to the Hejaz by ancient routes that were frequented by their caravans. The Quraish therefore had good reason to be concerned about the vulnerability of newly prosperous Medina and Mecca to attack by either the Byzantines or the Ghassanids. The moment seemed propitious to eliminate this lingering threat by a preemptive attack, especially since the official Melkite church had cut off its onerous subsidization of Heraclius' troops in Syria. The latter had begun to disband as an organized force and soon left Damascus virtually defenseless and a tempting target for the Quraish.

Thus, at about the same time that the campaign of Khalid and Muthanna had begun against the Persian frontier in Iraq, Abu Bakr sent an army north in four columns to invade Byzantine territory. One wing attacked southern Palestine and overran the area of Beersheba. The other three columns proceeded to Moab, on the eastern bank of the Jordan, but ran into stiff Byzantine opposition at the Yarmuk river gap near Deraa that blocked the road to Damascus. Khalid was recalled from the Euphrates front in December 633 to take command of the Arab armies and to break through the Byzantine bottleneck, leaving Muthanna to carry on against the Persians as best he could with the limited forces remaining under his command.

Khalid attempted to outflank the Byzantines by attacking Damascus from the east after a forced march across the desert from Iraq, but the attack failed when the Byzantines simply refused to budge. Heraclius then sent a force south from Homs to outflank the Arabs, but it was defeated in the summer of 634 at Ajnadain, about twenty miles west of Jerusalem. Buoyed by their victory against the regular Byzantine forces, the Arabs soon broke through the Yarmuk bottleneck at Marj as-Suffar, forcing open the door to Syria. By early March 635, they had marched up the Hauran plain along the east bank of the Jordan and laid siege to Damascus. Then, in September, with the help of a disgruntled Christian bishop who was probably a persecuted Monophysite, the gates of the city were opened and the Byzantine governor soon surrendered on the basis of the following rather generous terms offered by Khalid: "In the name of Allah, the compassionate, the merciful. This is what Khalid ibn-al-Walid would grant to the inhabitants of Damascus if he enters therein: he promises to give them security for their lives, property and churches. Their city wall shall not be demolished, neither shall any Moslem be quartered in their houses. Thereunto we give to them the pact of Allah and the protection of His Prophet, the caliphs and the believers. So long as they pay the poll tax, nothing but good shall befall them."[3]

After taking Damascus the Arab army moved farther north into Syria, capturing Baalbek, Homs, and Hama, and forcing Heraclius to withdraw to Antioch. Here, the Byzantine emperor mobilized a powerful army of some 50,000 men and marched southward to challenge the Arabs. The latter, following their basic operational strategy of avoiding pitched battles with regular armies whenever possible, quickly abandoned Damascus and the other Syrian cities and withdrew back into the desert. Byzantine forces reoccupied the Yarmuk gap at Deraa and once again closed that gateway to Syria. Half of the Byzantine army, however, was Armenian and there was a great deal of dissension in its ranks. Moreover, its continued effectiveness became seriously jeopardized as the Arab forces raided its supply convoys, took prisoners, and generally demoralized the troops. Then, on August 20, 636, the main Arab force attacked the Byzantine positions from the east, under the cover of a heavy dust storm that blew in from the same direction. At the same time, other detachments were sent north to cut off the Byzantine path of retreat. The element of surprise was decisive—there was no expectation of a major assault from the direction of the desert and the Byzantine troops were overwhelmed. The Byzantine expeditionary force, which had been mobilized and financed by Heraclius with great difficulty, was annihilated.

Plagued by a host of other higher priority problems at the time, Heraclius concluded that the cost of maintaining Byzantine control of Syria was simply more than he could afford. Accordingly, he decided to abandon the country, ending a 1,000-year period of Graeco-Roman domination there. He applied a scorched earth policy to the frontier region of Cilicia, presumably intending that it serve as an uninhabitable buffer zone between the contending armies, and then withdrew across the Taurus Mountains into Anatolia, making the mountain range Byzantium's southern boundary in Asia.

Following their victory at the Yarmuk, the Arab forces swept through Syria, quickly taking the major cities of Antioch and Aleppo. With Syria under their control, the remaining Byzantine possessions in Mesopotamia were easy prey for the Arab armies. Edessa, Constantina, and Dara were all taken in 639, effectively completing the conquest of northern Mesopotamia, the Jazira. From there the Arab armies continued to march north toward the Caucasus. However, they encountered considerable trouble in Armenia, where their advance ran into heavy opposition and ground to a halt in the difficult mountainous terrain. Similar problems were encountered in Palestine where Jerusalem stubbornly held out until 638, and Caesarea, which was supplied from Byzantium by sea, did not succumb until October 640.

As soon as the Arab forces emerged victorious from the second battle of the Yarmuk, Umar (634–644), who succeeded Abu Bakr as caliph upon the latter's death, ordered that part of the army from Syria be deployed to the Persian front. The new Sassanid king Yezdegird III (634–652) had mobilized a substantial force under the veteran commander Rustam to confront the Arabs. Rustam fully understood the Arab strategy of always fighting with the desert to their backs and sought to exploit it by adopting a fundamentally defensive strategy. He wanted to deploy his forces along the east bank of the Euphrates, effectively conceding the western bank to the Arabs. He was confident that the Arab forces would easily be defeated if they crossed the river into the alluvial plain that was intersected by canals, a battlefield terrain that was quite unfamiliar to them. On the other hand, if they remained on the western bank, they posed no further threat to Persia. Yezdegird, however, saw a defensive strategy against what he considered a bunch of marauding Bedouin as unbecoming for the king of Persia, and ordered Rustam to cross the Euphrates and drive the Arabs back into the desert.

Against his better judgment, Rustam carried out the king's orders and engaged the Arab forces at Qadasiya on the fringe of the desert in early 637. The fierce battle went on for days, and it appeared that the Arabs would suffer a decisive defeat. By the third day, however, the main body of the Arab army that had marched east from Syria arrived and turned the tide of battle. Rustam was killed and the Persian army was effectively wiped out. Two months later, after recuperating from the costly victory, the Arab forces crossed the Euphrates unopposed and blockaded the Persian capital at Ctesiphon. Yezdegird sued for peace, but his proposals were rejected and he withdrew to the Zagros Mountains in early 638, abandoning Iraq to the advancing Arabs. Although the Arab losses in the conflict had been no less severe than those suffered by the Persians, the extent of the booty that fell into their hands made it relatively easy to recruit new armies in Arabia.

Farther north, as already noted, the Jazira fell to the Arabs without much difficulty, in large measure because the indigenous Aramean Christian population was primarily Monophysite and had long been subjected to persecution by the official Melkite church. As a result, there was little local interest in supporting the Byzantine war effort. By the end of 640, the Muslims had occupied Mosul in the north and, in the south, had already crossed the Shatt al-Arab, the waterway into which the Euphrates and Tigris merge to empty into the Persian Gulf.

Umar, who was a cautious man, appeared to be content with the new Quraish Empire as it now stood. His commanders, on the other hand, had tasted the joys of conquest and were hungry for more. Amr ibn al-Aasi, who had been responsible for the conquest of Palestine, is alleged to have invaded Egypt in the latter part of 639 on his own initiative. Once the Arab forces had been committed to the enterprise, however, the caliph had little practical choice other than to lend his full support to the invasion. There is also another interpretation of the events, however, that suggests that the invasion was necessitated by the explosive growth of Mecca and Medina and the need to accommodate the burgeoning numbers of pilgrims visiting the cities by garnering the grain and other supplies that Egypt produced in large quantities. In any case, Amr's forces took Farama (Pelusium) in January 640, with the cooperation of the indigenous Copts who, as Monophysite Jacobites, resented their subordination to the Melkite Greeks. Then, bolstered by reinforcements sent from Medina, Amr defeated a Byzantine force at Heliopolis in July and laid siege to the fortress of Babylon. After a seven-month siege, the Byzantines withdrew in April 641, retreating down the Nile in boats.

Although the Byzantine forces probably could have withstood the Arab sieges for years, the political situation in the Byzantine capital would not permit it. Constantinople was in an uproar following the death of Heraclius in February 641. The regents for his successor Constans II (641–668), who was only eleven years old at the time, decided that the troops were needed more urgently to maintain order in the capital, as well as to battle the Lombards in Italy. Accordingly, the new Byzantine rulers were prepared to abandon Egypt if such became necessary, as it did when the Arab forces subsequently crossed the Nile and laid siege to Alexandria.

On November 8, 641, the patriarch Cyrus signed an agreement surrendering all of Egypt to the caliph, with the understanding that the Muslims were to cease the demolition of churches in the country and that the people were to be granted the freedom to practice their own religion. In addition, the treaty provided for an eleven-month armistice period during which those Greek citizens who chose to leave the country would be permitted to do so undisturbed. With the evacuation completed in September 642, the Arab army occupied Alexandria. Amr soon cleared the ancient pharaonic canal that connected the Nile north of Babylon with Qulzum (Suez) on the Red Sea, opening a direct maritime connection between Arabia and Egypt. Although, in response to appeals by the populace of Alexandria, the Byzantines sent a fleet of some 300 ships to Egypt and retook the city in 645, they were driven out again for all time the following year.

With the fall of Egypt, the remaining Byzantine provinces of North Africa were left virtually defenseless, and it was not long before Amr moved into Libya, initially to secure his western flank against attack from the desert. However, it soon became apparent that if the Arabs wanted to defeat the Byzantines decisively, they could not do so exclusively on the basis of their prowess in desert warfare. It would be necessary for them to exploit the maritime skills of the Egyptians and the Syrians in developing a significant naval capability with which they could challenge Byzantine control of the eastern Mediterranean. This led to the construction of a powerful fleet. Moreover, to protect their maritime flank in the Mediterranean, the Arabs seized Cyprus, the principal Byzantine naval base commanding the waters off the Syrian coast, in 649. By 655, the combined Syrian-Egyptian fleet was able to defeat a Byzantine armada of some 500 ships off the Lycian coast of Anatolia, thereby threatening although not destroying Byzantium's regional naval supremacy.

In the meanwhile, on the Persian front, Umar had forbidden his commander, Saad ibn abi Waqqas, from crossing the Zagros into the Persian heartland. In response to a request from the latter for permission to do so, Umar is reported to have stated: "I desire that between Mesopotamia and the lands beyond, the hills shall form a barrier, so that the Persians shall not be able to get at us, nor we at them. The fruitful plains of Irac suffice for all our wants; and I would rather the safety of my people than spoil and further conquest."[4] Yezdegird, however, was of a rather different mind in this regard. Having withdrawn into the Persian heartland, he still harbored dreams of driving the Arabs out of what had been Persian territory for centuries. He began the mobilization and training of a large army to undertake the re-conquest. This helped Umar ultimately decide to listen to the advice of his counselors who insisted that there could be no peace in the east as long as an independent Sassanid state existed. He dispatched an army across the Zagros to deal with Yezdegird, and, in a decisive battle at Nehawand in 642, the Persian forces were completely routed. However, in contrast to the situation that prevailed in Syria and Egypt, where all resistance collapsed immediately upon the defeat of the Byzantine armies, it took ten years of continual fighting to pacify Persia.

The remnants of the Persian army retreated to the fortified cities and continued to resist the Arab conquest. Isfahan, to which Yezdegird had withdrawn, fell in 643, and the king withdrew farther inland to the Caspian region to seek support, unsuccessfully, for a new offensive against the invader. Nonetheless, the Persian resistance movement received a substantial boost from the assassination of Umar by a Persian slave in Medina in 644. That event precipitated a widespread rebellion that lasted for the first five years of the reign of the new caliph Uthman (644–656). In 650, a new campaign of conquest was launched that saw the submission of Kerman and Sistan the following year, and soon reached Nishapur, the capital of the northeastern province of Khorasan. Finally, after Yezdegird was assassinated in 652, Persian resistance to the Arab occupation came to an end. Nonetheless, Arab settlement in Khorasan was very sparse and the territory continued to be ruled by indigenous chieftians who were nominally subordinate to the caliph, whose religious influence was considerably more extensive than his actual political control.

Uthman, with western Persia firmly in his grasp, and Muawiya, his chief lieutenant in Syria, became acutely sensitive to the vulnerability of the country to attack through Armenia, a geostrategic fact that Persians and Romans had grappled with and fought about for centuries. Accordingly, Uthman and Muawiya, in time-honored fashion, sought to transform Armenia into a client state that would serve as an effective buffer separating the Arabs and Byzantines along the frontier between the Taurus and the Caspian Sea. To achieve this, Uthman was prepared to offer Armenia rather generous terms. He proposed a treaty for an indeterminate period that for all practical purposes would give the country autonomy under nominal Arab suzerainty. He promised to levy no fixed tribute on the country for a period of seven years; in return, the Armenians were to vow that they would pay a token sum of their own choosing. Furthermore, no Arab chiefs or officers were to be garrisoned at Armenian strongpoints. Armenia was to establish and maintain a cavalry force of 15,000 men. Although this contingent would not be required to serve in Syria, it would be obligated to deploy to any other location at the discretion of the caliph. Finally, Uthman stipulated that "no enemy might enter Armenia. If the Greeks march against you, I will dispatch forces to your aid as soon as you request them."[5]

This offer, which was far more generous than anything ever received from the Sassanids, was accepted by Armenia since it essentially guaranteed its independence from both Byzantium and the Arabs. Constans II reacted forcefully to this development by marching into Armenia with a force of some 100,000 men to reestablish his authority there. But no sooner did he regain nominal control of the country than he withdrew. By the time Constans returned to his capital, the officials he had installed in Armenia to rule the country in his behalf had all been forcibly removed from office. It was clear that the Armenians were determined to pursue an independent political course. Capitalizing on this sentiment, in 654, with the cooperation of Theodorus, who had been deposed as ruler of Armenia by Constans the preceding year, Muawiya sent an Arab army into the country to compel its acceptance of Arab suzerainty. That same year, Arab forces reached into the Caucasus as far north as Tbilsi (Tiflis).

The rapid expansion of the Arab Empire throughout the Middle East tended to exacerbate some internal problems that were to have far-reaching consequences for its long-term viability. The early caliphs were quite concerned about the exposure of their relatively rustic troops to the more sophisticated cultures they would encounter in the course of their conquests. Umar had therefore decided to prevent his forces from fraternizing freely with the conquered peoples by establishing military cantonments away from the cities and confining the Arab troops to them. However, with the sudden end to the frenetic pace and exhilaration of the years of conquest, the ensuing tedium began to sow dissension and open disaffection in the Arab camps that threatened the centrality of the caliphal government in Medina. These problems were further aggravated by the unrelenting competition for influence and preferment between the two major houses of the Quraish, the Hashemites (the family of Muhammad) and the Umayyads. Uthman, who was an Umayyad, appeared to be very much under the influence of his kinsmen and was accused of nepotism. The resulting volatile situation erupted in rebellion early in 656 when mutinous Arab armies set out simultaneously from Egypt and the Jazira to march on Medina.

On June 17, 656, a mob of rebellious soldiers murdered Uthman in Medina while he was sitting on the floor reading the Koran. It is noteworthy that Muawiya, the governor of Syria, who was also an Umayyad, evidently played no part in these events. He had already unilaterally discarded the system of segregation of the Arab troops in military cantonments. Instead, he established his government in Damascus and allowed his men to fraternize freely with the indigenous population.

The murder of Uthman brought an end to the centrality of Medina in the Arab political constellation. The mutiny ended with the accession of Ali (656–661), the cousin and son-in-law of Muhammad, and therefore a Hashemite, to the caliphate. However, Ali's elevation did not go uncontested even among the Quraish, and he had to quell an open insurrection in Iraq in December 656 before his investiture could be considered firm. Because of the challenges to his rule, Ali was compelled to abandon Medina and locate his capital closer to the major population centers of the empire, from which he would be in a better position to exercise control over events. He moved his government to the military cantonment at Kufa in Iraq, and it was never to return to Medina, which was also perceived as politically and economically vulnerable because of its heavy reliance on grain shipments from Egypt. The center of gravity of the empire had now definitely shifted away from Arabia, and the question of its ultimate location would be determined by the outcome of the struggle between Syria and Iraq for predominance in the Arab world.

While Ali was busy establishing himself in Kufa, Muawiya was planning his own bid for supreme power in Damascus. He shrewdly refused to acknowledge Ali as caliph until the murderers of Uthman were punished. This he knew Ali could not do without grave political risk. Concerned that such a move on his part would probably rekindle the mutiny that brought Uthman down, the caliph was in no position to satisfy Muawiya's demand. Ali therefore concluded that he had no option other than to try and impose his authority on Syria by force. He challenged Muawiya on the battlefield at Siffin along the upper Euphrates in July 657.

The results of the military confrontation, however, were inconclusive and it was decided to submit the dispute to arbitration, a process that dragged on until January 659. Unable to find a satisfactory solution to the problem, the arbitrators appear to have concluded that both Ali and Muawiya should be excluded from the caliphate, leaving the position open for a compromise candidate. From Ali's perspective, this was hardly an equitable solution since he would lose the caliphate while Muawiya retained control of Syria, of which he was the governor. Ali therefore rejected the results of the arbitration, leaving Muawiya free to pursue his ambitions.

Ali's position, even in Iraq, had become weakened as a consequence of his having agreed to the arbitration in the first place. Many of his puritanical followers in Iraq, the Kharijites, became disenchanted over the fact that he had been prepared to bargain over a matter that they believed should have been left to divine dispensation on the field of battle. As a result, a number of rebellions broke out against Ali that kept him preoccupied while his adversary Muawiya was taking steps to consolidate his position in preparation for a major bid for power.

With the support of Amr ibn al-Aasi, Muawiya gained control of Egypt in 658. That same year, he secured his northern flank against a Byzantine attack by concluding a truce with Constans in return for the payment of an annual tribute. Then, in May 660, Muawiya proclaimed himself caliph in Jerusalem on the basis of his assertion that Ali was unfit for the position. Ali was preparing to undertake a campaign against Muawiya when he was assassinated in the mosque of Kufa in January 661, by a Kharijite who had never forgiven him for agreeing to arbitrate the question of the caliphate. This left the field open to Muawiya, who soon became undisputed caliph (661–680) and moved the capital of the empire to Damascus, where the character of the Arab Empire of the Quraish soon underwent a radical transformation.

NOTES

1. A. A. Vasiliev, *History of the Byzantine Empire*, vol. 1, p. 207.
2. Kamal S. Salibi, *Syria under Islam*, p. 19.
3. Philip K. Hitti, *History of the Arabs*, p. 130.
4. William Muir, *Annals of the Early Caliphate*, p. 189
5. Rene Grousset, *Histoire de l'Armenie*, p. 301.

2

The Umayyad Empire

Although the people of Damascus and its environs were ethnically Arab for the most part, they were very different culturally from the Arabs of Iraq, the majority of whom had just recently emerged out of the desert. The Damascenes had been settled in the ancient metropolis for centuries and were intimately familiar and quite comfortable with Byzantine political and administrative practices. Accordingly, Muawiya decided to build his caliphal regime along those familiar lines. In some instances, the same Christian officials who earlier had served the Byzantine government were retained in their positions.

Muawiya was viewed by the Syrians as being as much the legitimate heir of the indigenous Ghassanids as caliph of the Muslims, an advantageous perception he did nothing to dispel. Following Byzantine practice, Muawiya also changed the institutional character of the caliphate itself by making it dynastic rather than elective, designating his son Yazid to be his successor. The essentially non-Hejazi character of both his regime and its political base in Syria, exacerbated by the smoldering enmity between the Umayyads and the Hashemites, remained a bone of contention in the Arab sphere that was suppressed only temporarily while Muawiya held the caliphate. As observed by one scholar:

So long as the central government remained in Medina, Islamic influences were predominant, and the faithful Companions of the Prophet could attempt to organize the new society in accordance with the teaching of their dead master. But when in 661 Mu'awiyah made Damascus the capital of the empire, the old heathen sentiment of the Arabs was able to assert itself. In place of the theoretical equality of all believers in the brotherhood of Islam, we find the Arabs asserting themselves as a dominant aristocracy ruling over subject peoples. . . . During the whole of the Umayyad period, pious circles in Mecca and Medina which clung to the primitive apostolic traditions felt that Mu'awiyah instead of preserving the piety and primitive simplicity of the Prophet and his Companions, had transformed the Caliphate into a temporal sovereignty, animated by worldly motives and characterized by luxury and self-indulgence. The Umayyads were accused of having secularized the supreme power in the very midst of Islam, and of having exploited the inheritance of the Muslim community for the benefit of the members of their own tribe and family.[1]

Once he had consolidated his position as caliph, Muawiya renewed the expansionist war against Byzantium. During the reign of Constantine IV (668–685), forces from Syria took Rhodes in 672 and Crete in 674, threatening the Byzantine position in the Aegean and eastern Mediterranean. In 674, a powerful Arab fleet penetrated the Aegean, passed through the Dardanelles unopposed and landed a few miles from Constantinople. They mounted repeated assaults on the walls of the city, but were simply unable to break through. After several months, the Arab force withdrew to Cyzicus on the Sea of Marmara, some eighty miles from Constantinople. From this base, they plundered the countryside on both shores of the sea and made repeated attempts over a period of seven years to take the Byzantine capital. The failure of these assaults to succeed in breaking through the city's defenses have been attributed largely to the effective use by the Byzantines of the newly invented "Greek fire" as a defensive weapon. Frustrated by his inability to penetrate the walls of the Byzantine capital, coupled with the substantial losses in men and ships he experienced during the long siege, Muawiya finally abandoned the campaign in 680.

It had been widely believed in Europe at the time that if Constantinople had fallen to Muawiya, there was no European power that could have prevented the Arab armies from sweeping through Greece, Italy, and France. The withdrawal of the Arab fleet from Constantinople was therefore greeted with a great sigh of relief in Europe.

A change of regime in autocratically ruled states typically provides a moment of internal weakness as contenders scramble for power, and the death of Muawiya in May 680 triggered a renewal of civil strife among the Arabs as his son Yazid I (680–683) assumed the caliphate. The event that triggered the conflict was an aborted attempt to resurrect the caliphate of the house of Ali by his younger brother Hussein, which ended with the latter's death and the massacre of his followers at Karbala in Iraq in October of that same year. The death of Hussein ended the trouble in Iraq. However, the situation in the Hejaz proved to be more intractable.

Taking advantage of the unstable situation caused by the demise of Muawiya, one of the leaders of the Hejazi opposition to the Umayyads, Abdullah ibn Zubair (683–692), was proclaimed as a rival caliph in Mecca. His legitimacy was quickly recognized in the Hejaz, Iraq, South Arabia, and parts of Syria, effectively dividing the Muslim world into two camps. Medina openly revolted against Yazid's rule in the fall of 682, driving the Umayyad party out of the city. Reacting strongly to these challenges to Umayyad authority, Yazid dispatched a Syrian army to the south to pacify the Hejaz. The revolt in Medina was suppressed and the city was sacked in August 683. The Syrian force then laid siege to Mecca, and was engaged in driving Ibn Zubair out of the city in November of that year when the news arrived that Yazid had died. His young chronically ill son Muawiya II (683–684) had been acclaimed caliph in Damascus over the objections of the Qaisites, who refused to swear allegiance to him. In anticipation of the disorders that were expected to accompany the contested succession, the siege of Mecca was lifted and the Syrian forces were withdrawn.

The situation in the empire became further confused with the untimely death of Muawiya II shortly thereafter, a victim of the plague. Yazid's other sons were considered too young for such an appointment, and the choice to replace him as caliph in Damascus fell on Marwan ibn al-Hakam (684–685), an aged cousin of the caliph Uthman. The selection met with strenuous opposition and had to be ratified on the battlefield at Marj Rahit, north of Damascus, in July 684 by the defeat of the opponents who were prepared to contest his election. The struggle had the unintended consequence of dividing the Arabs of Syria into two principal camps, the Qaisi and the Yamani, a circumstance that prevented the unity of the Syrians when it was critically needed later on. In any case, Marwan also died from the plague (some suggest by foul play) in April of the following year and was succeeded by his son Abd al-Malik (685–705).

The caliphate of Abd al-Malik, however, was recognized only in Syria, Palestine, and Egypt. His Hejazi rival, Abdullah ibn Zubair, was still firmly in control in Mecca, and the rest of the empire in the Middle East was in a state of anarchy. No one seemed to be in control of affairs in Persia. In Iraq, the Kharijites and Shiites, that is, the Shiat Ali (the party or supporters of the house of Ali), were in open rebellion while the brother of Abdullah ibn Zubair was in control of the Arab military cantonment at Kufa.

It took six years before Abd al-Malik was sufficiently strong to take to the field and attempt to impose his control over the region by force. On the Byzantine frontier he was being harassed by the Mardaites—a group of Monothelite Christian Syrians that retreated to the north in advance of the Arab conquest—who formed a "brass wall" blocking access to Anatolia from the south. To secure this frontier, Abd al-Malik concluded an agreement with Justinian II (685–695) in 689. Under its terms, the Mardaites were to be relocated elsewhere in the Byzantine Empire in exchange for a payment of tribute and an agreement to share the revenues derived from Armenia, Iberia, and Cyprus. It seems rather remarkable that Justinian would deliberately weaken his defenses against the Arabs for a monetary consideration. However, aside from his preoccupation with events taking place simultaneously in the Balkans, it appears that Justinian's distaste for the Mardaites' religious profession was so strong that it caused him to lose sight of the strategic implications of their removal from the frontier zone.

With his northern flank secure, Abd al-Malik invaded Iraq in 691 and gained control of the country by the end of that year. This left the rival caliphate in Mecca without allies of any consequence, and the city fell to a Syrian army in October 692. Abdullah ibn Zubair was killed and Abd al-Malik became recognized as the sole caliph of the Muslims.

In the meanwhile, Justinian had been successful in his war with the Bulgarians and had taken a large number of Slavonian captives. He transplanted some 30,000 of these to Anatolia to replace the Mardaites as the protective barrier to Arab access to the strategic passes through the Taurus. With the Balkan situation under control, at least for the moment, and overly confident of the loyalty of his Slavonian troops, Justinian decided that the peace agreement with Abd al-Malik was no longer in his interest. He therefore sought to precipitate a crisis that would justify the scrapping of the treaty, particularly so that he might be free to reoccupy Cyprus. He found such a justification in 692, when he refused to accept the regular tribute payment from Abd al-Malik in coin carrying the caliph's image rather than that of the Byzantine emperor, something that was to be expected as the caliphate began to mint its own currency. Abd al-Malik protested that he had fulfilled his obligation under the treaty and wanted peace. But, according to Theophanes, "Justinian thought Abd al-Malik's request was caused by fear. He did not understand that what the Arabs wanted was to stop the Mardaites' inroads, and then to break the peace with a pretext that seemed plausible. This is just what happened."[2]

The Arab forces engaged the Byzantines near Sebastopolis in Cilicia. To Justinian's surprise and chagrin, some two-thirds of the Slavonian troops upon whom he depended so heavily betrayed him and joined the enemy, turning the affair into a complete debacle. Justinian was forced to flee to the Bosphorus for safety. The Byzantine defeat at Sebastopolis also precipitated a revolt by Symbatius, an Armenian patrician, that handed over southern Armenia to the Arabs as well. Now, with the Mardaite "brass wall" permanently removed from the Taurus frontier, Abd al-Malik was readily able to renew the campaign against Byzantium that had been sidetracked for some fifteen years. He initiated a series of incursions into Anatolia and maritime raids against the Byzantine coasts. But war with Byzantium was not among his highest priorities. Abd al-Malik was far more concerned with the consolidation of Arab control of the vast empire and it was primarily on this goal that he concentrated his efforts. One of the strategies he pursued as a major means of achieving his aim was Arabification. By imposing a uniform Arab culture on the diverse peoples of the empire he hoped to eliminate challenges to Arab minority rule. In 699, he made the use of the Arabic language obligatory for all public communications throughout the empire.

His son and successor Walid I (705–715) oversaw the subsequent expansion of the Umayyad Empire into Spain in the west and Central Asia in the northeast. In the latter, the frontier was extended to the Syr Darya River, bringing Islam into direct confrontation with Buddhism for the first time. To the southeast, Walid's forces pushed through Baluchistan as far as modern Hyderabad in the Indus delta. It is noteworthy that Umayyad religious policy underwent a significant modification as it was applied to India. Under Muslim law, Jews and Christians, "people of the Book," were to be permitted to continue to practice their faiths; and by a strained extension of this principle, undertaken for practical reasons, even Parsees were tolerated as people of the "Book of Zoroaster." Idolatry, on the other hand, was to be rooted out entirely. This policy was pursued vigorously in Central Asia with respect to Buddhism, shamanism, and other religions. In relatively wealthy India, however, the notion of "holy war" was completely set aside. As long as lucrative tribute was paid, traditional religions were permitted to flourish.

Walid was succeeded by his brother Suleiman (715–717), who resumed the incursions into Anatolia, pressing as far westward as Sardis and Pergamon. His fleet passed through the Dardanelles and approached Constantinople. Blocked from entering the Golden Horn by a chain that stretched across the entrance to the city from the sea it had to anchor in the Sea of Marmara and the Bosphorus. Suleiman landed his army and placed the city under siege in 717 but was unable to penetrate its massive walls, the Arab forces once again suffering heavy losses from the defender's use of the "Greek fire." According to one writer, "It would be no exaggeration to say that it was the Greek Fire which frustrated the plans of the Omayyad Caliphate to conquer Europe by way of Constantinople, and put an end to its projects with regard to the Eastern Roman Empire and the east of Europe."[3]

The Arab siege army also suffered heavy losses during the particularly severe winter that year. Then, in the spring of 718, the Byzantine emperor Leo the Isaurian (714–741) persuaded Khan Tervel of the Bulgars to attack the Arabs in their rear, inflicting additional heavy losses on them and making their military situation increasingly hopeless. In the meantime, Suleiman had died and his cousin and successor Umar II (717–720) decided to abandon the campaign entirely. The siege was lifted on August 15, 718, and what was left of the army returned to Syria.

The Arabs were subsequently prevented from making any serious attacks on Byzantium for more than another two decades because of the threat they confronted on their Caucasian frontiers from the Khazars of southern Russia. Leo had concluded an alliance with the latter that was sealed by the marriage of his son and successor Constantine V (741–775) to the daughter of the Khazar khagan. Nonetheless, the Arabs continued their forays into Anatolia, sometimes penetrating as far as Nicaea. Toward the end of his reign, however, Leo succeeded in inflicting a significant defeat on

Umar's forces in Phrygia that forced them to withdraw completely from western Anatolia.

One of the key issues that Umar II had to deal with concerned the financial resources of the empire. Muhammad had forbidden the persecution of Christians and Jews, but had required them to pay a head tax in return for the protected status they received. Muslims, of course, were not to be required to pay such a tax. As a result, the revenues of the original Muslim state were derived to a large extent from such taxation. However, during Muhammad's time there was no Arab empire to administer; also, indeed, there also was neither a government nor a full-time army to support. Now, some eighty-six years later, the situation was radically different. The Muslim domain no longer consisted of the relatively small communities of Mecca and Medina, and the tribes of the desert. The empire that was administered from Damascus was vast and demanded ever larger amounts of money to keep it going. As a practical matter, the ruling of Muhammad was frequently ignored and many converts to Islam were forced to pay the head tax anyway. The exemption had become primarily an Arab privilege, a fact that nurtured resentment among many non-Arab Muslims. Nonetheless, piously and somewhat naively, Umar decided that the explicit ruling of Muhammad had to be observed strictly and that the head tax was no longer to be extracted from any Muslim, whether Arab or not. As he anticipated, the edict became very popular and generated considerable support for the dynasty outside Arab circles. At the same time, however, its impact on the treasury was immediate and disastrous. Large numbers of adherents of other religions, particularly in Transoxiana, who were brought into the empire through conquest now voluntarily converted to Islam in droves to avoid paying the onerous tax.

Umar's decision regarding the head tax was soon reversed by his successor Yazid II (720–724) who sought to restore the solvency of his government. The immediate consequence of the restoration of the tax on non-Arab Muslims was a rebellion in Khorasan in eastern Persia. As the caliphate moved to suppress the revolt, the rebels appealed to the paramount khan of the Turks for help.

The Turkish tribes of Central Asia had recently formed a powerful confederation in the Ili valley, and welcomed the invitation to expand southward. The Turks invaded Khorasan, and it took Yazid's successors, Hisham (724–743), Walid II (743–744), Yazid III (744), and Marwan II (745–750), a decade of hard fighting between 738 and 748 to restore Umayyad authority in the region. A similar revolt broke out simultaneously among the Berbers in North Africa that lasted from 740 to 743, placing further strains on the resources of the caliphate.

The reign of Marwan II witnessed serious internal convulsions resulting from sectarian differences, tribal rivalries, ethnic distinctions, and the ongoing competition between the Umayyads and the Hashemites for preeminence. The latter struggle was to take on a new dimension in 743 with the accession of Ibrahim as head of the Hashemite Abbasid clan, which had been living in obscurity in Homeima, south of Kerak in Trans-Jordan. Spurred on by the obviously declining fortunes of the Umayyads, Ibrahim sent a loyal Persian agent, Abu Muslim, to Khorasan to promote Abbasid political aspirations. By June 747, conditions seemed right and Abu Muslim precipitated another revolt in Khorasan for the purpose of restoring the caliphate to the Hashemites. Since this encompassed the house of Ali by definition, the Shiites enthusiastically joined the rebellion. Indeed, in addition to broad sympathy for the Shiite cause in Persia, the Persians also harbored a festering grievance against the Umayyads who had kept them in a state of humiliation notwithstanding the fact that they had become Muslim. There was deep and growing resentment over Arab primacy in the Muslim world.

Marwan was unable to respond to the pleas for help from his governor at Merv, which fell to Abu Muslim in February 748, because of his preoccupation with an uprising at home in Syria that had spread from Palestine as far as Homs. He did, however, have Ibrahim seized and exiled to Harran in northern Syria, where he soon died, but it was already too late to stop the rebellion. By 749, the rebel forces had succeeded in seizing control of all of Persia, and had reached as far east as Herat, and as far west as Kufa, which was occupied by them in October of that year. In the meantime, the Abbasid clan secretly crossed the desert from Transjordan. Once arrived in Kufa, the rebel army hailed the Abbasid leader Abul-Abbas (750–754) as the rightful caliph. The Shiites, feeling betrayed because he was not a descendant of Ali, rejected Abul-Abbas' election and attempted to install an Alid, an effort that led to their harsh suppression. With Persia and Iraq in their hands, the Abbasids were now in a position to challenge the Umayyads for control of the rest of the empire.

In January 750, Marwan left Harran with a sizable army of some 120,000 men and marched east to confront the Abbasids on the banks of the Greater Zab River. Unfortunately for Marwan, his forces consisted largely of Yamani and Kharijite troops who approached the conflict with little enthusiasm. Having no significant stake in the outcome of the struggle, they were reluctant to take the offensive. Marwan made the mistake of telling the tribal leaders that there was treasure in his camp that would be distributed later to reward those who acquitted themselves bravely on the battlefield. Upon hearing this, some deserted the front lines and headed for the caliph's headquarters to avail themselves of the booty that was to be found there. To forestall this, Marwan sent a force under his son to the rear to protect his base camp. The latter troop movement was widely misinterpreted as signaling a retreat, and the entire front soon collapsed. Marwan was decisively defeated and forced to flee for refuge, first to Syria where he found little support. He attempted to raise a new army in Palestine, but this only provoked another uprising, forcing him to flee to Egypt with the Abbasids in hot pursuit. He was eventually found and killed in the Fayyum in August 750, bringing a definitive end to the Umayyad Empire.

NOTES

1. Thomas W. Arnold, *The Caliphate*, pp. 24–25.
2. Theophanes, *The Chronicle of Theophanes*, p. 63.
3. Muhammad A. Enan, *Decisive Moments in the History of Islam*, pp. 112–113.

3

The Abbasid Empire

The Abbasid seizure of the caliphate and political power in the Muslim world represented far more than a mere change of dynasty. It precipitated an even more dramatic change than the subjugation of the early Hashemites by the Umayyads and the transfer of power from Medina to Damascus. The Umayyad Empire was essentially a Mediterranean power. Syria, Palestine, and Egypt had been part of the Graeco-Roman world for more than a millennium, and Persia, Turkestan, and the Punjab had been colonies of this Mediterranean-centered empire. The Abbasids, on the other hand, had ridden to power on the shoulders of the Persians and had established their capital at Kufa, which had been part of Persia for a millennium. In essence, then, the Abbasid Empire represented a resurgence of Persian influence in the Middle East. The Abbasid Empire was no longer Arab in the sense that the Umayyad Empire had been. Although the Abbasids themselves were ethnic Arabs, and Arabic remained the official language of the empire, political advancement was open to all. The Arab imperium had been transformed into a Muslim state where Arab ethnicity no longer automatically assured preferment. This radical reorientation was bound to have serious repercussions in the Arab-dominated western part of the empire.

Abul-Abbas' brother and successor Mansur (754–775) soon moved the seat of the empire from Kufa to the small Christian village of Baghdad on the western bank of the Tigris, which was reconstructed to serve as the imperial capital. Baghdad was more strategically located than Damascus for communications with the far reaches of the empire. It was located on a main road to Persia, and at the site of the interconnection of the Euphrates and the Tigris through a navigable canal. It was also perhaps more than a merely remarkable coincidence that Baghdad, the capital of the new Persian-oriented Abbasid Empire, was established on the ancient frontier between the former Roman and Persian empires.

The political implications of the shift of the center of gravity of the Abbasid realm from the Mediterranean to the Persian frontier were soon realized. Rebellions against the Abbasids broke out throughout the western marches of the empire. To a large extent, these outbreaks were a direct consequence of Abbasid policy. The Abbasids were determined to eradicate every trace of Umayyad rule and influence, and this included the wholesale slaughter of those who had opposed, or who might threaten, their ascendancy. Indeed, Abu Muslim himself, who had been critical to the Abbasid success, was executed by Mansur as a potential threat to his unquestioned rule. By the time of the death of Mansur in 775, the western provinces of the empire in North Africa and Spain were already well along in the process of breaking away from effective control by Baghdad. Another consequence of these events was a resurgence of Byzantine military activity along the frontier to the north.

Taking advantage of the disarray in the Arab camp resulting from the Abbasid-Umayyad conflict, Constantine V (741–775) seized control of the Taurus passes and began pushing the Arabs down into the plains, extending the Byzantine frontier into Armenia once again. Mansur's successor, Mahdi (775–785), became determined to restore the situation along the northern frontier to that which existed under the Umayyads. He invaded Anatolia with a sizable army in 782 and swept across the Byzantine territory almost unopposed, setting up camp on the Bosphorus directly across from Constantinople. It appears that the empress Irene, who served as regent for the twelve-year-old Constantine VI (780–797), had sent a large number of troops to suppress the Slavonic revolt in Macedonia, Greece, and the Peloponnesus that same year. These troops had been drawn from duty along the eastern frontiers, making the Byzantine position there particularly vulnerable to Arab attack. As a result, Irene was forced to accept humiliating peace terms, including the payment of 70,000 gold dinars as tribute.

Under Harun ar-Rashid (786–809), the Abbasid Empire both shrunk in size and reached its peak of wealth and sophistication. Harun, it seems, had little interest in war and expansion, or even in retention of all of the farflung empire. He took no active measures to prevent the secession of Spain and North Africa. As a result, the empire was now confined entirely to the Middle East, and devoted its energies primarily to trade and commercial development. Nonetheless, Harun found it necessary to take additional steps to secure his northern frontiers in Armenia, where the Khazars posed a serious threat, as well as in Anatolia where the Byzantines had become active once more during the reign of Irene (797–802). Harun launched incursions into Anatolia that brought his forces as far as Ankara in the north and Ephesus in the west.

Once again distracted by internal crises, the Byzantines were unable to mount an effective defense and Irene was forced to pay tribute in return for a four-year truce. Her successor Nicephorus I (802–811), however, repudiated the terms of the treaty she had negotiated. He wrote to Harun, using the simile of a chess match: "Irene hath parted with the castle, and contented herself with the pawn. She hath paid thee moneys, the double of which thou shouldest have paid to her. It was but a woman's weakness. Wherefore, return what thou hast taken, or the sword shall decide."[1] Harun responded with a series of attacks that ravaged Anatolia, culminating in the capture of Heraclea and Tyana in 806. The net results of the conflict were the re-imposition of a requirement for an annual payment of tribute as well as a humiliating direct head tax on members of the Byzantine imperial household. However, Harun made no attempt to retain a foothold beyond the Taurus, something that might have made it more difficult for the Byzantines to attempt to extend their frontier south of the mountains. As it was, the Byzantines returned to the offensive again in 807 and moved into Cilicia, taking Tarsus, which gave them control of the strategically important Cilician Gates. Harun was forced to abandon his advantageous position in Tarsus because of his increasing preoccupation with the revolts that were erupting throughout his realm.

Following Harun's death, the question of the succession triggered a major civil war. His son Amin (809–813) had been designated as caliph, while a second son Mamun (813–833) was made governor of Khorasan. Mamun, however, refused to accept his brother's ascendancy, and proclaimed himself caliph. In June 811, at the head of the army of Khorasan, he defeated Amin's forces at Rai, at the foot of the Elburz Mountains, and marched on to Hamadan. Then, on September 1, 812, he laid siege to Baghdad, which held out until September 25, 813, when Amin was killed and Mamun's army occupied the capital. Mamun's seizure of the caliphate was accompanied by Shiite revolts in Mecca, Medina, and Iraq, presumably because of his especially close Persian connections; his mother was a Persian and it was a Persian army that put him on the throne.

With the crisis over his succession resolved, Mamun was able to direct his attention to the turbulent Byzantine frontier. At the beginning of the reign of Michael II the Stammerer (820–829), a serious rebellion broke out in Anatolia under the banner of Thomas the Slav, a pretender to the Byzantine throne. Mamun sought to take advantage of this situation by allowing Thomas to be crowned emperor in Antioch in exchange for a promise of territorial concessions in Anatolia once he succeeded in deposing Michael. With the support of the Byzantine fleet in the Aegean, Thomas and his forces crossed into Thrace and Macedonia and laid siege to Constantinople. However, with the aid of the Bulgarian nobility, the rebel forces were pushed

back and Thomas was captured and executed in 823, bringing down the
curtain on Mamun's attempt to mix in Byzantine politics.

Presumably because of his preoccupation with disposing of the numerous rebellions and other challenges to his succession, Mamun remained in
Khorasan for several years before finally relocating to Baghdad in 819. On
his arrival he found that the commander who had taken the city, Tahir
al-Hussein, had become extremely powerful in Mamun's absence. Tahir,
apparently aware that he was being perceived as a threat to the caliph, contrived to have Mamun grant him the governorship of Khorasan, thereby removing him from the intrigues that plagued the imperial capital. To
compensate him for what amounted to a voluntary internal exile, Mamun
gave Tahir virtually autonomous powers to govern the distant province as
he saw fit. Then, when Tahir died soon after his appointment, Mamun felt
obliged to recognize his son Talha as the governor of Khorasan in his place.
This was to prove to be a serious error in political judgment. By this act of
apparent generosity, Mamun unwittingly laid the basis for the establishment of a minor dynasty in eastern Persia, the Tahirids, which soon asserted in practice its complete independence from Baghdad.

Khorasan, which stretched as far to the northeast as the Oxus, was a primary source of recruits for the Abbasid army. The Arabian tribesmen who
had made up the core of the earlier caliphal armies were essentially equali-
tarians, in the Bedouin tradition, and cared little for formal ranks or titles.
Leadership, for them, depended on personal qualities and not official appointment. Their consequent individualism made them difficult to discipline within the context of a standing regular military establishment,
particularly as the tenor of the regime turned more despotic in the traditional Persian mode. The Khorasanis came to be considered more reliable
as imperial troops since they were not participants in the incessant plots
and sedition of the turbulent and troublesome Arabs. It was not long, therefore, before the Abbasid army completely lost its original Arab character, as
it became increasingly composed of Khorasanis. However, the heavy reliance on Khorasan for troops created a serious problem for the Abbasids in
the wake of the province's growing autonomy. The recruitment of troops
from Khorasan virtually ceased as the Tahirids began to absorb most of the
available indigenous manpower into their own provincial army.

Mamun's brother and successor, Mutasim (833–842), found a solution to
this problem in the procurement of large numbers of young slaves from
Turkestan to fill the ranks of the Abbasid army. Before long, these Turkish
recruits (mamluks) made up the core elements of the army, 10,000 of them
constituting the caliphal bodyguard. This prepared the ground for the
eventual loss of control of the state to this praetorian force. The traumatic
impact of these mamluk troops on the realm was soon felt. Whereas the Persians of Khorasan were Muslims and had had close links with the Arabs for
200 years, the Turks were mostly heathen and had little interest in even

learning the official Arabic language. As observed by one modern student of the period: "For two centuries the Empire of the Arabs had been fighting back against the pressure of the northern barbarians just as Rome had done. Mutasim introduced into the very citadel of the empire an army of complete foreigners. . . . Thereby he sold the pass to the enemy and committed the fate of the empire into the hands of men who were bound to it by no emotional or spiritual bond."[2] The mamluks alienated, and were alienated from, the public, and their presence in the capital created serious tensions there. Indeed, the popular hostility toward his caliphal guard was so great in Baghdad that Mutasim felt it necessary to move the capital to a new site on the Tigris, Samarra, about sixty miles north of the city.

Mutasim also inherited from his predecessor a rebellion centered in Azerbaijan that threatened to destabilize the entire northern frontier. For two decades, Babak, leader of an obscure religious sect known as the Hurramites, wreaked havoc in the area between the Caspian Sea and Hamadan with Byzantine support and military cooperation, killing perhaps as many as 200,000 people. In 837, when Mutasim's forces were closing in on him, Babak wrote to the Byzantine emperor Theophilus (829–842) informing him that the caliph had sent all his armies to Azerbaijan, leaving Syria and the Jazira especially vulnerable to attack. He suggested that if Theophilus should seize the opportunity to invade the region, he would meet with very little opposition. According to al-Tabari, "He hoped by writing to him in that way that the Byzantine King would bestir himself, and thus some of his [own] calamities would be drawn away from him because al-Mu'tasim would, perforce, recall some of those troops who were facing him and send them against the King of the Byzantines and thus would be occupied elsewhere than with himself."[3]

Although Babak's ploy did not save him, it does appear to have been instrumental in precipitating a major Byzantine incursion into northern Syria and the Jazira in 837. Theophilus' forces ravaged Zaperta, slaughtering the male population, and sacked Malatya and Samosata before withdrawing back to Byzantine territory. After disposing of Babak, Mutasim retaliated against the Byzantines with a punitive strike into Anatolia in 838, during which he destroyed the ancient city of Amorion (Ammuriya), the major communications center on the route between the Cilician Gates and Constantinople, before withdrawing back across the Taurus.

The increasing involvement of the Turkish mamluk generals in Abbasid politics began to be felt as they consolidated their control of the army. Under Mutasim's son and successor Wathiq (842–847), the mamluk general Ashnas was accorded the title of sultan, suggesting that his role extended beyond the strictly military sphere into the political. The implications of these developments for the survival of the Abbasid Empire were not fully recognized at the time, but were to be realized in practice two decades later. After the murder of Mutawakkil (847–861), it was the mamluk guard that determined, much as did the earlier praetorians in Rome, who might next succeed to the throne of the caliphate.

The involvement of the mamluks in the matter of the succession to the caliphate was not the result of any clearly thought through plot. They had merely become involved in one of an endless series of court intrigues and cabals, which in this particular instance led to the overthrow of Mutawakkil. Indeed, after acclaiming Muntasir (861–862) as caliph, they simply withdrew to their barracks. However, the mamluk commanders recognized that they could wield extraordinary power over the state if they should choose to do so. It was not long before they so chose, and began to exploit their positions of power for their own purposes. Six months after they had placed Muntasir on the throne they murdered him as well, appointing Mustaeen (862–866), a grandson of Mutasim, as caliph in his place. Then, in 865, the mamluk commanders quarreled among themselves, creating a split in the state. One faction continued to support Mustaeen and relocated the seat of the caliphate back to Baghdad, taking the caliph there with them. The other faction considered Mustaeen deposed and acknowledged Mutazz (866–869) as caliph in his place. They then successfully laid siege to Baghdad to give effect to their decision. Mustaeen was killed and Mutazz was installed as undisputed caliph. However, Mutazz soon fell out of favor with the imperial mamluks and was also murdered and replaced by Muhtadi in 869. Muhtadi, evidently anxious to introduce greater stability into the governance of the empire, made the laudable but naive mistake of seriously attempting to put an end to what was in fact the military dictatorship of the mamluks. He was rewarded for his efforts with assassination before the end of his first year on the throne, and was succeeded by Mutamid (869–892). Early in the latter's reign, a satisfactory power-sharing arrangement with the mamluk commanders was worked out that placed the actual exercise of caliphal power in the hands of his brother and vice-regent, Muwaffaq, thereby accounting for Mutamid's relatively long tenure as caliph. It was during his reign that the capital of the empire was moved back to Baghdad from Samarra.

One clear but unintended consequence of these decades of mamluk intervention in and manipulation of palace politics was that the earlier allegiance to the caliphate began to dissipate. When it was recognized that the caliph was merely a figurehead, a pampered prisoner in his own palace under the control of Turkish mercenaries, the provinces of the empire began to break away from Baghdad's control. The army itself had little interest in the preservation of the empire as such, and interposed no serious opposition to the defection of its more remote components.

In 869, the year of Mutamid's accession, a new Alid claimant to the caliphate arose. Ali ibn Muhammad, who claimed descent from Ali and Fatima, the daughter of the Prophet, emerged from northern Persia and began to seek followers from among those social classes that had most to gain from a revolt against the ruling Abbasids. He directed his appeal especially to the masses of black slaves who labored in the marshes of southern Iraq, most of whom had been imported from Zanzibar (Zenj) by slavers. Ali cast himself in the role of a messiah, a deliverer who would bring them relief from their harsh involuntary servitude to the Abbasids. He soon succeeded in precipitating a major insurrection, the so-called Zenj Rebellion, the intent of which was the overthrow of the Abbasid caliphate. The revolt quickly spread throughout the entire Euphrates-Tigris delta region. It also traveled along the banks of the Karun River as far north as Ahwaz. For a time the rebels cut off Baghdad, the heart of the empire, from communications with the south and even threatened the blockade of the city. The rebellion, which lasted until 883, had particularly disastrous economic consequences for the empire. It put an end to the highly profitable sea trade from India and Southeast Asia that came up the Persian Gulf to Basra, and which formed the basis for much of the legendary wealth of Baghdad. The loss of revenue derived from this trade further destabilized the Abbasid state itself, since it now had difficulty in paying the mercenary troops that were critical to its continued viability.

The lucrative maritime trade began to be diverted from the Persian Gulf region to the Red Sea and Egypt. Ahmed ibn Tulun (868–884), a young Turkish officer who had been designated by the caliph to be the governor of Egypt, used the new influx of wealth from this trade to make Egypt effectively independent of the central government in Baghdad, to which it merely paid tribute. Since he was fully preoccupied with the ongoing slave revolt, the caliph could do little to prevent Ahmed from consolidating his power in Egypt. The caliph's problems in southern Iraq and Persia also presented a welcomed opportunity for the Byzantines to begin to encroach further on Abbasid territory in Cilicia. Unable to mount an effective defense of the region himself, the caliph authorized Ahmed to undertake the defense of Syria on his behalf. Ahmed rose to the occasion and, in 877, exploited the existing power vacuum along the Mediterranean littoral to establish himself as overlord there as well, once again linking Syria, Palestine, and Egypt in a common political constellation comparable to that which had existed repeatedly in earlier times. Ahmed also established a naval base at Acre to assist in the defense of the territory and seized control of Damascus and Antioch, over the violent objections of their respective Abbasid governors. Although he did actually proceed to Tarsus to confront the Byzantines, he quickly decided that it served his interests more to focus his efforts on seizing control of the rest of Syria, and perhaps the Jazira as well. Accordingly, he abandoned Tarsus to the Byzantines and marched on Harran instead. He then headed for Mosul, but had to terminate his campaign in order to return to Egypt to deal with a domestic crisis foolishly precipitated by his son Khomaria, whom he had left in charge of the country during his absence.

Ahmed's death in 884, and his replacement by the not very competent Khomaria (884–895), left both Egypt and Syria in a state of virtual limbo, with the regime in Baghdad too weak to reassert its own control there. An inconclusive struggle between Khomaria and the caliph for domination of the provinces continued for two years before a peace treaty was concluded in 886. The agreement provided that the Tulunids would retain the governorship of Egypt and Syria for a period of thirty years in return for the annual payment of a small tribute. Although the caliph Muktafi (902–908) subsequently managed to re-impose his control over Egypt and Syria in 905, when the Tulunids were betrayed by the commander of the Egyptian army, the empire clearly seemed to be coming apart at the seams.

To the north, a new and aggressive ruler, Basil I (867–886), mounted the Byzantine throne. Since Heraclius' withdrawal behind the Taurus Mountains in the seventh century, the Arabs had maintained effective control of the strategic passes, the most important of which was the Cilician Gates leading from Heraclea to Tarsus. This enabled them to raid into Anatolia virtually at will. Basil was determined to change this situation and succeeded in occupying and fortifying the Taurus passes. Then, in 879, a Byzantine army swept down from the mountains into the Jazira and laid waste the countryside, reestablishing a Graeco-Roman presence there for the first time in 200 years.

With Basil's death in 886, the situation along the frontier became frozen until the accession of Constantine VII Porphyrogenitus (913–959) to the Byzantine throne. The Byzantines then renewed the drive to regain their former position in Syria, and incursions across the Taurus became an annual summer event. The Abbasids were in no position to offer any effective opposition to them. What remaining strength the dynasty had was sapped by the revolt of the Qarmatians that had broken out in Arabia in 900. The Qarmatians (the followers of Hamdan Qarmat) were a puritanical and equalitarian sect whose rising was in large measure a reaction to the imposition of Persian despotism and Turkish militarism on the Arabs. The following year, the Qarmatians took Homs and Hama, and placed Damascus under siege, establishing their control over most of Syria. They then turned southward and seized the Yemen. In 906, the Qarmatians captured Kufa and threatened Baghdad itself. Although the caliph Muktafi soon blunted the Qarmatian drive and managed to suppress the movement, he was unable to regain control of the Arabian Peninsula, where an independent state arose in the region of Bahrain. His authority was severely damaged and he was unable to reestablish it unequivocally in what remained of the empire.

A new and serious challenge to the Abbasids, the full implications of which were not to be fully understood for some two decades, arose in Syria about 890 in the person of Muhammad al-Habib, a Shiite of the Ismaili sect who claimed descent from Ali and Fatima. He announced the coming of a redeemer, the Mahdi, who would restore the caliphate to the house of Ali.

Muhammad al-Habib gained some adherents among the Berbers of North Africa who, under the leadership of one Abu Abdullah, defeated the last of the Aghlabids in Tunisia in 909 and took over their capital at Raqqadah. The following year, Muhammad's son Ubaidallah (909–934) fled to Africa where he portrayed himself as the awaited Mahdi, claimed the caliphate, and began a campaign of conquest that soon brought him as far west as Morocco. In 914, Ubaidallah turned eastward and marched on Egypt and, for a short period, occupied Alexandria and the Fayyum region. In 921, his son Abul-Qasim extended his rule as far south as Upper Egypt before being defeated decisively by the forces of the caliph Muqtadir (908–932), ending the threat from the emerging Fatimid dynasty for the moment.

NOTES

1. William Muir, *The Caliphate: Its Rise, Decline and Fall*, p. 480.
2. John B. Glubb, *The Empire of the Arabs*, p. 349.
3. al-Tabari, *The Reign of al-Mu'tasim*, pp. 58–59.

4

Abbasid Decline and Imperial Disintegration

At the eastern extremity of the Abbasid Empire, a new power emerged from Sistan, in southeastern Persia, in the person of Yakub ibn Leith as-Saffar (867–878). After making himself master of his native province, Yakub moved north and crossed the frontier into Khorasan in 867, wresting control of Herat away from the Tahirid ruler Muhammad (862–873). He then appealed to the caliph Mutazz for appointment as governor of neighboring Kerman to the west. His application was contested by Ali ibn Hasan, the son of the warlord of Fars (Persis), who had similar aspirations. Ali attempted to preempt the possibility of an unfavorable decision by occupying the capital of Kerman before Yakub could reach it. The forces of Ali were subsequently defeated by Yakub, who then decided to bypass Kerman and head for the richer province of Fars. He took its main center, Shiraz, in April 869, but withdrew later that year because he simply wasn't capable of sustaining an occupation of the province. However, Yakub's growing power became a matter of concern in Baghdad, and the caliph Mutamid, in an attempt to channel Yakub's ambitions, formally designated him as lord of Kerman, Sistan, and Balkh. Mutamid also urged him to direct his attention to the conquest of the pagan lands farther to the east on behalf of the caliphate, hoping thereby to keep him away from Fars, which was much too close to Iraq for comfort.

In the meanwhile, the autonomous Tahirid dynasty that had ruled Khorasan since 821 was beginning to disintegrate. Hasan ibn Zaid, the ruler of Tabaristan (Mazanderan), seized control of Gurgan (Hyrcania), while other local chiefs began to nibble away at the fringes of the Tahirid realm. At this point, Yakub decided that the time was ripe to take what remained of Khorasan away from its Tahirid ruler, Muhammad. The grandees of the Tahirid state had become quite disenchanted with Muhammad and were unwilling to fight to ensure the survival of his regime. Yakub was therefore able to march unopposed into Nishapur in August 873 and put an end to the Tahirid dynasty in Khorasan. The next year he defeated Hasan ibn Zaid of Tabaristan and added that province to his rapidly growing empire as well. Alarmed at his movement westward, the caliph tried to undermine Yakub by challenging his legitimacy. He disseminated propaganda throughout the territories under Yakub's control, by means of pilgrims returning there from Mecca, to the effect that Yakub was a usurper and therefore did not merit the loyalty and obedience of the peoples he ruled. The net effect of this was that Yakub decided to invade Fars in the summer of 875. At that point, the regime in Baghdad went into panic out of fear that Yakub would join forces with the Zenj rebels, with whom he had begun negotiations. Fortunately for the caliphate, Yakub found that he was unable to agree to an alliance with the Zenj for practical reasons. They were considered by many to be Muslim heretics and he was evidently unwilling to risk having an alliance directed against the caliph tainted by charges of heresy. He therefore marched on Baghdad alone in 876. For his part, Mutamid declared a holy war against Yakub and went out to confront the Saffarid forces with a far superior army that he had managed to raise. After a fierce but indecisive battle, Yakub was compelled to retreat to nearby Susiana, where he set up his headquarters.

Under Yakub's brother and successor, Amr ibn Laith (879–901), the Saffarid Empire soon became a victim of his unbridled ambition. After a period of very troubled relations with the caliphate, Amr emerged stronger than ever and began to petition the caliph Mutadid (892–902) to grant him a charter for the lands of Transoxiana, traditionally considered a dependency of Khorasan. Mutadid, who became increasingly concerned about Amr's growing power, saw this as a golden opportunity to cut the Saffarids down to size. In February 898, the caliph sent the requested tokens of investiture to Amr. At the same time, however, he contrived to instigate a conflict between the Saffarids and the Samanids, who had actually ruled Transoxiana for some time and had transformed it into a relatively prosperous region. It has been suggested that Mutadid not only reconfirmed Samanid rule over Transoxiana, but also asked for their assistance in eliminating Saffarid control of Khorasan.

When Amr sent an army across the Oxus in October 898, it was soundly defeated. Then, when he decided to take to the field personally, against the advice of his counselors, Amr suffered another defeat at the hands of the Samanid Ismail and was taken captive in April 900. Amr was sent as a prisoner to Baghdad, where the caliph had him murdered the following year. Khorasan now came under Samanid rule, although the Saffarids continued to be a significant power in Sistan and Kerman for another decade.

The Samanids originated from a Persian family of Balkh (Bactria) that had accepted Islam in the early eighth century. Around 819, the four grandsons of the founder of the dynasty, Samankhudat, were installed as governors of Samarkand, Ferghana, Shash, and Herat by the caliph Mamun, under the overlordship of the Tahirid rulers of Khorasan. The Samanid governor of Ferghana, Ahmed, soon gained control of Samarkand as well, and he later turned both over to his son Nasr (874–892), who was given command of all Transoxiana by the caliph in 875 and then made his brother Ismail the ruler of Bukhara. It was Ismail (892–907) who intervened in Khorasan against the Saffarids. However, instead of handing the province back to the Abbasids, he established Samanid rule over Khorasan, which lasted for a century. In 902 he also added Tabaristan, including Rai and Qazvin, to his growing domain.

As Baghdad, which had become the capital once again in 892, continued to decline in importance as the center of Abbasid culture, Bukhara rose to great prominence as a center of Muslim civilization under the Samanid rulers Nasr II (913–942) and Nuh I (942–954). During the reign of Nasr, control over the Samanid domains was consolidated and his reach expanded even farther to include Tashkent. The Samanids, however, trod the same path as the Abbasids and suffered a similar fate. They too became dependent on an army of Turkish recruits who soon became its officers and administrators. Indeed, by the end of the reign of Abd al-Malik I (954–961), a Turk, Alptigin, had been made supreme commander in Khorasan and, as will be seen later, set in motion a series of events that soon brought the Samanid dynasty to an end.

During this same period, the Dailamite tribesmen of the Elburz Mountains in northern Persia, who had been converted to Shiite Islam and were extremely hostile to the Abbasids, broke out of their mountain strongholds in 913 and began to plunder the region from Qazvin to Rai. When Baghdad proved unable to stop them, they extended their sway as far as Hamadan. In 932, the Dailamites, now under the leadership of the Buwayhid or Buyid family, seized Isfahan, moved into Fars, and made themselves masters of all Persia west of the Salt Desert. Joined by his brothers, one of which took control of Media, Ahmed ibn Buwaih also conquered Kerman and established the Buwayhid capital at Shiraz. In the meanwhile, the security situation in Baghdad under the caliphs Radi (932–940) and Muttaqi (940–943) had deteriorated to the point where it was ripe for outside intervention to restore some semblance of order. In 945 Ahmed ibn Buwaih marched into Baghdad unopposed and took control of the city. The caliph Mustakfi (943–946) was compelled to acknowledge his authority and to award him the honorary title of Muizz ad-Dowla. Ahmed, however, was not satisfied with the power-sharing arrangement and, at the end of January 946, broke into the palace, blinded the caliph, and threw him into prison where he died five years later. He then appointed Muti (946–974), the son of the caliph

Muqtadir, as caliph on the condition that he remain in the palace and make no attempt to interfere in the running of the government. Henceforth, it was the Buwayhids who actually ruled in Baghdad. However, the Buwayhid capital remained in Shiraz, which now replaced Baghdad as the real power center of the empire.

The assumption of power by the Buwayhids in Iraq had other significant consequences as well. In 890, Hamdan, the emir of the Arab Taghlib tribe, seized the fortress of Mardin in the Jazira and used it as a base for the establishment of an independent dynasty. In 905, his son Abu al-Hayja was made governor of Mosul under the nominal authority of the caliph Muqtadir and ruled there until his death in 929. His son and successor Hasan extended Hamdanid control over virtually all of Mesopotamia and northern Syria. Then, in 941, when the caliph Muttaqi was forced to flee Baghdad and seek refuge in Mosul because of incursions from Khuzistan by the Baridi brothers, who held control of the province, the Hamdanids became the power behind the caliphate. Hasan was given the title of Nasir ad-Dowla, while his brother Alim became known as Saif ad-Dowla. However, when the Buwayhids entered Baghdad in 945, they subjugated the Hamdanids who then became their vassals.

The Hamdanid Saif ad-Dowla, dissatisfied with his now subordinate status in Iraq, decided to move into Syria, which was at the time under the control of the Turkish ruler of Egypt, Muhammad ibn Tughj (935–946). The latter had come to Egypt in 935 and within two years became sufficiently powerful to receive the princely title of Ikhshid from the caliph Radi. Wishing to distance himself from the growing anarchy in Iraq, he sought to secure control of the land approaches to Egypt. He was able to demand and obtain from the caliph a grant legitimizing his seizure of the Sinai and Palestine as far north as Ramle. Before long, Muhammad ibn Tughj attempted to insulate himself further from the machinations of the mamluk generals in Baghdad by extending his frontiers into both Syria and Arabia. In 941, the caliph Muttaqi formally recognized the Ikhshidid viceroyalty over Egypt and Syria, as well as over Mecca and Medina. Thus it happened, at the same time that Muhammad ibn Tughj was attempting to consolidate his position in Syria, that Saif ad-Dowla was moving into the country to escape control by the Buwayhids. The two met in confrontation at Damascus and Saif ad-Dowla was forced to withdraw to the north. As a result, Saif ad-Dowla had to be satisfied with control of Aleppo and northern Syria, which placed him squarely on the troubled frontier with the Byzantines, with whom he soon became involved in a lifelong struggle. Indeed, for the next two decades, it was Saif ad-Dowla alone that blocked the southward thrust of the increasingly aggressive Byzantines.

Nicephorus Phocas (963–969) had faced Saif ad-Dowla more than once since he had become commander in chief of the Byzantine army in the East in 954. Six years later, while he was engaged in the re-conquest of Crete, Saif ad-Dowla mounted a massive incursion into Anatolia, raiding and looting virtually unopposed for several weeks until his army was trapped and decimated by Nicephorus' brother Leo. Saif ad-Dowla just barely escaped capture. Then, in 962, Nicephorus Phocas crossed the Taurus frontier and invaded and conquered most of Cilicia. He also seized the Amanus range to protect Cilicia from the south, and then set out for Aleppo, circling around the army that Saif ad-Dowla had sent against him. Aleppo fell to the Byzantines before the end of that year, and was thoroughly looted before they withdrew behind the Amanus.

Nicephorus had not yet reached Cappadocian Caesarea when the death of Romanus II in March 963 was announced, and he was proclaimed emperor by his officers. As Byzantine emperor, he became determined to undertake the re-conquest of Syria. In 965, a Byzantine expedition under the patrician Niketas re-conquered Cyprus, ending the Arab occupation of the island after seventy-seven years. With Cyprus under Byzantine control, the maritime approaches to the Cilician coast were now secure. Nicephorus then sent an army to conquer the Muslim emirates of Mopsuestia and Tarsus, which had been bypassed in the earlier invasion of Cilicia. He emptied Tarsus of its Muslim population and resettled it with Christians, mostly Armenians. After these initial successes, Nicephorus became distracted by wars in Sicily and Bulgaria for several years, giving the Hamdanids and Aleppo a brief respite.

When Saif ad-Dowla died in 967 all opposition of any consequence to Byzantine expansion southward ceased. The Buwayhids, having completely written off Syria, never even attempted to deter or repel the Byzantine incursions. As a consequence of these onslaughts from the north, a power vacuum was created in Syria and along the Euphrates that resulted in the emergence of a number of increasingly independent principalities, in addition to that of Aleppo. The Euphrates valley in the region of Kufa came under the rule of the Beni Mizyed, the ruling house of the Beni Asad tribe, while Mosul and the southern Jazira came under the control of the Beni Uqail. The ancient strategic crossroad city of Harran was ruled by the Beni Numair, and northern Jazira came under the control of a Kurdish emir, Ibn Marwan.

After the death of Muhammad ibn Tughj in 946, the situation in Egypt and southern Syria remained relatively secure and stable for another two decades. His faithful retainer, the Ethiopian eunuch Kafur, promptly took over control of the Ikhshidid regime on behalf of Muhammad ibn Tughj's sons and heirs. He managed to successfully defend both Egypt and Syria against the Fatimids and Hamdanids respectively, who sought to take advantage of the traditional weakness of a regime during the transition period to a new reign. However, with Kafur's death in 968, the situation changed dramatically. The eleven-year-old Ikhshidid heir Ahmed abu al-Fawaris (968–969) succeeded him and simply was incapable of dealing with the challenges confronting him in the north from the Hamdanids, in the east from the resurgent Qarmatians, and, most important, in the west from the Fatimids who had proclaimed their own caliphate.

The Fatimid caliph Muizz (952–975) took advantage of the loss of effective leadership in Egypt with the death of Kafur to resume the long-delayed campaign of conquest. In February 969, his general Jahwar, a former Greek slave, set out from Tunisia with an army and marched on Alexandria, which submitted without a fight. In June of that year, an Egyptian army made a feeble effort to stop Jahwar but was easily defeated in a battle near the pyramids at Gizah. Egypt thus came under Fatimid rule almost without a struggle, and was to be ruled by that dynasty for the next 200 years from Cairo, which was established as the new capital of the country in 973.

Egypt experienced a long period of relatively stable government under the Tulunids, Ikhshidids, and now the Fatimids. During this same period, there emerged a number of independent and apparently solidly based principalities in southwestern Arabia, at a time when the rest of the Middle East had been embroiled in seemingly continuous turbulence for nearly a century, beginning with the Zenj Rebellion of 869. The relative stability that prevailed in the Red Sea region resulted in a dramatic change in the pattern of international trade and commerce, with far-reaching consequences. Trade between the Indian Ocean and the Mediterranean began to bypass almost entirely the troubled Persian Gulf region and once again shifted back to the ancient Red Sea maritime and coastal routes, making Egypt the major entrepôt for the trade passing from Asia to Europe. This gave renewed commercial importance to the coastal strip of Palestine and ancient Phoenicia, and brought an economic revival to Syria. In addition to its traditional strategic interests in control of the approaches to the country from Asia, Egypt now sought to gain undisputed control of the African-Asian land bridge and the caravan routes passing through it, as well as the ports along its Mediterranean coastline. With Syria itself in political disarray as a consequence of the Byzantine incursions and the collapse of Ikhshidid power in the south, the attempts by the autonomous rulers of Damascus to stop the Fatimids from proceeding north into Syria soon proved fruitless. Palestine and central Syria were soon added to the growing Fatimid Empire.

The death of Kafur in 968, and the subsequent collapse of Ikhshidid power, also set in motion significant developments in northern Syria. That same year, having already secured control of Cilicia and Cyprus, the latter protecting his flank from attack from the sea, Nicephorus Phocas turned to the East once more with a massive invasion of Syria from Anatolia. Initially bypassing Antioch, he laid waste the coastal region from Tarsus as far south as Tripoli, sacking Latakia, Homs, and Hama before returning to Antioch, which was thenceforth to remain in Byzantine hands for more than a century. Yahya of Antioch, an eleventh-century historian, wrote: "The incursions of Nicephorus became a pleasure for his soldiers, for nobody attacked them or opposed them; he marched wherever he pleased, and destroyed whatever he liked, without encountering any Muslim, or anyone else who would divert him and prevent him from doing that which he wished. . . . Nobody could resist him."[1]

At the same time, the Hamdanid heir in Aleppo, Saad ad-Dowla (967–991), was faced with a challenge from a cousin, Abu Firas al-Harith, who sought to set up an independent dynasty in Homs. He was ultimately defeated and killed by Qarghuwayh, Saad ad-Dowla's Turkish mamluk, who soon seized power in Aleppo himself. Saad ad-Dowla withdrew to his territory in the Jazira while another of his mamluks, Zuhayr, went to war against Qarghuwayh on his behalf. When he came to believe that the security of his position in Aleppo was threatened, Qarghuwayh appealed to Nicephorus for help. The emperor, intent on further asserting his sway in northern Syria, was only too pleased to oblige and marched on Aleppo. At his approach, Saad ad-Dowla's army abandoned its assault on the city and withdrew farther south. Nicephorus, however, seized the opportunity presented and entered Aleppo himself in 969, forcing Qarghuwayh to agree to humiliating peace terms in exchange for a Byzantine withdrawal. According to Ibn al-Adim:

It was specified that Qarghuwayh, and after him Bakjur [his mamluk], would be the emirs of the Moslems. After them, the Byzantine emperor would choose an emir from among the inhabitants of Aleppo; the Moslems themselves would not have the right to elevate anyone [to this position]. . . . Should a Moslem army arrive there with the purpose of raiding Byzantine territory, Qarghuwayh was to stop it and say: "proceed from elsewhere, and do not enter the territory of the peace." . . . Should the emperor or [his] army commander undertake to raid the land of Islam, Bakjur was to meet them at an appointed place and escort them through the localities [covered by] the peace. . . . Should the Byzantines raid a non-Moslem community, the emir was to assist them with his own troops. . . . Byzantine caravans proceeding to Aleppo . . . [had to be properly] escorted and compensated for any losses suffered because of brigandage.[2]

Aleppo was thus transformed, at least for the moment, into a Byzantine vassal state. However, the treaty was subsequently repudiated by Saad ad-Dowla, and was scrapped entirely when he regained independent control of Aleppo in 977.

Shortly after his withdrawal from Aleppo, Nicephorus Phocas was overthrown and murdered by his nephew John Tzimisces (969–976). Preoccupied in the north for the next several years, John did not return to the Middle East until 974, when he invaded the Jazira and marched down the Tigris to the gates of Baghdad. The city was saved when the caliph and the Buwayhid chief of the palace offered to pay a large indemnity and an annual tribute in return for his withdrawal. In the following year John swept across the Jazira again, taking Nisibis and Edessa, and then marched into

Syria and Palestine, conquering Damascus, Tiberias, Nazareth, Acre, Sidon, and Beirut. As one Byzantine chronicler wrote: "All nations were horror-stricken by the attacks of John Tzimisces; he enlarged the land of the Romans; the Saracens and Armenians fled, the Persians feared him; and people from all sides carried gifts to him, beseeching him to make peace with them; he marched as far as Edessa and the River Euphrates, and the earth became filled with Roman armies; Syria and Phoenicia were trampled by Roman horses and he achieved great victories."[3]

The Byzantines, however, were unable to retain their hold on the territories because of their lack of the manpower needed for a permanent occupation force. Accordingly, they had to satisfy themselves with sacking and wasting the country mercilessly, and with taking large numbers of women and children as captives to be sold in the slave markets. Fortunately for Syria, the succeeding Byzantine emperor Basil II (976–1025) was too preoccupied with long wars against the Bulgarians to give much attention to Asia. The toll exacted by the Byzantine depredations on Syria and its people was horrendous. In 985, the Arab writer Muqaddasi observed: "The people of Syria live in terror of the Greeks, who have driven many from their homes and devastated the country districts."[4]

At the same time, Hamdanid Syria was faced with encroachment from the expanding Fatimid Empire to its south. Said ad-Dowla (991–1001) was forced to appeal to Basil for aid in stopping the Fatimid advance. The appeal struck a responsive chord since the Byzantine emperor had no interest in seeing the frontier region falling under the control of a more powerful adversary than the Hamdanids. Basil rushed a relief force of some 17,000 men to Aleppo in 995 to assist in its defense. The Byzantine intervention was successful and the Fatimids were forced to abandon their siege of the city. They returned to the Orontes valley in 999, and Basil intervened once again, this time forcing the Fatimid caliph Hakim (996–1021) to sign a peace treaty in 1001 that confirmed Hamdanid independence in Aleppo.

Said ad-Dowla died or was murdered that same year and his guardian Lulu, ostensibly acting as regent for Said's sons who were subsequently sent to Cairo in 1003, usurped the throne. When Lulu died in 1009, his son Mansur attempted to mount the throne but was opposed by a brother of Said ad-Dowla, Abu al-Hayja. The Fatimids exploited the opportunity presented by this succession crisis and dispatched a force to support the claim of Mansur, in return for which he recognized Hakim as suzerain over Aleppo. This act brought the Hamdanid dynasty in northern Syria to an end. The Fatimids subsequently abandoned Mansur and supported his opponents when his rule was challenged by a rebellion in 1012. Mansur was forced to flee for his life to the Byzantines in 1015, and Aleppo finally came under direct Fatimid rule.

The nominal Abbasid Empire was coming apart on all its fronts, and the Buwayhids clearly were incapable of preventing disintegration or even maintaining public order as it took place. The power of the Buwayhids had reached its high point under Adud ad-Dowla (949–983). In 977, he succeeded in uniting the several petty kingdoms that had arisen under Buwayhid rulers in Persia and Iraq, forming them into a single large state that stretched from the Caspian to the Persian Gulf and from Isfahan to the Syrian frontier. Adud ad-Dowla sought to enhance the prospects for the dynasty by linking it through marriage to the Abbasids, thereby creating the possibility of a Buwayhid becoming a legitimate candidate for the caliphate. Accordingly, he married the daughter of the caliph Ta'i (974–991), and had the caliph marry his own daughter. However, Adud's sons, Sharaf ad-Dowla (983–989), Baha ad-Dowla (989–1012), and Samsam ad-Dowla, became involved in a series of internecine struggles that, coupled with the continuing squabbles among their descendants, soon effectively destroyed the Buwayhid Empire.

THE RISE OF THE GHAZNAVIDS

The fate that awaited the Buwayhids had already struck the Samanids. With the death of the Samanid Abd al-Malik in 961, Alptigin, the Turkish commander of his forces in Khorasan, attempted a coup that would have placed his own candidate on the throne. The attempt failed and Alptigin prudently decided to withdraw to the eastern fringes of Khorasan. With a contingent of loyal followers, he laid siege to the Afghan citadel of Ghazni, which fell four months later, and established himself there as the Samanid governor (961–963). Some fifteen years later, his mamluk and son-in-law, Subuktigin (977–997), was chosen by the Turkish soldiery to become governor, thereby setting the stage for a new dynasty to emerge. Once established in the position, Subuktigin began to build an autonomous power base in Ghazni, although he remained nominally subordinate to the Samanids. He conducted successful expansionist campaigns against India, and forced King Jaypal of the Punjab to cede the strategic border area of Kabul, which controlled the passes through the mountains into the rich Indian plain.

Subsequently, during the reign of the Samanid Nuh II (977–997), which coincided with Subuktigin's own period of office, one of Nuh's Persian military barons, Abu Ali, rebelled, setting in motion a series of events that had dramatic consequences for the eastern marches of the Middle East. Abu Ali appealed for help against Nuh to the chief of the Qara-Khanid Turks, Bughra-khan Harun, who ruled at Balasagun on the Chu River in Central Asia. Bughra-khan responded positively and mounted an expedition that reached Bukhara in May 992, but he soon withdrew back into Turkestan. However, to counter the threat from the Qara-Khanids, Nuh appealed for assistance from Subuktigin, who promptly agreed to help and effectively established a Ghaznavid protectorate over Khorasan, making his son Mahmud commander of the army there in 994. Upon Subuktigin's death in 997, Mahmud (998–1030) made himself the effective ruler of all the lands previously governed by his father as a Samanid vassal. He then demanded that Mansur II (997–999), who had succeeded Nuh in Bukhara as head of the Samanids, relinquish his title to Khorasan. However, before Mansur could work out an accommodation with Mahmud, he was deposed and blinded by his own mutinous mamluks in February 999, in favor of his brother Abd al-Malik II. This presented Mahmud with the opportunity to exploit the confused situation to his advantage. He now rose to the defense of the incapacitated Mansur as the legitimate Samanid ruler, and inflicted a decisive defeat on the Samanid army that supported Abd al-Malik at Merv in May 999. As a practical matter, this brought an end to the Samanid dynasty in Khorasan as well as in Transoxiana. In October 999, Mahmud sought to obtain legitimacy for his power grab by declaring his allegiance to the caliph in Baghdad. In the words of one writer, Mahmud of Ghazni had "a devouring ambition, and the temper of a zealot. . . . Mahmud was a staunch Muslim, and if his campaigns against the idolators brought him rich store of treasure and captives, it was in his eyes no more than the fit reward of piety. . . . The caliph of Baghdad [al-Qadir], who had probably outgrown such illusions, was not the man to baulk a willing sword. He sent Mahmud his pontifical sanction and the official diploma of investiture as rightful lord of Ghazni and Khurasan."[5] Along with the caliph's imprimatur that gave his regime the aura of legitimacy in the Muslim world that he needed as a matter of practical politics, Mahmud received the honorific title of Yamin ad-Dowla.

In the meantime, Abd al-Malik had flown to Bukhara, hoping to continue the Samanid dynasty there. However, it was already too late to salvage the Samanid state. The final blow was delivered by the Qara-Khanid Ahmed Arslan Khan (998–1014), who took Bukhara in October 999, made Abd al-Malik a prisoner, and annexed Transoxiana. Ismail al-Muntasir (1000–1004), the last of the Samanids, attempted unsuccessfully to restore the fortunes of the dynasty and was killed around 1004. Ahmed Arslan soon reached an accord with Mahmud of Ghazni that established the Oxus as the common boundary of their adjoining realms. According to one assessment of these developments:

The events of this year 999 in the land of Beyond-the-River [Transoxiana] were of world significance. From time immemorial, the land between the Oxus and the Jaxartes [Syr Darya] had been disputed between the Persian (or Aryan) race and the Turanian or Turkish. In the days of Cyrus and Darius the Persians had held the line of the Jaxartes. In the days of Chosroes, immediately before Islam, the boundary of Persia had been west of the Oxus, but Beyond-the-River had been a neutral area, ruled by a number of local dynasties. . . . In this year, 999, the great Turkish advance began. It was to end seven hundred years later beneath the walls of Vienna. For the first time, in the person of Mahmood of Ghazna, a Turkish chief was ruling East Persia, while Trans-Oxiana under the Qara Khans became virtually incorporated in Turkestan.[6]

Mahmud continued to expand the Ghaznavid state. In 1001, he conquered Kabulistan, which he followed with the seizure of Kashmir and the Punjab in 1004 and 1005. However, he was constantly under threat from the Qara-Khanids who looked with envy upon the increasingly magnificent Indo-Persian empire Mahmud was building from Ghazni. Thus, while Mahmud was occupied in India, the Qara-Khanid Ahmed Arslan Khan invaded Khorasan in 1006 and sacked Balkh and Nishapur. Forced to abandon his campaign in India, Mahmud returned and defeated the Qara-Khanids near Balkh in January 1008. Following this, he launched another series of campaigns in India that lasted until 1025. Before he was through, Mahmud had extended the Ghaznavid frontier as far as the Ganges and the Malwa Rivers. To some extent, the security of his Central Asian flank was improved as a consequence of the attacks on the Qara-Khanid rear by the Khitan kings of China who had sent an army into Kashgaria in 1017. Although these attacks were successfully repelled, they distracted the Qara-Khanids from their protracted warfare along the Ghaznavid frontier. In 1025, Mahmud returned from India to deal with yet another Qara-Khanid threat from Ahmed Toghan Khan (1024–1026) who had invaded Transoxiana. Ahmed Toghan withdrew at Mahmud's approach but returned with an army the following year and reoccupied Bukhara and Samarkand, while Mahmud was engaged farther west in the defeat of the Buwayhid Majd ad-Dowla (997–1029) at Rai, and in the conquest of Georgia. It was already evident that the seemingly irrepressible flow of peoples and armies from Central Asia would have a major impact on the history of the broader region.

NOTES

1. A. A. Vasiliev, *History of the Byzantine Empire*, vol. 1, p. 309.

2. Kamal S. Salibi, *Syria under Islam*, p. 71.

3. Vasiliev, *History of the Byzantine Empire*, vol. 1, pp. 310–311.

4. John B. Glubb, *A Short History of the Arab Peoples*, p. 127.

5. Stanley Lane-Poole, *Medieval India under Mohammedan Rule 712–1764*, pp. 17–18.

6. Glubb, *The Course of Empire*, pp. 101–102.

5

The Rise of the Seljukids

Seljuk, chief of a clan of the Turkish tribe of the Oghuz, moved from the Kirghiz steppe in Central Asia to Jand in about 970. Jand was a border town situated on the frontier between the lands of the Turks and Muslims in the area where the Syr Darya (Jaxartes) empties into the Aral Sea. Here Seljuk, who was a politically astute and ambitious leader, decided to abandon the traditional shamanism of the Turks and adopt Islam. Obtaining support for his conversion and that of his loyalists from the religious officials of nearby Muslim countries such as Bukhara and Khwarizm, Seljuk maneuvered himself into a position where he was able to refuse to pay taxes to nonbelievers such as the Oghuz officials in Jand.

Establishing what amounted to an independent government on the frontiers of Samanid Transoxiana, Seljuk's clan soon became involved in the wars between the Persian Samanids and the Turkish Qara-Khanids. About 992, Seljuk's son Israil (Arslan) led the clan in support of the Samanids, attacking the Qara-Khanid ruler Bughra-khan Harun in Transoxiana. Nonetheless, time was running out for the Samanids. In November 999, Bukhara was taken by the Qara-Khanid Ilig-khan Nasr effectively wiping out the Samanid state. The Seljukids formed a brief alliance with the Samanid Abu Ibrahim al-Muntasir and continued the struggle with the Qara-Khanids, inflicting a series of defeats on them in August 1003 and June 1004. After breaking with al-Muntasir, the Seljukids effectively took control of the Samanid lands in Khorasan, using them as the basis for the empire they would build over the next several years.

Once established in the former Samanid territory, the Seljukids began raiding ever more deeply into the region and soon reached as far to the west as Azerbaijan and the Jazira. In 1016, Israil's son Chaghri Beg led an incursion into eastern Anatolia that lasted several years, after defeating the Armenian forces near Lake Van. Then, in cooperation with the Qara-Khanid Ali-Tegin, Israil seized Bukhara in 1020–1021. The Ghaznavids watched the irrepressibility of the Seljukid depredations in neighboring Khorasan with increasing apprehension. It would only be a matter of time before the two clashed.

In 1025, a meeting was held in Transoxiana between the khagan of the Qara-Khanids, Yusuf Qadir Khan, and the sultan of the Ghaznavids, Mahmud. It was decided to have the Seljukids rounded up and transferred away from Turkestan and Transoxiana before they caused any more problems to the Ghaznavid state. Following this agreement, Israil was apparently lured to Samarkand, arrested, and sent into exile in India where he died in 1032. The sudden collapse of authority among the Seljukids resulted in their being scattered throughout the surrounding territories. However, it was at best a temporary reprieve for the Ghaznavids. By 1029, Israil's brother Mikail was able to reconstitute the Seljukids as a cohesive force and to challenge the Ghaznavids for control of Khorasan. Within a few years, the Seljukids shocked the Ghaznavids by being able to inflict a serious defeat on them for the first time at Nasa in 1035. This development forced the Ghaznavids to attempt to reach an accommodation with the Seljukids by offering them three provinces in Khorasan as part of a treaty that included a grant of tribal autonomy within the Ghaznavid state. The Seljukids, however, were not to be bought off in this manner and continued to raid as far as Balkh and Sistan.

The Ghaznavids were apparently unable to cope effectively with the hit-and-run tactics of the weaker but more mobile Seljukids, who avoided pitched battles whenever possible and had no reluctance whatever to retreat immediately upon being confronted by superior enemy forces. This put the Ghaznavids at a distinct disadvantage. The mobility of the Ghaznavid army was severely hampered by its heavy dependence on fixed bases in the larger towns, where their supplies and war materiel were concentrated. The Seljukids, on the other hand, simply bypassed these strongpoints, making no attempts at siege warfare for which they were ill equipped. Instead, they ravaged the outlying oases, cutting off the food supplies and starving the cities and fortified towns into submission. The Seljukids are reported to have argued in their deliberations regarding the prosecution of their conflict with Masud (1030–1040), Mahmud's son and successor as sultan of Ghazni: "It is unwise to seek a pitched battle with this sovereign. Let us keep to our own way [of fighting] and not be burdened with baggage and impedimenta. In this way we will gain the preponderance. We will not disperse, unless some difficulty arises, so let him go backwards or go forwards, just as he wishes. Winter has passed and summer has begun; we are steppe-dwellers and are well able to endure extremes of heat and cold, whereas he and his army cannot, and after suffering this distress for a while, will have to turn back."[1]

Seljuk's grandson, Tughril Beg Muhammad (1037–1063), with the help of his brother Chaghri Beg, inflicted a second major defeat on the Ghaznavids near Sarakhs in May 1038, with many of Masud's *ghulams* (slave soldiers) defecting to fight with their Oghuz kinsmen. In effect, this victory not only gave the Seljukids complete control of Khorasan, but also it gave them political independence and sovereignty in the territory, the Ghaznavids having been driven entirely out of the country. When Masud, who had gone off to conquer India, found out what had taken place in Khorasan, he quickly marched toward Sarakhs with an army of some 50,000 troops and 300 war elephants. Seriously outnumbered, the Seljukids were forced to withdraw to the desert from which they conducted a hit-and-run war of attrition that bled the Ghaznavid army, which was unprepared for a desert campaign. Ultimately lured into the desert in the spring of 1040, the Ghaznavid army, under the command of Masud, soon found itself without water as the Seljukids destroyed the wells and continued their relentless attacks. It was not long before the toll of casualties and morale reached the point where the Seljukids felt that they were ready to challenge the Ghaznavids in open battle. Between May 22–24, the two armies clashed at the fortress of Dandanqan near Merv. The Seljukids emerged victorious after destroying a large part of the Ghaznavid forces, and proclaimed Tughril Beg as sultan of the new Seljukid state.

Although Masud managed to escape with a small number of his men, they murdered him while he was trying to reach India. Taking advantage of the dynastic succession struggles that broke out among the aspirants to the Ghaznavid throne, which inhibited their ability to mount an adequate defense of their northern territories, Tughril Beg's forces were soon able to seize Khwarizm (Khiva) and Tabaristan as well. In 1043 he took control of most of northern Persia, eliminating the Buwayhids, and established the headquarters of the Seljukid clan first at Rai (Tehran) and later at Isfahan after it was captured in 1051.

In the meantime, the Byzantine emperor Constantine IX Monomachus (1042–1055), following the expansionist policy of his predecessors, sent an army to the Caucasus with instructions to stop the Seljukid raids that were destabilizing the region. In response, Tughril Beg dispatched an army under Qutalmish (Qutlumush) to challenge the Byzantines. The armies clashed near Ganja in 1046, with the Byzantines experiencing their first defeat at Seljukid hands. Ganja was placed under siege, but the Seljukids were unable to compel its surrender. Breaking off what was apparently a fruitless siege, Qutalmish joined forces with another army dispatched by Tughril Beg to challenge a large Byzantine force reinforced by Georgian and Abkhazian troops at Hasan-Kale in the plain of Erzerum in September 1048. Once again, the Byzantines were defeated. Erzerum was occupied and the Seljukids now had access to the entire area between Lake Van and Trebizond, on the Black Sea coast. As a consequence of these setbacks at the hands of the Seljukids, Constantine Monomachus was forced to reach an accommodation with Tughril Beg. According to the treaty agreed to in 1050, the emperor undertook to repair the mosque in Constantinople and allow the *khutba* (the Friday sermon) to be read in the name of the Seljukid sultan. The sultan's name was invoked in the mosques of Ganja and Tabriz in Azerbaijan as well by 1054.

Observing the rise of this new power in the east from his vantage point in Baghdad, the caliph Qaim (1031–1075) saw this development as an opportunity to replace the declining Buwayhids with the Seljukids as protectors of the caliphate. Aside from the practical consideration that there appeared to be no way of stopping the westward advance of the Seljukids, making it politically necessary to reach some accommodation with them, the matter of their religious orientation was a particularly significant factor in this decision. The Buwayhids were Shiites. Consequently, for more than a century the Abbasid caliphs had suffered the humiliation of being under the control of people who fundamentally rejected the very legitimacy of their caliphate. The Seljukids, on the other hand, were mainstream Sunni Muslims who fully accepted the appropriateness of Abbasid primacy. In January 1055, at the invitation of the caliph, Tughril Beg arrived in Baghdad even though the last of the Buwayhid princes, Malik ar-Rahim (1048–1055), was still in nominal control of the city.

An incident involving the death of several Seljukid soldiers in Baghdad served as justification for a confrontation with the Buwayhids, and Tughril Beg issued an ultimatum demanding Malik ar-Rahim's surrender. The latter was in no position to defend the city against the overwhelmingly superior Seljukid forces, and had no choice but to yield. He was subsequently sent to a prison in Rai where he died in 1058, bringing an end to the Buwayhid dynasty. Tughril Beg and the Seljukids became protectors of the caliphate and the effective rulers of what remained of the Abbasid Empire, while their Oghuz tribesmen were permitted to follow the traditional custom of the steppe and pillage and plunder at will.

The Abbasid decision to seek Seljukid assistance was to be vindicated shortly after Tughril Beg withdrew from Baghdad. No sooner had he departed than the former military governor of the capital, Basasiri, seized the city in an attempt to overthrow Qaim and install the Fatimid Mustansir (1035–1094) as caliph in Baghdad. This cabal was thwarted, and the Abbasid caliphate preserved, by Tughril Beg who was designated by the caliph as the "Right hand of the Commander of the Faithful," that is, the second in command of the Abbasid caliphate, in January 1058.

Upon his death in 1063, the childless Tughril Beg was succeeded by his nephew Alp Arslan (1063–1072). However, Qutalmish contested the succession and refused to acknowledge his supremacy. Although Qutalmish was defeated and killed after a short struggle in December 1063, the long-term implications of the incident were significant. Resentment over the affair ultimately led to the breakaway of Qutalmish's descendants and their establishment of a Seljukid sultanate in Anatolia that was entirely independent of the state centered in Rai.

Alp Arslan continued the expansion of the Seljukid domain in all directions. Politically astute, although illiterate, he married his eldest son to the daughter of the Qara-Khanid ruler of Transoxiana and another son to a daughter of the sultan of Ghazni, thereby securing at least temporary stability on his eastern frontiers as he undertook a campaign of conquest in the west. Strategically, he sought to prevent a Byzantine-Fatimid alliance by driving a wide wedge between their contiguous frontiers, the Fatimids having earlier taken advantage of Constantinople's preoccupation with Europe to restore their grip on Syria and Palestine. In pursuing this strategy, Alp Arslan alternately attacked the Byzantines and the Fatimids, apparently unable to conduct simultaneous campaigns against both. He attacked Syria in 1065, pillaging Antioch and Edessa, and took Aleppo in 1070, pushing the Fatimids as far south as Damascus. His actions against Byzantium will be described later.

In the east, the frontier separating the Seljukids and the Qara-Khanids along the Oxus heated up once again during the reign of Buritigin's son and successor Shams al-Mulk Nasr (1068–1080) in Transoxiana. Although Alp Arslan was killed during the Seljukid invasion of the territory in November 1072, his son and successor Malik Shah (1072–1092), acting under the guidance of his powerful guardian and vizier Nizam al-Mulk, managed to impose Seljukid suzerainty over Transoxiana. He drove the Qara-Khanids out of the country and forced their Ghaznavid ally, Zahir ad-Dowla Ibrahim, to seek terms.

During the reign of Malik Shah, who moved the capital of the empire to Isfahan, the boundaries of the Seljukid Empire underwent further extension. Of particular significance for the subsequent history of the Middle East, the Seljukids captured Jerusalem in 1077, an event that was broadcast far and wide throughout Europe in lurid detail by returning Christian pilgrims. In 1087 Malik Shah married off his daughter to the caliph al-Muqtadi (1075–1094), further consolidating the Seljukid grip on the caliphate. In 1089–1090, he returned to Transoxiana, subjugated Bukhara and Samarkand, and transformed Qara-Khanid Transoxiana into a virtual dependency of the growing Seljukid Empire.

However, at the same time that Malik Shah was raising the empire to new heights, he also made a fateful administrative decision that was to prove to be a principal cause of the decline of Seljukid power. He divided the empire into essentially autonomous provinces that were ruled by Turkish chiefs in a typically feudal arrangement. This resulted in a fundamental change in the character of the military organization that served as the foundation of the Seljukid state. The sultans had achieved empire through the aggressiveness of their powerful Oghuz horse-archers. Now, with the empire divided into fiefdoms, the Turkish feudal lords were compelled to raise their armies locally from the inhabitants of their respective territories who were Turks, Arabs, Persians, and Kurds. These fighting forces were very different in character from the irrepressible Oghuz cavalry and could not provide the military power base necessary to sustain the decentralized empire.

In the meanwhile, the Fatimids were driven entirely out of Syria and Palestine, where minor vassal principalities emerged in all the cities of any consequence. Tutush (1078–1095), a younger brother of Malik Shah, carved a Seljukid fiefdom out of Syria and established his regime in Damascus. Marching north, Tutush was about to found an independent Seljukid kingdom of Syria when Malik Shah intervened and forced him to return to Damascus. Malik Shah, who was assassinated as a result of a conspiracy involving his wife Terken Khatun and the caliph al-Muqtadi over the planned succession, was nonetheless succeeded by his minor son Berk-Yaruk (1093–1104). It was during the period of uncertainty that attended the early years of the latter's reign that Tutush regained control of Aleppo and soon attempted to seize Persia. But the accomplishment of that feat proved to be beyond his capabilities and he was defeated and killed near Rai in February 1095. His Syrian kingdom became divided between his warring sons Ridwan (1095–1113), who ruled the north from Aleppo, and Duqaq (1095–1104), who controlled the south from Damascus. Both quickly lost their Turkish character as they became Arabified. However, the internecine squabbles in Syria soon weakened the Seljukid position in the Mediterranean coastal region to the point where the Fatimids were able to regain control of Jerusalem once again in 1098, after their capture of all the coastal towns between the Egyptian frontier and Byblos.

The coherence of the fledgling Seljukid Empire was shattered further in 1099 by the rebellion of Berk-Yaruk's half brother Muhammad Tapar, supported by the latter's brother Sanjar, the governor of Khorasan. This family squabble developed into a civil war that lasted almost five years. According to the peace agreement concluded among the parties in December 1101, Muhammad was to become king of Azerbaijan, the Jazira, and Diyarbekir, and Sanjar was to continue to rule Khorasan. Berk-Yaruk was to remain nominal overlord of the Seljukids, retaining the title of sultan and directly ruling the remainder of the empire. Upon the premature death of Berk-Yaruk at the age of twenty-five, Muhammad (1105–1118) became sultan and head of the Seljukid clan.

Although it entered a period of relative tranquility during Muhammad's tenure, the Seljukid Empire as a whole soon began to disintegrate into its component elements, primarily as a result of the internal dynastic struggles that drained its energies. As noted by one writer: "Each prince in an effort to secure allies disposed of resources and territories and thus weakened himself by that much. They died young and left their infants in the care of military chiefs [atabegs] whom they judged, or rendered, strong enough to be able to defend their rights; inevitably, these atabegs worked above all to secure for themselves the real power and expected some day to liquidate a nominal dynasty which had become useless."[2]

The Seljukid Empire that Malik Shah left to his successors was ultimately partitioned into several independent states that expended much of their energies and resources in seemingly counterproductive struggles with each other at a time when mounting external pressures required their unity and mutual support. As a result, the several Seljukid states experienced varying life spans.

In the east, the frontiers of the Seljukid realm were guarded by Sanjar (1096–1156), the youngest son of Malik Shah, who had been made ruler of Khorasan, which included all of Persia east of the Salt Desert. In 1102, Khorasan was invaded by the Qara-Khanids under Qadir-khan Jibra'il, the ruler of Kashgaria, but they were turned back by Sanjar who then proceeded to reassert Seljukid suzerainty over Transoxiana, appointing the local Qara-Khanid leader Arslan-Khan as vassal ruler of the territory. Sanjar also intervened in the dynastic quarrels among the Ghaznavids in Afghanistan, effectively imposing his suzerainty over that land as well. He seized Ghazni in 1117, deposed the Ghaznavid Arslan-Shah, and replaced him on the throne with another member of the same dynasty, Bahram-Shah. In 1130, Sanjar had a falling out with Arslan-Khan, into whose hands he had entrusted Transoxiana, and he invaded the territory, captured Samarkand, and deposed the khan, replacing him first with Hasan-Tigin (1130–1132) and later with Rukn ad-Din Mahmud (1132–1141). Sanjar also imposed his suzerainty on Ala ad-Din Atsiz (1127–1156), the Turkish ruler of Khwarizm who revolted against Seljukid domination in 1138. Although Atsiz flooded the banks of the Oxus to impede the advance of Sanjar's forces, he nonetheless was decisively defeated at the fortress of Hazarasp. However, Sanjar subsequently pardoned him and restored him to his former position in 1141.

It was at about that time that Sanjar began to experience significant reversals of fortune. Transoxiana was invaded by Ye-l Ta-shih (c. 1130–1142), the khan of the Qara-Khitai, a horde of Sinicized Buddhist Mongols who had migrated to Turkestan from China and established their dominance over the eastern Qara-Khanids in Kashgaria. They now attacked the western Qara-Khanids, defeating Rukn ad-Din Mahmud in the spring of 1137 at Khodzhent in Ferghana. Sanjar, who later attempted to come to the rescue of his Qara-Khanid vassals, met the Qara-Khitai in battle near Samarkand on September 9, 1141, and suffered a serious defeat. He was forced to withdraw into Khorasan, effectively surrendering all of Transoxiana to the invading forces. That same year, the Qara-Khitai also raided Khwarizm, compelling Atsiz to pay them tribute.

Taking advantage of the disarray among the Seljukids caused by the Qara-Khitai onslaught, Atsiz not only repudiated Seljukid suzerainty over Khwarizm once again but also went on the offensive and invaded Khorasan, occupying Merv and Nishapur. However, Atsiz was unable to hold these advanced positions against Sanjar's counterattacks, which drove him back across the frontier. Sanjar then invaded Khwarizm in 1143 and 1147 where he succeeded in re-imposing Seljukid suzerainty over the county.

Notwithstanding his success in Khwarizm, Sanjar was being worn down by the seemingly endless challenges to which he was being subjected. The situation reached a critical point in 1153, when he tried to impose Persian-style administrative and fiscal regulations on the Oghuz tribes, the parent stock of the Seljukids. The Oghuz responded by pillaging Merv, Nishapur, and the other main towns of Khorasan, taking Sanjar prisoner in the process. Without an effective leader, the Seljukid army remained virtually powerless to prevent other ambitious local rulers from asserting their autonomy, thereby critically weakening the Seljukid sultanate. Sanjar remained in captivity until 1156, when he finally managed to escape, but he died the following year as his Seljukid state crumbled.

Sanjar left no heirs, and Khorasan became a virtual no man's land in which the Oghuz chiefs could do as they pleased while nominally acknowledging the suzerainty of the ruler of Khwarizm, Arslan (1156–1172), the son and successor of Atsiz. Upon Arslan's death in 1172, his two sons, Takash (1172–1200) and Sultan-Shah, fought over the succession to the throne. Takash, the loser in the contest, sought refuge with the Qara-Khitai in December 1172. The latter were quite prepared to invade Khwarizm and reinstate Takash on its throne as their vassal. However, no sooner had this been done than Takash rebelled against the Qara-Khitai who now reversed alliances and took up the cause of the deposed Sultan-Shah. But, as a practical matter, it was too late to replace Takash with Sultan-Shah on the throne of Khwarizm without a very costly struggle. As an alternative, the Qara-Khitai gave Sultan-Shah an army with which he undertook the conquest of Khorasan, capturing Merv, Sarakhs, and Tus in 1181. Sultan-Shah continued to reign over Khorasan until his death in 1193, after which Khorasan reverted to Takash and was incorporated within the Khwarizmian Empire.

With Khorasan as his base of operations, Takash soon invaded and conquered most of western Persia. He defeated and killed the last of the Seljukid sultans of Persia, Tugrul III (1175–1194), in a decisive battle fought near Rai on March 19, 1194, thereby adding the districts of Rai and Hamadan to his expanding realm.

NOTES

1. Clifford E. Bosworth, *The Ghaznavids: Their Empire in Afghanistan and Eastern Iran 994–1040*, p. 248.

2. Claude Cahen, "The Turkish Invasion," in *A History of the Crusades: The First Hundred Years*, p. 162.

6

The Period of the First Crusades

The death of Gagik I Bagratuni (989–1020), the ruler of Greater Armenia, was followed by disorders that destabilized the country, making it ripe for foreign intervention once more. Basil II (976–1025) of Byzantium took advantage of the confused situation to attempt to re-impose Byzantine hegemony in the country. At the same time, reverberations from the movement of the Seljukid Oghuz in the direction of Anatolia were being felt there as well. Unable to cope with these simultaneous pressures, the ruler of the eastern Armenian province of Vaspurkan agreed to cede the territory to Basil in exchange for an appointment to the governorship of Cappadocia. As a result, Vaspurkan as well as a part of Iberia were annexed by Basil in 1021, extending the Byzantine frontier east of Lake Van as far as the present Turkish-Persian border.

Basil permitted the remainder of Greater Armenia to remain under the nominal rule of the son and successor of Gagik, John Smbat (Sempad), during his lifetime with the understanding that it was to revert to the Byzantine emperor upon his death. The subsequent complete annexation of Armenia by Constantine IX Monomachus (1042–1055) had the effect of extending the Byzantine frontier in Asia to northern Mesopotamia once again. However, it actually resulted in a weakening of the imperial defense system because it eliminated Armenia as a buffer zone between Byzantium and the encroaching Seljukids. It had now become the sole responsibility of the Byzantines to defend the Armenian frontier, there being little incentive for the Armenians to do so themselves. To make matters worse, this increased defense burden came at a time when the political climate in Constantinople was hardly conducive to financing additional military expenditures.

During the reign of Constantine X Ducas (1059–1067), drastic reductions were introduced in the regular Byzantine military budget in response to powerful internal political pressures. This led to a cut in the salaries of the active officers and to a decrease in the number of paid reservists. The net results of the budget cuts included a significant reduction in the size of the imperial armed forces and a serious impairment of Byzantine military capabilities. The frontier garrisons became virtually depleted of Byzantine troops, and many Greek residents began to relocate away from the frontier regions. Moreover, having essentially weakened its own military infrastructure, Byzantium became even more heavily dependent on the employment of foreign mercenaries to meet even its minimal defense needs. As a consequence of these developments, the Byzantines were caught quite unprepared by the sudden appearance of Alp Arslan and his powerful Oghuz army on the doorstep of Armenia.

Alp Arslan, as indicated earlier, was pursuing the strategy of driving a territorial wedge between the Byzantines and the Fatimids, hoping thereby to prevent an alliance between them that might be able to block his advance. In 1064 he crossed the Araxes, and in the following year he managed to seize Ani, the capital of the last independent ruler of the Armenian province of Kars. Alp Arslan then struck at Cilicia, which he laid waste. Having toppled the Byzantine frontier defenses, the Seljukids then forced their way into Anatolia and stormed Kayseri (Caesarea) in 1067, defeating the Byzantine armies at Levitane and Sebaste (Sivas). The following year, Alp Arslan led his army farther into Byzantine territory, breaking through as far as the walls of Konya (Iconium). Then, turning west, he mounted a campaign that brought him as far as the Aegean coast in 1069.

At this critical point in time, Constantine Ducas died, leaving his young son Michael as his heir and the empress Eudocia as regent of the empire. The Byzantine politicians, who now saw an impending disaster on the horizon, insisted that a stronger hand was needed at the helm of the state to salvage the situation. Accordingly, Eudocia married Romanus IV Diogenes (1068–1071), a distinguished Cappadocian general, who became emperor in place of Michael.

As far as Romanus was concerned, control of Armenia was the key to the containment of the Seljukids. As long as Armenia was in Byzantine hands, the Seljukid flank would be exposed. This would make it dangerous for Alp Arslan to remain in Anatolia since his lines of communication to the east could be cut. Romanus' strategy therefore called for the recovery of Khliat and the surrounding fortresses, the gateway to the main invasion routes through Armenia that passed to the north of Lake Van. He quickly mobilized a large army consisting primarily of foreign mercenaries, mainly Patzinaks (Pechnegs), Oghuz, Normans, and Franks, and launched a drive eastward across Anatolia toward Armenia. His offensive met with some initial successes in 1068 and 1069, when the Seljukids were preoccupied farther south with a campaign against the Fatimids in Syria. However, as soon as Alp Arslan learned that a Byzantine army was approaching Armenia, he left the campaign against the Fatimids in the hands of a trusted vassal, Atzis ibn Abaq, and sped north to intercept and confront Romanus.

In August 1071, the opposing armies met in battle near the fortress at Manzikert (Malazgird), north of Lake Van. By feigning a withdrawal, Alp Arslan contrived to lure the Byzantine army into a nearby valley, where it was trapped and at the mercy of the Seljukid forces. At this juncture, the Patzinaks, Oghuz, and other Turkish mercenaries concluded that discretion was indeed the better part of valor and decided to defect to the Seljukids. To make matters worse, the Norman contingent refused to engage the Seljukids in combat. This effectively sealed the fate of the remaining Byzantine forces, which proved to be no match for their Turkish adversaries. The Byzantines' mercenary army was defeated and Romanus was taken prisoner.

While in captivity, Romanus concluded a treaty with the Seljukids that obligated him to pay a substantial annual tribute, as well as a ransom of 1.5 million gold dinars in exchange for his freedom. Romanus, however, was unable to fulfill his obligations under the treaty because the Byzantine throne had been usurped during his absence by Michael VII Ducas (1071–1077), a fact that was exploited by the Seljukids later in justifying their assault on Byzantium. Notwithstanding these developments, Alp Arslan took no further steps at the time to secure and strengthen his position in the Mediterranean littoral. Instead, he was forced to turn eastward once again, crossing into Central Asia in 1072 to deal with the threat to his position in Persia that was emerging from Khwarizm.

While Alp Arslan was engaged in his campaigns far to the east, the Oghuz tribesmen that he left behind in Anatolia continued to raid and ravage the countryside. It was not long before Constantinople was goaded into doing something about the depredations. In 1073, a primarily Norman mercenary force, under Roussel of Bailleul, was dispatched to Anatolia to deal with the problem. However, intrigued by the opportunities presented by the power vacuum and the consequent anarchy and turmoil that he found in the peninsula, Roussel soon turned on his employers and before long made himself master of all of northern Anatolia. The emperor Michael sent an army against him, but it was defeated and its leader, Caesar John Ducas, taken prisoner. Roussel then demanded formal recognition by the emperor of his conquests in Anatolia. When Michael refused, Roussel challenged the legitimacy of his succession to the throne by proclaiming the captive Caesar John Ducas as emperor and threatening to march on Constantinople. Without an army with which to defend the city, Michael made the fateful decision to appeal to the Seljukids for assistance. He turned to Suleiman, the son of Qutalmish who had been killed by Alp Arslan during the struggle for the Seljukid succession. Suleiman, who had already estab-

lished a Seljukid power base in Anatolia that was independent of Alp Arslan, agreed to help. With his assistance, Roussel and his Normans were
defeated. At the same time, Suleiman exploited the opportunity presented
by the campaign to expand and consolidate his own independent position
in the peninsula. From this point on, the Seljukids of Rum (Anatolia) became a highly significant factor in the regional power equation and intervened repeatedly in Byzantium's domestic politics.

In January 1078, Nicephorus Botoniates (1078–1081), the Byzantine military governor of Asia Minor, revolted against Constantinople with the support of Suleiman and his Oghuz army and succeeded in having himself
crowned emperor that March. Toward the end of 1080, another claimant to
the throne, Nicephorus Melissenus, gathered a mercenary army made up
mostly of Turks, and declared himself emperor in Nicaea (Iznik). He too appealed to Suleiman for support. In this case, however, the involvement of
Suleiman in the succession struggle backfired. Before long, Suleiman induced the Turkish mercenaries who had hired out to Nicephorus Melissenus to abandon him and join the Seljukid forces. This enabled Suleiman to
add the provinces of Lydia and Ionia to his growing domain, without the
necessity of having to fight a major war of conquest for them. By the time
that Alexius I Comnenus (1081–1118) seized the Byzantine throne, Suleiman had overrun virtually all of Anatolia.

Although the independent Seljuk sultanate of Rum established by Suleiman (1077–1086) remained nominally under Byzantine suzerainty, it was
already clearly lost to Byzantium as a practical matter. From his new capital
at Nicaea (which was relocated to Konya after 1097) Suleiman was well positioned to make his influence felt at Constantinople, only some eighty
miles distant.

Interestingly, neither Alp Arslan nor any of his successors to the Seljukid
sultanate of Persia took any steps to bring Anatolia under the control of the
government at Isfahan. The explanation appears to be that, as the Seljukid
elite became increasingly assimilated to Persian culture, a significant gap
began to develop between them and their freebooting Oghuz tribesmen,
who continued to live and fight according to the customs and traditions of
the Central Asian steppe. As a result, the Seljukid leaders were only too
pleased to see the undisciplined bands of Oghuz warriors carry on their
raiding and pillaging as far as possible from Persia proper, and Anatolia
was sufficiently large and remote to fully absorb their destructive energies.
Indeed, by virtue of its altitude, climate, and vegetation, the Anatolian pla-
teau may be considered as an extension of the steppe zone of Central Asia
that held a natural attraction for the Oghuz nomads of the Kirghiz steppe.
This helps explain why Anatolia became Turkified, whereas the center of
the Seljuk Empire retained its primarily Persian character, language, and
culture, although strong Turkic elements took root in Azerbaijan and Khorasan.

To compound Alexius' problems, Tzachas (Chakan Beg), a Turkish adventurer who had spent part of his youth at the court of Nicephorus Botoniates, fled to Anatolia where he took over Smyrna and some other coastal cities and Aegean islands with his pirate fleet. Tzachas decided to attack Constantinople from the sea, cut it off from its sources of supply, and force it to capitulate to him. In pursuit of this ambition, he entered into negotiations with those Turkish elements that were already in one stage or another of conflict with Byzantium, mainly the Patzinaks and the Seljukids, for the purpose of mounting a coordinated assault on the Byzantine Empire that would bring it to its knees.

Tzachas' ambitions were far reaching. He envisioned the emergence of a new Turkish empire that was to be built on the ruins of Byzantium, with himself as emperor. According to one historian, "in the person of Tzachas there appeared a foe of Byzantium who combined with the enterprising boldness of a barbarian the refinement of a Byzantine education and an excellent knowledge of all the political relations of eastern Europe of that time; he planned to become the soul of the general Turkish movement and would and could give a reasonable and definite goal and general plan to the senseless wanderings and robberies of the Patzinaks."[1] Abu al-Qasim succeeded Suleiman in 1086, after the latter was killed in an unsuccessful attempt to conquer Aleppo. He decided to cooperate with Tzachas and to help himself at the same time by attacking Nicomedia.

Alexius was critically short of manpower, having lost almost all of Byzantine Asia Minor, the traditional recruiting ground for the Byzantine armed forces. Accordingly, as his predecessors had done, Alexius sent agents to western Europe in 1091 in search of mercenaries to help thwart the serious and growing immediate threat to Constantinople. While his representatives were scouring Europe for help, Alexius managed to deal successfully with the imminent threat by employing the time-honored method of Byzantine diplomacy, that is, getting one group of adversaries to destroy the other. In the case at hand, he was able to enlist the help of the khans of Cuman (Polovtzi), who all but annihilated their traditional enemies, the Patzinaks, in the battle of Levunium on the banks of the Maritsa River in April 1091.

With the Patzinaks out of the way, Alexius disposed of Tzachas by stirring up Qilij Arslan (1092–1107), who had just succeeded to the sultanate of Rum, against him. Alexius pointed out to Qilij Arslan that Tzachas' ambitions were as much a danger to him as to Byzantium and offered to conclude a treaty with Rum that would assure the security of both states. The Seljukid ruler accepted the logic of this argument and soon disposed of Tzachas by having him murdered. The peace treaty that was concluded between Alexius and Qilij Arslan effectively eliminated the immediate threat to Constantinople.

In the meanwhile, Alexius' appeals to the western European states for mercenary troops, although no longer a matter of urgency, struck a deeply responsive chord with Pope Urban II. The pope was committed to carrying on with the idea of organizing a crusade to the East that had been advocated earlier by Pope Gregory VII. The primary purpose of the crusade, as originally conceived, was to engage in a decisive struggle against the religious schismatics of the Greek Christian East. However, Byzantium's weakness in face of the external threats confronting it, and its evident need to plead for assistance from the Latin West, presented opportunities for a papal initiative that far transcended the very limited purposes Alexius had in mind. For one thing, the pope was acutely aware that the final schism between the Greek and Roman churches had taken effect only as recently as 1054. It was therefore quite conceivable that, at least from his perspective, a significant Latin response to the Byzantine appeal might actually result in a reunification of Christendom. On November 27, 1095, the pope issued a call to arms at the Council of Clermont. According to the chronicler Fulcher of Chartres, the pope declared, in part:

You must with all speed take to your brethren in the East the help so often promised and so urgently needed. The Turks and Arabs have attacked them and advanced into the territory of Romania [Byzantium] as far as that part of the Mediterranean known as the Sound of Saint-George [the Bosphorus]. And now, penetrating ever further into the land of those Christians, they have vanquished them seven times in battle, killing and taking captive a great number; they have destroyed the churches and ravaged the kingdom. If you do not resist them they will extend their sway still further over the faithful servants of God.[2]

Nonetheless, it seemed quite unlikely that sufficient interest could be generated in western Europe to cause very many people to voluntarily risk their lives merely in order to save Constantinople. On the other hand, Jerusalem and the other holy sites of Christianity in Palestine were also under a less than benign Turkish control. It thus became understood by the promoters and organizers of the crusade that it was being launched for the primary purpose of wresting the Holy Sepulchre from Muslim hands. To achieve this, the armies of Christendom would have to assemble at Constantinople, from where they would cross into Anatolia and move south to Palestine, pushing the Turks before them. In the process of this more extensive campaign, Constantinople would receive the relief that it sought from the Turkish threat.

The response to the pope's appeal was dramatic, although there can be little doubt that not all of those who volunteered for the crusade did so out of selfless religious commitment. Many were motivated by the prospect of the fabulous booty that was to be garnered from the fabled lands of the East, while others, particularly among the leaders, saw the crusade as an unparalleled opportunity to acquire distant lands, and the power that went with them, for themselves.

Under the leadership of Peter the Hermit, a People's Crusade, a vast rabble of simple peasants inspired by religious fervor, reached Constantinople in August 1096. Some 20,000 men, women, and children were ferried across the Bosphorus only to be massacred by the Turks near Nicomedia on October 21. One highly significant outcome of this debacle was that Qilij Arslan came to believe that it was no longer necessary to take the crusaders seriously. He therefore concluded that his foothold in western Anatolia was sufficiently secure for him to be able to march off to the eastern part of the peninsula to confront the Danishmends, a Turkish clan that had been deliberately stirred up by the Byzantines to distract the Seljukids. The Danishmends had made claim to Malatya (Melitene), a town of strategic and commercial importance that served as the gateway from Anatolia to both Seljukid Iraq and Persia. This was a claim that Qilij Arslan felt obliged to challenge most forcefully.

It soon became clear that Qilij Arslan had no inkling of how serious the situation was becoming. By the spring of 1097, some 150,000 Christians, mostly Franks and Normans (the crusaders would generally become known as Franks regardless of country of origin), had assembled at Constantinople in four armies. These were led by Godfrey of Bouillon, duke of Lorraine and of Lower Lotharingia; Robert, duke of Normandy; Raymond de Saint Giles, count of Toulouse and marquis of Provence; and Bohemond, the count of Apulia. Alexius Comnenus was sufficiently concerned about the real intentions of this group of adventurers to insist that they take an oath of fealty to him before crossing the Bosphorus. He made it particularly clear that Byzantium claimed any territory they might recover from the Turks that had been under Byzantine rule before the battle of Manzikert in 1071. With regard to the matter of the intentions of the crusaders, Alexius' daughter, Anna Comnena, wrote: "The simpler-minded were urged on by the real desire of worshipping at our Lord's Sepulchre, and visiting the sacred places, but the more astute, especially men like Bohemond and those of like mind, had another secret reason, namely the hope that while on their travels they might by some means be able to seize the capital itself, looking upon this as a kind of corollary."[3]

The crusader armies crossed the Bosphorus into Anatolia and marched on Nicaea, which they placed under siege on May 14, 1097. When he discovered what had occurred, Qilij Arslan raced back to relieve the siege of Nicaea, but it was already too late. With his forces divided and unable to break through the crusader lines and gain access to the city, by May 21 he was forced to concede the loss of Nicaea and withdraw. Nonetheless, the Franks were unable to take Nicaea by storm. It was only after the Byzantines brought ships overland and then floated them on the lake approaches to the city, completing its total blockade, that the garrison surrendered to the Byzantine admiral Butumites in June. The loss of Nicaea was followed by another defeat of Qilij's forces at Dorylaeum (Eskisehir) at the end of the same month. After this, the Turks were forced to evacuate the western part of Anatolia for fear of finding themselves cut off there; they withdrew farther eastward into the interior. Alexius took advantage of the situation and quickly occupied Smyrna, Ephesus, Sardis, and a number of other towns in what was once Lydia, thereby restoring Byzantine control over the western half of Anatolia.

After crossing the Taurus, a detachment of Franks under Baldwin of Bouillon detoured eastward into Armenia where they captured the strategically important fortresses of Ravendal and Turbessel, from which they were able to control the territory of Armenia west of the Euphrates. On the eastern bank of the river, the Turks were still the dominant power, although they permitted Thoros, an Armenian vassal, to rule in Edessa under their suzerainty. Hoping to exploit Baldwin's presence in the region as a means of gaining independence from the Turks, Thoros invited him to enter Edessa in February 1098, where he adopted Baldwin and made him his heir and co-ruler. Early in the following month, with Baldwin's evident approval, Thoros became the victim of a conspiracy and was lynched. On March 10, Baldwin had himself enthroned as the ruler of the area, the county of Edessa, which became the first of the crusader-created states in the Middle East.

Another column, under Tancred the Norman, detoured to the west and conquered Cilicia as far as Tarsus. The main body of the crusader army continued on its planned march southward and laid siege to Antioch on October 21, 1097. After holding out for more than seven months, the city fell on June 3, 1098, following an unsuccessful attempt by Ridwan of Aleppo to break the siege. However, no sooner had the Franks entered the city than they found themselves under siege by the army of Karbuqa, the Turkish emir who had taken Mosul from the Arab Beni Uqail in 1096 and annexed it to the Seljukid Empire. Fortunately for the Franks, Karbuqa had squandered three precious weeks in a vain attempt to take Edessa and therefore failed to arrive at Antioch before the crusaders were able to enter the city. Had the latter been caught still besieging Antioch, it is quite likely that the Turkish relief forces would have defeated them. As it was, Karbuqa's attempt to reverse the situation by dislodging the Franks from Antioch failed and the siege was broken on June 28. After this, Antioch was to remain in Christian hands for close to two centuries.

The crusader march on Jerusalem was halted for another six months as the Provencals and Normans, under Raymond and Bohemond respectively, argued over who should have control of Antioch. Ultimately, Bohemond (1098–1104) was declared prince of Antioch and Raymond became commander in chief of the army that was to conquer Jerusalem. According to the understanding reached with Alexius Comnenus, Antioch should have been transferred to Byzantine control since it came under the category of lands that had been under Constantinople's rule before 1071. However, Bohemond had no intention whatever of honoring his commitment and subordinating himself to the emperor. Indeed, he promptly undertook a siege of Latakia, to prevent the nearby port from being used by Alexius in the event that he intended to transport an army by sea to attack Antioch. The territory of the principality of Antioch was extended to include Cilicia in 1108, when it was wrested from Byzantine control by Tancred after having changed hands several times during the preceding decade.

Departing from Antioch in mid-January 1099, Raymond led the crusader army southward along the coastal strip without encountering any significant opposition. The local rulers were unable to mount any effective resistance and were prepared to pay tribute to avoid being attacked. It also appears that after the disaster at Antioch, the Sunni Muslim rulers of Mosul, Aleppo, and Damascus preferred to remain on the sidelines, particularly since the Christian army was marching against the Shiite Fatimids who had themselves advanced into Palestine again during the previous year. As long as the Franks did not attempt to move into their territories, they would do nothing to hinder their advance. This attitude would seem to reflect a perception of the purposes of the crusade that was very similar in nature to that suggested by the Arab historian Ibn al-Athir as one possible explanation of the Frankish invasion of Syria. That is, "that the Fatimids of Egypt were afraid when they saw the Seljukids extending their empire through Syria as far as Gaza, until they reached the Egyptian border and Atsiz [Malik Shah's general who attacked Egypt from Palestine in 1076] invaded Egypt itself. They therefore sent to invite the Franks to invade Syria and so protect Egypt from the Muslims."[4]

Raymond proceeded along the Palestine coast as far south as Jaffa before turning inland. Ramle was abandoned in anticipation of the arrival of the crusaders, who reached Bethlehem on June 6, 1099. The following day they arrived at the gates of Jerusalem with some 40,000 men, greatly outnumbering the Egyptian garrison defending the city. Jerusalem was stormed on July 15, and the Franks carried out an indiscriminate slaughter of the inhabitants. The crusader Kingdom of Jerusalem was established under Godfrey of Bouillon (1099–1100).

Godfrey's most immediate military task was that of securing the coast, without which his position in Jerusalem would be highly precarious since his maritime lines of communication with Europe could easily be interdicted at the water's edge. The problem was further exacerbated by the loss of the overland route to Europe. Once the crusader armies had crossed Anatolia, the Seljukids succeeded in regaining firm control of the Taurus passes, thereby effectively severing the land route to Europe across the peninsula and making the Kingdom of Jerusalem particularly vulnerable as long as it did not control the coast. To fully secure the coast it was necessary to take the major Fatimid naval base at Ashkelon, an objective that Godfrey was unable to achieve. The Egyptian fleet therefore remained in a position to come to the aid of the other coastal towns and deny the crusaders effective control of their Mediterranean flank. However, the Egyptian fleet proved to be rather ineffective if not completely inactive throughout the crusader campaign. It was perhaps not to be expected that the Shiite Fatimids would make any particular effort to help the Sunni Seljukids in Syria. However, for reasons that are quite unclear, the Egyptian fleet also did little to protect the coast of Palestine, which had been under Fatimid control.

The Franks never had a fleet of their own to speak of and, without a naval capability, they could neither effectively contain Egypt nor impose their control over the coastal cities. The Byzantines, on the other hand, were the other major maritime power in the region but were unwilling to use their ships to further Frankish expansionism at the expense of their own geopolitical interests. Consequently, Godfrey had to solicit the cooperation of the Italian maritime powers in this effort. The Pisans and Venetians clearly perceived the tangible commercial benefits to be derived from control of the Mediterranean ports, especially the anticipated tax-free passage of goods that would increase the profits of their oriental trade. Accordingly, they were quite pleased to enlist in Godfrey's campaign to seize the major coastal towns of Palestine. In 1099, the Pisans took Jaffa, in which they received special trade rights, while the Venetian fleet captured Haifa shortly afterward, butchering both the garrison and the populace. Godfrey's forces defeated an Egyptian relief army near Ashkelon in August 1099 and the Fatimid fleet abandoned its base in Palestine and returned to Egypt. Nonetheless, Ashkelon itself was to hold out until 1153. Caesarea, the last of the remaining Egyptian-held ports of Palestine, surrendered to a Genoese fleet in 1101.

When Godfrey died on July 18, 1100, his brother Baldwin I (1100–1118) was called from Edessa to ascend the throne of the Kingdom of Jerusalem. Baldwin soon expanded the bounds of the realm to reach from Aqaba on the Red Sea to Beirut, and from the Mediterranean to the Jordan River. The prevailing geostrategic situation made it highly desirable that the Franks attempt to push the Muslims beyond the habitable areas in the south and east so that the surrounding desert might be made to serve as a *cordon sanitaire*, protecting the flanks of the Frankish states. The key to achieving this objective lay with the capture of Damascus. However, the accomplishment of this goal eluded the Franks. The most they were able to achieve was the transformation of the Hauran district farther south into a no man's land that they exploited, as did Damascus. In the south, the situation appeared well under control as Fatimid Egypt became fully preoccupied with its own internal political crises, and no longer posed a credible military threat to the crusader states. Farther north, by contrast, strategic considerations urged that Frankish control should be extended to Aleppo to protect their exposed flank in Syria, but this too proved beyond their capacity.

In 1104, Bohemond attempted to capture the ancient strategically located fortress town of Harran, which controlled the gateway to Mosul. Had Bohemond succeeded in this venture, a wedge would have been driven between the three Seljukid centers of the west, Anatolia, Syria, and Iraq. Even though the success of such a move would have cut off Damascus from its links to the rest of the Seljukid world, its rulers would not join with Aleppo and Mosul in challenging the Frankish advance. For Damascus, Frankish Antioch and Edessa served as useful buffer states between it and the other Seljukid provinces, and it had no interest in doing anything to alter the regional balance of power in a way that might reduce the value of those buffers. In other words, from Damascus' perspective, it was not at all clear that the other Seljukids were natural allies and the Franks natural enemies. It seems evident, at least in this case, that religion and ethnicity were rather minor factors in the regional geopolitical equation.

As it turned out, the assault on Harran failed as the Frankish army was cut to pieces on the banks of the Balikh River. However, they had greater success to the west where they finally managed to secure control of virtually the entire Mediterranean coastal region. Tripoli fell to the Franks in July 1109 and became an autonomous county under the nominal suzerainty of the king of Jerusalem. Thus, in a little more than a decade, four small Latin states were established in Syria and Palestine: Jerusalem and Edessa, which were Burgundian; Antioch, which was Norman; and Tripoli, which was Provencal. As a practical matter, Frankish rule never really extended very far inland from the coast, even though cities such as Aleppo and Damascus occasionally paid tribute to the Franks to mitigate the lingering threat of attack.

By 1110, the Seljukid sultan of Persia, Muhammad, had succeeded in restoring order in his turbulent empire and assigned to Mawdud (1108–1113), the governor of Mosul, the responsibility for dealing with Edessa and Antioch. In May of that year, Mawdud laid siege to Edessa, forcing Baldwin to come to the rescue of the city. Mawdud returned to Syria the following year where he engaged Baldwin and the combined armies of the Frankish states, some 16,000 men, at Shaizar north of Hama. After two weeks of indecisive skirmishing, Mawdud withdrew to Mosul. He returned to Syria again in May 1113. This time he received the cooperation of the atabeg Tughtigin (1095–1128), a former slave of the Seljukid sultan Tutush and regent for his son Duqaq, who was now the lord of Damascus, which had become independent of the Seljukid Empire in 1109.

With the consolidation of Frankish control of the coast, the local balance of power was upset to the clear disadvantage of Damascus. Thus, when Baldwin decided to break the existing truce with Damascus, the latter found itself threatened by the Frankish states on its three flanks. It was now prepared to align itself with the Seljukids once again. With Tughtigin's help, Mawdud inflicted a sharp defeat on Baldwin south of the Sea of Galilee, but was forced to withdraw upon the arrival of Frankish reinforcements that threatened his dominance on the battlefield. The overall Seljukid campaign fizzled, however, after Mawdud was assassinated in Damascus that September.

Two years later, the sultan sent Aqsonqor il-Bursuqi, the atabeg of Mosul (1113–1126), and Bursuq ibn Bursuq, the lord of Hamadan, to continue the struggle against the Franks. Bursuq's efforts were effectively sabotaged by the rulers of Aleppo and Damascus who, again fearful of being forced to surrender their local autonomy to the emissary of the sultan, joined forces with the Franks to completely defeat Bursug's forces at Tel-Danith, southwest of Aleppo, in September 1115. This defeat marked the last serious effort by the Seljukids to re-conquer Syria.

Sultan Muhammad died in April 1118 and was succeeded by his minor son Mahmud, who became almost totally engrossed in the civil wars that erupted between him and his three brothers. As a result, he proved to be incapable of imposing effective control on the Turkish lords of Mosul, the Jazira, and Syria.

In the meanwhile, Roger of Antioch (1112–1119) was able to apply such pressure on Aleppo that it was forced to seek the assistance of the Ortoqid emir Ilghazi of Mardin. Ilghazi took control of Aleppo (1118–1122) and promptly seceded from the Seljukid Empire. He then formed an aggressive alliance with Tughtigin of Damascus and invaded Antioch in 1119, soundly defeating Roger's army. Luckily for the Franks, Ilghazi failed to follow up his victory with an occupation of the city, reportedly because of an illness contracted as a result of too much strong drink—presumably imbibed in celebration of his victory. He thereby forfeited the significant advantage he had achieved on the battlefield, enabling the reinforcements that subsequently arrived from the Kingdom of Jerusalem to force him to withdraw from Antioch. The threat to the Frankish state from Aleppo diminished considerably after Ilghazi was defeated in a war with King David II (1089–1125) of Georgia near Tiflis in 1121.

Baldwin I also died in April 1118, leaving behind only a small number of knights and colonists in Palestine who would have to struggle hard to maintain their positions while awaiting reinforcements that could only come by sea, since the land routes were no longer open to them. The patriarch Gormond described their situation in a letter written about 1120:

We are besieged by Saracens from all parts: from Babylon in the east, from Ascalon in the west, from Assur [i.e., Tyre] on the sea-coast, from Damascus in the north. We are every day invaded, slaughtered, enslaved; beheaded, our corpses are the prey of beasts and birds; we are sold, like sheep on the market. . . . What of the sufferings of the foot-soldiers? They are locked in the towers and in the walls of Jerusalem, and in the caves of the country. . . . Nobody, indeed, dares go for a mile or even less outside the walls of Jerusalem and other places . . . because the Saracens are not afraid to approach nearly as far as the gates of Jerusalem.[5]

Nonetheless, they managed to persevere. During the reign of Baldwin's cousin and successor, Baldwin II (1118–1131), the Kingdom of Jerusalem was expanded by the addition of Tyre, which fell to the Venetians in July of 1124. This took place while the king himself was being held prisoner after falling into the hands of Balak, Ilghazi's successor in Aleppo, in April 1123. He was subsequently released after agreeing to certain conditions that he ignored once he obtained his freedom.

After a decade and a half of continuous struggle it seemed that the regional balance of power in Syria had been restored. Aleppo counterbalanced Antioch, Damascus counterbalanced Jerusalem, and the minor emirates in the Upper Orontes valley counterbalanced Tripoli. In 1125, however, the balance was upset once again as Aqsonqor il-Bursuqi took over control of Aleppo in addition to Mosul. The emergence of a relatively large Muslim state centered in Aleppo was seen as a serious threat to the security of the Frankish states. Baldwin II went to war, primarily to restore the situation that had prevailed earlier, and succeeded in inflicting a significant defeat on il-Bursuqi at Azaz in northern Syria in May 1125. Il-Bursuqi was assassinated the following year, and the moment seemed ripe for the Franks to finally capture Aleppo, particularly in light of the chaos that had erupted following the death of the atabeg.

Bohemond II (1126–1130) had just arrived from Europe to take over his inheritance in Antioch from Baldwin, who acted as its guardian in the interim, and was expected to lead the initiative against Aleppo. However, he quickly became preoccupied with the now traditional civil war between the Frankish states of Antioch and Edessa and allowed the opportunity to seize Aleppo to lapse. The Franks were not to have a second chance.

NOTES

1. A. A. Vasiliev, *History of the Byzantine Empire*, vol. 2, p. 384.
2. Regine Pernoud, ed., *The Crusades*, p. 23.
3. Anna Comnena, *The Alexiad*, X.5.
4. *Arab Historians of the Crusades*, p. 4.
5. Jean Richard, *The Latin Kingdom of Jerusalem*, vol. 1, p. 17.

7

The Era of the Zengids

In 1127, Imad ad-Din Zengi (1127–1146) became atabeg of Mosul and adopted an aggressive external policy designed to consolidate Turkish rule in the region. He quickly seized the strategically important towns of Nisibis, Sinjar, and Harran, following which he took Aleppo in 1130. With the latter as his base, he began to mobilize the military capability with which to challenge the Franks for control of northern Syria. For the next decade, Antioch repeatedly came under threat of attack by Zengi's forces.

Antioch's security situation began to appear particularly tenuous after Zengi succeeded in forcing the surrender of the fortress of Montferrand in the Upper Orontes valley in July 1137. Nonetheless, Zengi's higher priority at the time was to bring Damascus under his control. He had attempted to do so through intimidation in 1130 but was unsuccessful. He was subsequently diverted from giving the necessary attention to this goal by his involvement as a partisan of Masud in the lingering succession crisis in Iraq that followed the death of the sultan Mahmud in 1131. During the height of that struggle in 1133, he even attempted to seize Baghdad but was prevented from doing so by the caliph Mustarshid (1118–1135), who retaliated with a siege of Mosul that same year.

Chastened by this experience, Zengi avoided any further involvement in Iraq, at least for the time being, and returned to the Jazira. He broke off his campaigns in the north in 1135, when he was invited to intervene in Damascus by its ruler Shams al-Muluk Ismail, who was facing a mutiny of his own troops. Zengi was only too pleased to oblige and sped toward the city. However, by the time he arrived, Ismail had already been overthrown and replaced by his brother Mahmud, who now prevented Zengi from entering Damascus. He was about to lay siege to the city but was diverted from doing so by a call from the caliph in Baghdad to intervene in Iraq once again by joining in an alliance against the sultan. As with his earlier venture into the politics of Iraq, this one also turned out poorly and Zengi eagerly withdrew and returned to the north.

At this point in time, however, the political balance in northern Syria had undergone a significant change as a consequence of the resurgence of Byzantine power in the region under the emperor John II Comnenus (1118–1143). He restored Byzantine control over Armenian Cilicia (or Lesser Armenia), which was established as a principality at the end of the eleventh century by Ruben Bagratuni (1080–1095) and was populated primarily by refugees from Armenia who had fled south in advance of the Turkish invasion. Next, he undertook the reassertion of Byzantine authority over Antioch and northern Syria. John Comnenus arrived at Antioch with his army in August 1137, and forced Raymond of Poitiers, who had gained control of the city-state by marrying Bohemond's granddaughter, to acknowledge Byzantine suzerainty. He then put Shaizar under siege, withdrawing only after receiving payment of an indemnity and a commitment to pay an annual tribute to Constantinople.

Although he was himself campaigning in the area, Zengi was not prepared to take on the Byzantine army and therefore deliberately avoided coming into contact with it. John Comnenus seized the initiative and launched an offensive against Zengi in March 1138, but his attempt to take Aleppo failed and he was soon forced to withdraw from Syria entirely to attend to more pressing matters closer to home in Anatolia, where a war with the Danishmends was raging. Once the Byzantines departed from Syria, Zengi marched south and attempted to seize Damascus again in 1139. However, in anticipation on Zengi's attack, Muin ad-Din Unur, the military commander and effective ruler of the city, sought to assure its security through a renewal of its former alliance with the Kingdom of Jerusalem. The treaty that was concluded with Fulk (1131–1144), Baldwin's successor, provided for a payment to the Franks of 20,000 pieces of gold monthly for their expenses and the provision of hostages as a guarantee of good faith. Muin ad-Din Unur also promised to turn over the fortress of Banias that was controlled at the time by an emir friendly to Zengi, once the latter withdrew from the town. Banias was a point of great strategic significance because it dominated the road between the Galilee and Damascus, which in Zengi's hands would have made both districts highly vulnerable to attack. The treaty with the Franks gave the Damascenes the capability once again to thwart Zengi's long-standing ambition to extend the region under his control to include Damascus.

For the next five years, Zengi became increasingly preoccupied with events in Iraq and withdrew almost entirely from any further activity along the Syrian front. However, the deaths of John Comnenus in 1143 and Fulk the following year drew him back to the region. Zengi evidently perceived the uncertainty and political immobility that characterized the period of transition to new regimes in both Byzantium and Jerusalem as presenting a window of opportunity for purposes of territorial expansion that could be exploited without running the risks of triggering a major war with the Christian states. With neither Byzantium nor Jerusalem in a position to come to the immediate relief of northern Syria, Zengi decided to attack Edessa, which fell toward the end of December 1144 after a four-week siege. Zengi quickly followed up on this victory by also seizing all the territory of the county that lay to the east of the Euphrates, the first significant loss of territory suffered by the Franks. Even though they managed to retain control of the territory of Edessa west of the Euphrates for another half-dozen years, the first crusader state to come into being was also destined to be the first to disappear. Zengi himself was murdered in 1146, and was succeeded by his two sons; the eldest, Saif ad-Din Ghazi (1146–1149), became ruler in Mosul, while his younger brother, Nur ad-Din Mahmud (1146–1174), took control of Aleppo.

The fall of Edessa produced a sharp reaction in Europe, and generated the demand for a new crusade. Louis VII (1137–1180) of France and Conrad III Hohenstaufen (1138–1152) of the Holy Roman Empire became determined to exact retribution for this serious loss, and soon led their armies to the East. Conrad reached Constantinople in September 1147 and, without waiting for the arrival of the French forces, crossed the Bosphorus into Anatolia. He split his army into two contingents. One, that included most of the noncombatants, was to proceed along the extended but relatively secure route that followed the Aegean and Mediterranean coasts, while Conrad himself intended to lead the main body of the army along the shorter route directly across Seljukid territory to Edessa. He progressed without significant opposition as far as Dorylaeum (Eskisehir). There, in late October 1147, he ran into the forces of Masud (1116–1156), the Seljukid sultan of Konya, and suffered a serious defeat that cost him a good part of his army. Conrad was forced to return to Nicaea, where the French forces had just arrived. The second German contingent was also severely mauled by the Turks when it struck inland at Laodicea, and was later virtually destroyed in its entirety in February 1148 on the coast of Pamphylia. The few that survived ultimately made their way to Syria by ship.

Having learned a lesson from Conrad's misadventures, Louis followed the longer route through Smyrna and Ephesus and along the Mediterranean coast with his entire army, expecting little interference from the Turkish forces in the area. However, the French army met the same fate as its German predecessors. Early in 1148 they suffered a serious defeat west of Konya. They then managed to fight their way to the coast at Attalya. The few Byzantine ships that arrived to provide them with some relief could only accommodate the king, the clergy, and the barons, and it was only these few who were therefore able to reach the Syrian coast near Antioch in safety. The rest of the army tried to fight their way to Syria overland, but they were soon routed by the Seljukids, losing most of the French infantry in the process.

Louis eventually arrived at Jerusalem in May 1148, only to find that Conrad had already reached Palestine directly by ship from Constantinople with what remained of his army. Another French force under Alfonse Jourdain, count of Toulouse, also soon arrived by ship. These leaders, who were joined by Baldwin III (1144–1163) of Jerusalem, held a council of war in Acre on June 24, 1148, and decided on a course of action that was remarkably ill conceived, to say the least.

The regional power equation was plain. The Franks had been able to maintain their positions in Syria and Palestine for half a century because of the chronic disunity among the Turkish warlords. There could be little doubt that, were the latter to unite with the Turkish rulers of the Jazira, the Frankish forces would be hopelessly outnumbered. A critical factor that had contributed to preventing such unification was the alliance between Damascus and the Kingdom of Jerusalem.

The pact between Damascus and Jerusalem had been renewed by Fulk, but was violated by his successor Baldwin III early in 1148. It seems that the Frankish barons of Judea convinced him to lend his support to the emir of the Hauran who had revolted against the atabeg of Damascus. It was their hope to profit from the situation by gaining control of additional land east of the Jordan. This hostile act precipitated a brief war with Damascus during which Baldwin's forces were defeated handily. Nonetheless, Muin ad-Din Unur favored a renewal of the alliance with Jerusalem as a means of helping to ensure the continued independence of Damascus in the face of growing Zengid expansionism under Nur ad-Din of Aleppo. The latter had attacked Antioch in both 1147 and 1148 and had seized a good part of the Frankish territory east of the Orontes. Without a Damascus-Jerusalem alliance, he might well have no other alternative but to try and reach an accommodation with Nur ad-Din, something he was very anxious to avoid and something that the Franks had a vital interest in trying to prevent from taking place.

The objective of maintaining the regional balance of power clearly required that the threat posed by Nur ad-Din be eliminated, and the renewal of the alliance with Damascus was an essential step toward that goal. However, for reasons totally unrelated to the prevailing geopolitical realities, Louis and Conrad decided to mount a surprise attack on Damascus, their only potential Muslim ally of any military significance. Since they did not have the necessary equipment with them to place the well-fortified city under an effective siege, it could only be taken by a direct assault, which was attempted unsuccessfully on July 24, 1148. In the meanwhile, Muin ad-Din Unur had sent messages to all the regional Muslim leaders asking them to send reinforcements, some of which, under the command of the Zengid

Saif ad-Din of Mosul, began arriving in the vicinity of Damascus two days after the initial crusader assault. According to Ibn al-Athir, Muin ad-Din Unur sent the following message and warning to the commanders of the Frankish forces: "What reason have you for supporting these people against us when you know that if they [the Franco-German armies] take the city they will seize your possessions on the coast? I warn you that if I feel that I am losing the battle, I shall hand the city over to Saif ad-Din, and you may be sure that if he becomes ruler of Damascus you will not be allowed to keep a foothold in Syria."[1] Two days later, the crusaders were still unable to take the city. Faced by the prospect that Muin ad-Din Unur might make good on his threat to open the gates of Damascus to the army of Saif ad-Din, the Franks convinced their crusader allies to break off the campaign and return to Acre.

The crusader armies withdrew from Damascus after having suffered heavy losses, without any compensating gains other than Banias, which was finally turned over to the Franks in accordance with the terms of the earlier Damascus-Jerusalem treaty. To make matters worse, recriminations over the debacle precipitated a falling out between Louis and Conrad on one side and the Frankish states on the other, the latter only too well aware of the dangerous position in which they had been placed by the politically foolhardy attempt to conquer Damascus. As a result of the bitter feelings provoked by the affair, the monarchs of Europe simply disassociated themselves from the Frankish states for the next forty years, a policy that had very serious consequences for the latter.

Following the travesty of the Second Crusade, that is, the misadventures of Louis VII and Conrad III, Baldwin III made the serious mistake of diverting his attention away from the significant developments that were taking place in northern Syria. Instead, he occupied himself with an ill-conceived campaign against the Fatimids in southern Palestine. Baldwin seems to have become obsessed with the idea of conquering Ashkelon, the last major Fatimid outpost in the country, even though it posed no present threat to the security of the Frankish kingdom. By 1150, he had built a formidable fortress over the ruins of ancient Gaza that enabled him to gain control of the overland lines of communications between Ashkelon and Egypt, although he was unable to interdict the sea-lanes between them. In January 1153, he concentrated all his forces on a siege of Ashkelon that lasted until the fortress surrendered on August 19, 1153, effectively eliminating the Fatimid presence in Asia. However, the campaign for Ashkelon virtually depleted Baldwin's resources and seriously impaired his ability to defend adequately against the very dangerous threat to his interests that was emerging in Syria. Thus, when Nur ad-Din turned to the conquest of Damascus, thereby threatening a radical change in the regional balance of power, Baldwin simply was in no position to assist in its defense even though its continued independence was of vital importance to the security of his own domain.

Nur ad-Din, in addition to being an extremely shrewd political leader was also a zealous Muslim. He was only too familiar with the internecine struggles that had effectively immobilized the Abbasids as well as the Seljukids, and permitted the emergence of the crusader states. He decided to take a page from the crusaders' book and to employ religion rather than ethnicity as the unifying theme of his expanding state. Accordingly, he proclaimed a jihad, a holy war, against the Franks, a counter-crusade to realize the triumph of Islam against Christianity. Although there was a strong basis in Muslim jurisprudence for such a jihad, it was still a rather novel approach that took many by surprise. And it was the caliph in Baghdad rather than Nur ad-Din in Aleppo who had the nominal religious authority to proclaim a crescentade, something that the caliph could hardly do given the convoluted politics of the region. To create support for his holy war, Nur ad-Din undertook an intensive propaganda campaign that was designed to develop a strong public sentiment in its favor. This also served to severely limit the ability of the various Muslim emirs, upon whose loyalty he had to depend, to pursue an alternate independent political course. As reported by Ibn al-Athir, Qara Arslan (1144–1167), the emir of Diyarbekir, who had little enthusiasm for a holy war against the Franks, stated:

Nur ed-Din adopted such a policy toward me that if I did not provide him with troops my own subjects would rebel against me and drive me out. Even in my own household he kept up a correspondence with ascetics and holy men, explaining to them the sufferings which the Franks imposed on the Moslems of Syria, death, captivity, and plunder. He entreated them to help him with their prayers and asked them to rouse the faithful to the holy war. Each of those to whom he wrote would go and sit in the mosque with their followers and friends and there give them Nur ed-Din's letters to read. When they had read them they would burst into tears and curse me, calling God's vengeance on me. This is why I cannot help but march against the Franks.[2]

As early as 1149, Nur ad-Din attempted to win over the people of Damascus and thereby drive a wedge between them and the Franks. The following year, he returned to the vicinity of Damascus with his forces and sent a message to Abaq, the successor of Muin ad-Din Unur, and the other leaders of the city: "I desire no more than the well-being of the Muslims, jihad against the infidels, and the release of the prisoners they are holding. If you come over to my side with the army of Damascus, if we help each other to wage the jihad, my wish will be fulfilled."[3] The response of Abaq was to send for help from Baldwin, who quickly dispatched forces that camped at the gates of the city. Nur ad-Din prudently avoided a collision with the allies and withdrew from the area as he kept up a propaganda barrage against Damascene collaboration with the Franks. At the same time, he sponsored the organization of a network of agents within the city that actively undermined Abaq's position.

By 1153 Abaq found himself increasingly politically isolated with only a small coterie of emirs who continued to urge him to hold out against Nur ad-Din. The latter disposed of the remaining opponents to cooperation with him by arranging for false information to reach Abaq to the effect that a plot was being hatched against him from among those closest to him. Without bothering to corroborate the information, Abaq proceeded to execute or imprison his closest associates, leaving himself almost entirely isolated within Damascus. Nur ad-Din then began to intercept food convoys headed for the city, forcing prices up dramatically and raising the fear of starvation. It only remained to spread the word that all these hardships could have been avoided if Damascus had not aligned itself with the enemies of Islam.

Nur ad-Din returned to the gates of Damascus in mid-April 1154 and Abaq issued another call for help from Baldwin. This time, however, Baldwin had already expended most of his resources on the conquest of Ashkelon and was in no position to help Damascus against the common enemy. When Nur ad-Din mounted his final assault on the city a week later, the demoralized Damascenes offered only token resistance.

With the fall of Damascus, Nur ad-Din's sway extended over all the Muslim areas of Syria and the Jazira. At this stage, however, he deliberately avoided any attempt to complete his conquest of Syria with an assault on Antioch. He was well aware that Constantinople continued to consider Antioch part of its traditional domain, and understood that such an attack would assure a Byzantine intervention in northern Syria, something he did not want at a time when he was preoccupied farther south. Rather than risk a two-front war with Byzantium and Jerusalem, he made it his policy not to provoke Constantinople. He preferred to deal with Jerusalem first.

The volatile relations between Nur ad-Din and Baldwin reached a critical point in February 1157 when the latter, severely pressed financially, authorized the confiscation of the herds and flocks that the Damascenes and Turks had traditionally pastured near Banias, under Baldwin's protection. The accompanying goatherds and shepherds were all slaughtered in the process. This outrage provided Nur ad-Din with the excuse he had been seeking to declare war on Jerusalem, which he was now able to do with the enthusiastic support of the Damascenes. In June 1157, Baldwin's army suffered a severe defeat near Banias, where it was cut to ribbons. As William, the archbishop of Tyre, noted at the time: "This time Our Lord visited upon the King and his men what they had done to the Turkomans and to those of Arabia, when they treacherously killed and robbed those whom they had guaranteed upon oath."[4] However, the expected onslaught against Jerusalem was delayed by an earthquake that struck the length of Syria in August 1157, which caused a great deal of destruction. This natural disaster gave

Baldwin a needed respite during which to try to improve his defense posture.

Baldwin was deprived of any hope of assistance from Western Europe in coping with the growing threat that Nur ad-Din posed. He himself had created the untenable situation in which he now found himself by squandering his resources on an unnecessary campaign against Ashkelon. Baldwin therefore contrived to obtain support from Constantinople by marrying the niece of the Byzantine emperor Manuel Comnenus (1143–1180) in September 1158. The following month, the emperor unexpectedly arrived in Armenian Cilicia with a powerful army and proceeded to Antioch, which he reached in April 1159, ostensibly for the purpose of confronting and defeating Nur ad-Din.

Although the question of sovereignty over Antioch had long been a matter of serious contention between the Frankish state and the Byzantines, given the threat from Nur ad-Din, Antioch had little choice but to welcome Manuel Comnenus with open arms. Seizing the initiative, in May 1159 the combined Byzantine-Frankish armies marched toward Aleppo to deal with the Zengid ruler. Manuel, however, was ambivalent about the prospect of eliminating Nur ad-Din. He understood that he was welcomed in Antioch only because of the threat posed by Nur ad-Din and that, once the latter had been disposed of, the long-standing enmity between the Frankish state and Byzantium would come to the fore once again. On the other hand, a continuation of the threat posed by Nur ad-Din to Syria would enable Manuel to effectively transform Antioch into a Byzantine protectorate.

Nur ad-Din, for his part, continued to pursue his policy of avoiding a direct confrontation with the Byzantines. Accordingly, as the combined Byzantine-Frankish army reached within some twenty-five miles of Aleppo, Nur ad-Din appealed to Manuel to settle their issues peacefully. This provided Manuel with the opportunity he sought and he accepted Nur ad-Din's offer without even consulting his outraged allies, who had hoped to rid themselves of the threat from Aleppo for all times. As the price of peace between them, Manuel extracted a commitment from Nur ad-Din to support his campaigns against the Seljukids in Anatolia, an enemy of far greater concern to Constantinople than the Zengids. At the same time, the Frankish states were given to understand that, while Nur ad-Din was campaigning against the Seljukids in Anatolia, they were not to conduct any large-scale military operations against his Syrian bases. They were not to attempt to upset the balance of power that Manuel wished to see maintained in northern Syria. The arrangement negotiated between Manuel and Nur ad-Din generally remained in effect for the next two decades.

At the same time that the situation in northern Syria appeared to be stabilizing, the theater of conflict between Nur ad-Din and the Franks shifted southward to Egypt. The Fatimids had been preoccupied with seemingly endless internal power struggles and political crises for decades. As a consequence, Egypt, which was still immensely rich, was virtually defenseless and constituted a tempting target to both Nur ad-Din and the Franks. Indeed, it was this desire to avail himself of Egypt's wealth that contributed to Baldwin's obsession with the conquest of Ashkelon and the opening thereby of the gateway to the country. It seemed clear that the wealth of Egypt could help tip the regional balance of power in favor of whoever could gain control of it.

In 1154, the year that Nur ad-Din took control of Damascus, the Fatimid caliph Dhafir (1149–1154) was murdered by his vizier, who in turn was ousted by the governor of Upper Egypt, Talaia ibn Ruzzik, after Dhafir's five-year-old son Faiz (1154–1160) was proclaimed caliph. When he later died in 1160, he was replaced as caliph by his nine-year-old cousin Adhid (1160–1171). The following year, the vizier Ibn Ruzzik was assassinated. He was succeeded by his son who was subsequently overthrown by a *coup d'etat* in December 1162 by Shawar as-Saadi. Shawar himself was displaced by another coup the following August by Dirgham al Lakhmi. In October 1163, Shawar appealed to Nur ad-Din to reinstate him in power as vizier, promising to pay the costs of the campaign. Nur ad-Din welcomed the opportunity to intervene in Egypt and dispatched a force from Damascus commanded by the Kurdish mercenary Shirkuh in April 1164.

By contrast with the Franks of Jerusalem, who only had to be concerned about crossing an inhospitable part of the Sinai desert in order to reach Egypt, Shirkuh had to cross the length of the enemy Kingdom of Jerusalem as well. Accordingly, Nur ad-Din initiated a diversionary attack in the north of Palestine that drew Amalric (1162–1174), the brother and successor of Baldwin III as king of Jerusalem, and his forces to the Galilee. At the same time, Shirkuh marched south from Damascus along the east bank of the Jordan until he reached the southern end of the Dead Sea. From there, he marched westward across the desert to arrive at Bilbeis unheralded, and took the town on April 24. By May 1, he was outside the walls of Cairo, where the vizier Dirgham panicked and was killed while trying to flee the city. Acting on behalf of Nur ad-Din, Shirkuh reinstated Shawar as the *de facto* ruler of Egypt.

Shawar, however, had no desire to see Egypt under a permanent Zengid occupation and secretly invited Amalric to intervene in Egypt and drive Shirkuh and the Zengid forces out. Amalric, who was as pleased to intervene in the country as Nur ad-Din had been, agreed and the Franks trapped Shirkuh in Bilbeis, to which they laid siege. To Nur ad-Din this represented a clear violation of the balance of power agreement he had concluded with Manuel. He reacted forcefully by launching a major offensive against the Franks in northern Syria that was intended primarily to relieve the pressure on Shirkuh in Egypt, by forcing Amalric to withdraw in order to protect his northern flank. Nur ad-Din attacked and defeated the joint forces of Bohemond III (1163–1201) of Antioch and Raymond of Tripoli at Artah, capturing both. Bohemond was released a year later, but Raymond remained a prisoner for a decade while Amalric ruled Tripoli as regent. The Antiochan frontier was pushed back to its previous line along the Orontes. At the same time, Nur ad-Din was concerned about provoking Constantinople into another invasion of Syria. He could ill afford a Byzantine intervention when a significant part of his army was engaged in a conflict in Egypt. Accordingly, he once again declined the opportunity to attack and take the city of Antioch itself.

The diversionary attack mounted by Nur ad-Din succeeded in seriously weakening the morale of the Frankish forces in Egypt, contributing to a stalemate on the battlefield. Before long, both Shirkuh and Amalric concluded that it was in the best interest of both sides to withdraw their forces from Egypt, an apparent vindication of Shawar's policy of playing one side against the other. Shirkuh nonetheless continued to press Shawar to join Nur ad-Din's camp against the Franks. However, the Fatimid Shiite leadership was very wary of aligning itself too closely with the Sunni Turks, whom they feared as much as the Franks. Indeed, when Shirkuh suggested that Egypt join in the struggle against the Franks for the triumph of Islam, Shawar is reported to have responded: "No, for they are not *Firenj* [Franks], but *firej* [salvation]!"[5]

Shirkuh's continued pressure on Shawar to align with Nur ad-Din apparently convinced Shawar that he could retain his independence only by entering into an alliance with Amalric. This step precipitated another invasion by Shirkuh in January 1167. Shawar appealed to Amalric for help once again, and the latter soon responded by entering Egypt in force. The Turks and Franks fought each other indecisively along the Nile for seven months, although Amalric ultimately managed to blockade Shirkuh in Alexandria, forcing him to agree to a mutual withdrawal from Egypt. Amalric subsequently retained a small garrison in the country and received an annual tribute of 100,000 gold dinars from Shawar. He made no further attempt to take control of the government. Egypt had become a vassal state of the Kingdom of Jerusalem. This arrangement was acceptable to Nur ad-Din, at least for the time being, as long as no attempt was made to annex Egypt to the Frankish state.

NOTES

1. *Arab Historians of the Crusades*, p. 61.
2. Zoe Oldenbourg, *The Crusades*, p. 377.
3. Amin Maalouf, *The Crusades through Arab Eyes*, pp. 151–152.
4. Odenbourg, *The Crusades*, p. 350.
5. Ibid., p. 366.

8

Saladin and the Ayyubid Empire

In 1168, Amalric married the great-niece of the Byzantine emperor Manuel Comnenus and further strengthened his relationship with Constantinople by means of a new formal alliance with the empire. Assured of Byzantine support, Amalric decided to repudiate his treaty with Shawar and to invade and conquer Egypt. A joint Byzantine-Frankish assault on the country was planned to take place the following year, but Amalric was impatient and decided to initiate the campaign more expeditiously. Acting unilaterally, he launched an invasion of Egypt before the Byzantine forces were ready to join him, presumably because he wanted to ensure that he alone garnered the lion's share of Egypt's wealth. This proved to be a serious blunder on Amalric's part since he did not have the military forces necessary to conquer the country, let alone occupy it.

Amalric placed Cairo under siege and demanded payment of a tribute of 1 million gold dinars. Shawar promptly appealed to Nur ad-Din for help. This time he sent Shirkuh south with an army that clearly would have overwhelmed the Franks. Under the circumstances, Amalric was compelled to abandon his demands for tribute and simply withdraw from Egypt. Shirkuh entered Cairo unopposed in January 1169 and took control of the city. Having invited Zengid intervention, Shawar now became preoccupied with trying to figure out a way to rid Egypt of the Turkish forces. But it was already too late. Shawar was soon seized and executed, probably at the instigation of the young caliph Adhid who then appointed Shirkuh as vizier and effective ruler of Egypt.

Shirkuh, however, died suddenly on March 23, 1169, creating a power vacuum in the country. After a few days of palace intrigue, and against the wishes of some of the Zengid officers who did not wish to see another non-

Turk in such a position of power, Shirkuh's nephew Saladin (Salah ad-Din), a Kurd, managed to seize control of the state. He obtained formal appointment as vizier from the Fatimid caliph, a step that was necessary to give legitimacy to his rule.

Saladin's sudden rise to power in Egypt caused serious misgivings among the supporters and retainers of the Fatimids. The latter were Shiites, whereas Saladin and his Turks were Sunnis. To eliminate this source of potential trouble for his regime, Saladin soon replaced all the Fatimid officials with his own men. This proved to be a prudent move since some of those officials were already plotting with the Franks in Jerusalem to find a means of dislodging the Turks from Egypt.

In August 1169, Saladin was faced by a revolt of the caliph's personal guard, which consisted primarily of a corps of some 50,000 Sudanese and Nubian troops who were fiercely devoted to the man who was both their master and religious leader. Believing that Saladin was holding the caliph prisoner, the royal guards mounted an assault on Cairo that seriously threatened the security of the Zengid forces in the city.

Saladin decided to respond to this challenge by an act of wanton brutality that was calculated to shatter the morale of the royal guards and their ability to continue to function as a cohesive fighting force. He deliberately put the camp where the rebel troops kept their wives and children to the torch. This horrendous act had the effect that Saladin anticipated. The overwrought rebels dispersed in disorder, only to be hunted down and slaughtered. The caliph's Armenian Guard was disposed of in a comparably brutal fashion. The gates of their compound were sealed before they could get out, and their quarters were then set ablaze. By destroying the core elements of the Fatimid army, and thereby eliminating all effective opposition, Saladin (1169–1193) was able to achieve undisputed control of the country.

Amalric, beside himself with worry over the unanticipated consequences of his Egyptian adventure, attempted to regain a foothold in Egypt that same year with the support of a Byzantine fleet. He laid siege to Damietta, but the effort proved unproductive and ended in another defeat for him. In 1170, Saladin launched his own counteroffensive, capturing Gaza and the Frankish port at Aila (Aqaba) on the Red Sea.

Although he was the de facto ruler of Egypt, Saladin was careful always to portray his actions as taking place in the name of his nominal overlord, Nur ad-Din. The latter had recently become master of the Jazira, in addition to Syria, upon the death of his brother Qutb ad-Din, who had succeeded Saif ad-Din as atabeg of Mosul, thereby unifying the Zengid domains into a single powerful state. A staunch defender of Sunni orthodoxy, Nur ad-Din called upon Saladin to terminate the Shiite caliphate of the Fatimids, a demand that had significant political overtones. It was clear that despite Saladin's nominal subservience to Nur ad-Din, the former's barely disguised autonomous control of Egypt had become a matter of serious concern to the Zengid chief; Nur ad-Din began to view Saladin's ascendancy as a challenge to his own authority. Since Saladin's formal status as vizier was derived entirely from the authority of the caliph, the termination of the caliphate would surely raise a cloud over the legitimacy of Saladin's position in Egypt. To dispel this cloud, he would henceforth be forced to base his legitimacy on his appointment by Nur ad-Din, a grant of authority that could be revoked at any time. Furthermore, since Saladin was a Kurd, and not a Turk, the continued loyalty of some, perhaps many, of his Turkish troops might become subject to the whim of Nur ad-Din.

Understandably, Saladin was reluctant to comply with Nur ad-Din's order to eliminate the Fatimid caliphate, and he procrastinated. However, on September 10, 1171, an emissary of Nur ad-Din took the initiative and, climbing the pulpit in a Cairo mosque ahead of the Shiite preacher, recited the prayers in the name of the Abbasid caliph, effectively announcing the transference of allegiance to the Sunni caliphate in Baghdad. Once this occurred, Saladin no longer had any practical option other than to comply with Nur ad-Din's instructions. The Fatimid caliphate was abolished entirely, with Adhid dying three days later under suspicious circumstances. Egypt nominally became subservient to the Abbasids who, since the collapse of Seljukid power in the region, had once again become the real rulers of southern Iraq, a factor that enhanced the prestige of their caliphate throughout the Muslim world and made its imprimatur politically significant.

Somewhat surprisingly, instead of undermining Saladin's autonomous position in Egypt, the elimination of the Fatimid caliphate had the unanticipated consequence of actually strengthening it. Since he was in fact in control of the country, with or without a caliph's blessing, the Egyptians soon acknowledged Saladin as their undisputed independent ruler. This raised the serious threat of an intervention by Nur ad-Din, something that Saladin tried to forestall with all the means at his disposal. At one point, Saladin's father Ayyub, a trusted lieutenant of Nur ad-Din, interceded and prevented a split between the two that would have meant war. Nonetheless, concerned about his vulnerability to attack in Egypt, Saladin sent his brother Turan Shah to conquer Arabia and Yemen, providing for a refuge there in the event that Nur ad-Din decided to march against him. At the same time, this expansionist move enabled Saladin to establish his hegemony over the Red Sea region and the lucrative trade routes to India and East Asia.

Saladin's worst expectations were about to be fulfilled as Nur ad-Din prepared to invade Egypt and reassert his authority over his wayward lieutenant. According to Ibn al-Athir, "Nur ad-Din was making preparations to invade Egypt and take it from Saladin, in whom he divined a certain reluctance to fight the Franks as he should. He knew that it was fear of himself, Nur ad-Din, and of finding himself face to face with his Lord, that weakened Saladin's enthusiasm, and made him content to have the Franks as a bulwark between them."[1] War was averted only by the death of Nur ad-Din on May 15, 1174, which left his eleven-year-old son Malik as-Salih Ismail (1174–1181) as successor to the Zengid imperium.

When Amalric died two months later, on July 11, leaving the Kingdom of Jerusalem to the thirteen-year-old Baldwin IV (1174–1185), Saladin, suddenly and quite unexpectedly, found himself without any formidable competitors for the role of dominant power in the region, a role that he now pursued with determination. He began by first marching into Syria, occupying Damascus in late November 1174. From there he proceeded to challenge Nur ad-Din's successor for control of the country, and decisively defeated the forces of Malik as-Salih Ismail at the Horns of Hama in April 1175. Saladin was now master of Egypt and most of Muslim Palestine and Syria, with the notable exception of Aleppo, which remained in Zengid hands.

Farther north, in Anatolia, the tolerable relations that had been established between the emperor Manuel Comnenus and the Seljukid sultan of Konya, Qilij Arslan II (1156–1192), were breached by the Byzantines. After a long struggle, Qilij Arslan had managed to eliminate the Danishmend dynasty in 1175, and to incorporate all their lands into his realm. Manuel could not view the growing power of the Seljukids with equanimity and sought to interfere with their consolidation of power in eastern Anatolia by capturing their seat of government at Konya. Seizing the Seljukid capital would surely enhance significantly Manuel's prestige in Europe, especially since it would also give him control of the overland route to the Holy Land.

However, Manuel's plans went awry when, in the course of the campaign that he initiated, the Byzantine forces were outmaneuvered and trapped in a gorge near Myriocephalon in Phrygia. Manuel's army suffered a crushing defeat on September 17, 1176, with the emperor barely escaping with his life. The Byzantine historian Niketas Choniates wrote of the disaster: "The horrors that took place there defy all description. Since they could neither advance nor retreat (for the Turks took up positions in the rear and made the way forward impassable), the Romans, like cattle in their pens, were cut down in this gorge. . . . Indeed, the sight was worthy of tears, or, more accurately, the magnitude of the evil was too great for tears."[2]

Their decisive defeat at the battle of Myriocephalon put an end to any Byzantine hope of ever driving the Seljukids out of Asia Minor. On the contrary, with their position in Cilicia and northern Syria now completely undermined, it seemed more likely that it was the Byzantines that would ultimately be forced to abandon what remained of their once extensive empire in Asia. The Seljukids now had control of virtually the entire Anatolian peninsula, and the Frankish states to the south could no longer look to Byzantium for help in times of crisis.

Saladin sought to take advantage of these developments by attacking Palestine, but he was defeated by the forces of Baldwin IV at Tel al-Jazar near Ramle on November 25, 1177. However, the Franks were unable to muster the resources necessary to follow up on their victory. The most they could do was to attempt to prevent Saladin from attacking again, a strategy doomed to failure. Two years later, on June 10, 1179, the Franks were severely beaten by Saladin at Marjayoun, at the bend of the Litani River in southern Lebanon, a defeat that cost them half of their knights. Baldwin was forced to ask for a truce, a request that Saladin was pleased to grant for reasons of his own.

Saladin had become preoccupied with establishing his mastery over the Jazira, and he was therefore eager to be able to maintain a series of intermittent truces with the Franks that obviated the necessity of conducting military operations on two opposite fronts simultaneously. Establishing his rule over the Jazira was an objective of higher priority for Saladin than completing the conquest of Palestine. He could ill afford to get bogged down in a long war with the Franks while a new political force arose to fill the vacuum that was being created in eastern Syria and the Jazira as Zengid power there declined after the death of Nur ad-Din.

The opportunity for Saladin to advance his aims came with the death of Malik as-Salih Ismail of Aleppo in 1181. The young prince had bequeathed his domain to his cousin Izz ad-Din Masud (1176–1193) of Mosul. The latter, however, was more interested in adding the Sinjar Mountains to his realm and exchanged Aleppo for them with his brother Zengi II. However, before Zengi could establish himself as atabeg in Aleppo, Saladin intervened and occupied the city in June 1183, thereby uniting all of Muslim Syria and Egypt into a single state once again.

While this was taking place in the east, the truce with the Franks in the west collapsed, forcing Saladin to divert his attention away from his eastern campaign. In 1182, he managed to impose a temporary quarantine on Frankish Syria, effectively interdicting all maritime communications to and from its ports, thereby preventing the arrival of reinforcements for the perennially manpower-short crusader states. He then mounted a series of brief campaigns in 1183 and 1184 that, although militarily inconclusive, placed sufficient pressure on the Franks to make them amenable to a renewal of the truce, which was subsequently reinstated in 1185. This left Saladin free once again to devote his full attention to the Jazira.

He laid siege to Mosul in June 1185, but an assault on the city was delayed by his illness until the following year. Early in 1186, rather than risk certain attack, Izz ad-Din Masud made a peace overture to Saladin, which he accepted. By treaty of March 3, 1186, the atabeg of Mosul acknowledged Saladin's suzerainty. Under this vassalage agreement, Izz ad-Din Masud was able to remain as de facto ruler of Mosul while Saladin nominally added the northern Jazira and part of Kurdistan to his empire. Given the chronic instability on his frontiers with the Frankish states, Saladin had to be satisfied with this arrangement. It assured a modicum of security on his eastern flank while he focused his attention on western Syria and Palestine.

As a matter of general policy, Saladin preferred to achieve his strategic goals through political means rather than through war, whenever such was possible. Accordingly, he launched a sophisticated diplomatic campaign that was designed to completely isolate the Frankish states politically. He negotiated with the Italian maritime cities, encouraging them to divert their trade links from Syria and Palestine to Egypt in the hope of depriving the Franks of any support from them. Then, in 1185, he concluded a treaty with the Byzantine emperor Andronicus Comnenus (1183–1185). The emperor was under threat from the Normans and needed to secure his flanks against the Seljukids in Anatolia by forcing the latter to become preoccupied with a threat from Saladin on their southern frontier. Under this treaty, Andronicus was prepared to concede Palestine to Saladin on the condition that the latter recognize Byzantine suzerainty there. In addition, Saladin was to concede to the emperor any territory that might be conquered from the sultan of Konya as far south as the frontiers of Antioch and Lesser Armenia. It appears that Saladin was a consummate politician since he apparently was able to maintain simultaneous alliances with both the Byzantines and the Seljukids.

Shortly after the death of Baldwin IV, his brother-in-law Guy de Lusignan (1186–1192) ascended the throne of Jerusalem. Guy was a particularly weak ruler and was unable to restrain his own nobles from breaking the truce with Saladin. Renaud de Chatillon, the lord of Kerak in Moab, which dominated the ancient route from Damascus to the Hejaz, ignored Guy's instructions and began to plunder Muslim pilgrims travelling to Mecca. From Aila (Aqaba), he also launched a fleet of pirate ships that raided the coastal towns of the Hejaz. Saladin concluded that the truce he had made with Baldwin had outlasted its usefulness, and he exploited Renaud's criminal acts, which Guy seemed incapable of dealing with, as a justification for a renewal of the conflict. In March 1187, Saladin, adopting the tactic used by his mentor Nur ad-Din, proclaimed a holy war and sent word to his viceroys and vassals in Egypt, Syria, the Jazira, and Diyarbekir to mobilize for a campaign near Damascus. He then crossed the frontier into Palestine in June, laying siege to Tiberias at the end of the month.

The crusader states, from the very beginning, were faced with acute shortages of manpower. When confronted by Muslim invasions, they had to mobilize every available man, depleting the cities as well as the countryside. Without an assured reserve of manpower, the Frankish rulers understood that if one of their armies were to be destroyed, it could not be replaced. Accordingly, to the extent possible, they tried to avoid pitched battles that could become decisive. Their preferred tactic was to skirmish and maneuver, stalling until the arrival of winter, which would force an end to the hostilities until the following spring. Nonetheless, and notwithstanding the compelling logic behind this policy, Renaud and others convinced Guy to confront Saladin in a pitched battle that took place at Hattin on July 4, 1187. It turned out to be an unmitigated disaster for the Franks. They lost much of their army, which left their cities largely defenseless, while Guy himself was taken prisoner.

Saladin anticipated the possibility of a new crusade from Europe that might be generated as a consequence of the defeat at Hattin, as had occurred after the fall of Edessa. He therefore wished to take maximum advantage of the seriously weakened condition of the Kingdom of Jerusalem and sought to force it into submission. He marched into Acre unopposed. Although he failed to take Tyre, he quickly captured Sidon and Beirut, driving a wedge between the Kingdom of Jerusalem and the county of Tripoli. He then laid siege to Jerusalem on September 20, 1187, and accepted the surrender of the city on October 2. Throughout the following year, Saladin continued systematically to reduce the Frankish fortresses in Palestine.

The news of the defeat of the Franks at Hattin followed by the fall of Jerusalem had a profound impact in Europe. Frederick Barbarossa of Germany (who died in Cilicia before he could reach the Holy Land), Philippe Auguste of France, and Richard I of England all undertook the crusade that Saladin had correctly surmised would be forthcoming. In the meanwhile, Saladin had released Guy on the basis of his solemn promise not to take up arms against the Muslims again. Guy promptly reneged on his commitment and sought to recapture Acre in the summer of 1189 with a contingent of several hundred men, the most that he was able to muster. However, he could not hope to break into Acre with the small force at his disposal. He dug in east of the city, where he was able to withstand an initial attack by Saladin's forces. A few days later, on September 1, 1189, a crusader fleet arrived with some 10,000 Flemish and Danish troops. With these very substantial reinforcements the Franks laid siege to Acre. Saladin, in turn, brought up the main body of his army and laid siege to the besiegers of Acre, triggering a war of attrition between them that dragged on for almost two years. Finally, on July 11, 1191, after the arrival of the new crusader armies of England and France, as well as a smaller force of Germans (the army of Frederick Barbarossa had disintegrated for the most part under the command of his son, Frederick of Swabia), Acre was forced to surrender.

Following the fall of Acre, Philippe Auguste quickly returned to France, while Richard marched south along the coast with the intention of attempting the re-conquest of Jerusalem. Saladin also moved south parallel to Richard, harassing his forces along their route of march. Then on September 7, 1191, after having received reinforcements, Saladin engaged Richard in a pitched battle at Arsuf, north of Jaffa, hoping to duplicate his earlier victory at Hattin. This proved to be a serious miscalculation on Saladin's part, as the tide of battle went against him. Avoiding further pitched battles with

Richard, Saladin adopted a scorched earth policy and destroyed everything along the road to Jerusalem including the towns of Lydda and Ramle,
slowing Richard's advance by forcing his troops to spend valuable time for-
aging for supplies. By the time the crusader forces reached Ramle on December 8, the rains had already started, turning the roads into a quagmire.
Richard was effectively compelled to suspend military operations until the
following spring.

When the campaign was renewed in June 1192, Richard realized that he
was now courting disaster. Since Saladin was positioned defensively in the
Judean hills, an attempt by Richard to have his army march uphill some
2,500 feet through an area where the only water was to be found behind the
enemy's lines would truly be setting the stage for another Hattin. Richard
concluded that the logic of the situation demanded prudence and he withdrew back to Ramle on July 4, 1192, abandoning his goal of retaking Jerusalem.

Richard had succeeded in recapturing the coastal plain between Ashkelon and Tyre. Saladin, however, was still in control of Beirut, severing the
land connection between Tyre in the south and Tripoli and Antioch in the
north. Richard now set his sights on forcing Saladin to withdraw from the
coast so that he might reestablish the territorial contiguity of the Frankish
states. However, as Richard marched north toward Beirut, Saladin
marched south and attacked Jaffa in force, compelling Richard to return to
Jaffa by ship from Acre in order to prevent a new wedge being driven
through what remained of Frankish Palestine. Richard succeeded in holding Jaffa against Saladin's attacks, and it soon became clear that the conflict
had reached the point of stalemate. Richard therefore became anxious to
terminate the struggle and return to England. According to Imad ad-Din
(Saladin's retainer and chronicler), Richard sent the following message to
Saladin: "Now the time is close when the sea becomes unnavigable and the
crests of the waves swell up on high. If you agree to a truce and enable me
to, I shall fulfil my desire (to go); but if you fight and oppose me I shall pitch
my tents and fix my dwelling here. Both sides are tired, both companies are
exhausted. I have renounced Jerusalem and will now renounce Ascalon. . . . If we persist in our miserable conflict we shall destroy ourselves. So
fulfil my desire and win my friendship; make a pact with me and let me go;
agree with me and accept my response." Interestingly, Saladin was rather
reluctant to call off the conflict this time, apparently having undergone a
change of heart and perspective after many long years of virtually continual warfare. It seems that war itself had become his way of life. Imad ad-Din
records that he told his emirs and counselors that they were

in a strong position and within sight of the victory we have longed for. . . . We have
become accustomed to fighting the Holy War and in it we have achieved our aim.
Now it is difficult to break off what has become customary. . . . We have no other occupation and aim than that of making war, for we are not among those who are be-

guiled by games and led astray by dissipation. If we give up this work, what shall we do? If we destroy our hope of defeating them, what shall we hope for? . . . My feeling is to reject the idea of a truce, and in preferring war, to prefer my honour and make it my leader.[3]

Nonetheless, Saladin's counselors appear to have prevailed upon him to respond positively to Richard's offer and the Peace of Ramle was concluded on September 1, 1192. Under its terms, only the strip of coast between Jaffa and Tyre remained under Frankish control, a situation that was to continue for another century. Richard sailed for England and Saladin returned to Damascus in November 1192, where he died the following March 3. He left behind an Ayyubid empire that stretched from the Libyan Desert to Kurdistan.

NOTES

1. *Arab Historians of the Crusades*, p. 69.
2. Niketas Choniates, *O City of Byzantium, Annals of Niketas Choniates*, pp. 102–103, 107.
3. *Arab Historians of the Crusades*, pp. 234–235.

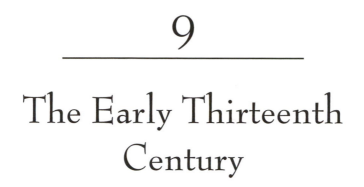

9

The Early Thirteenth Century

Saladin apparently had little confidence that the empire he had built would survive him intact. Presumably to reduce the probability of a counterproductive struggle over the succession among his heirs, he divided the empire among them before his death. However, if it was in fact Saladin's intention to assure a smooth transition to a stabilized territorial arrangement in this way, that intention was not destined to be realized by his family.

The empire was distributed as follows. The sultanate itself was awarded to Saladin's eldest son Afdal (1193–1196), who was to remain the nominal suzerain of the empire, as well as the ruler of Damascus and southern Syria. Egypt was assigned to his son Aziz (1193–1198), while Aleppo and northern Syria went to a third son, Zahir (1193–1216). Saladin gave the Jazira to his brother Adil (1193–1218). As he evidently feared, within a year of Saladin's death, his sons began quarreling among themselves, egged on by their uncle Adil who soon began to eliminate them one at a time. By 1200, Adil had succeeded in reuniting most of the Ayyubid Empire under his personal rule and he proclaimed himself its sultan. Even though separate dynastic offshoots continued to rule in Aleppo and the Yemen, Adil's authority had become generally acknowledged throughout the empire.

As discussed in the preceding chapter, Saladin had reduced the territory of the Kingdom of Jerusalem to the coastal strip between Jaffa and Tyre, with Acre replacing the city of Jerusalem as its capital. Guy de Lusignan died in 1192 and was ultimately succeeded by his brother Amalric II (1197–1205), who also became king of Cyprus. Richard of England had conquered the island while he was en route to Palestine during the Third Crusade and gave it to Guy, whose family was to continue to rule there for 300 years. On July 1, 1198, Amalric concluded a treaty with Adil that ceded Beirut to the Kingdom of Jerusalem, restoring contiguous Frankish control of most of the coasts of Palestine and Syria. At the time, Adil was still preoccupied with establishing his control over the Ayyubids and needed peace with the Franks in order to give that problem his undivided attention. To secure that peace, he was prepared to yield to Amalric what Saladin had denied to Richard. During the same period, the county of Tripoli was united with Antioch, reducing the number of remaining Frankish states to two.

To the north, although Ayyubid-Seljukid relations remained troubled, they had settled into a state of de facto non-belligerence and accommodation. They continued to quarrel over the fringe zones that separated their domains. However, as a practical matter, the Ayyubids were apparently fully prepared to concede that Anatolia lay beyond their sphere of interest, while the Seljukids had too many problems internally and on their eastern and western frontiers to harbor any serious ambitions in Syria.

The final collapse of Seljukid rule in Persia in 1194 had little immediate impact on the Seljukids of Anatolia. Qilij Arslan II had tried to resolve the potential succession issue among his sons by subdividing the sultanate several years before his death. As in the case of the Ayyubids, it didn't help much. As he lay dying in 1192, Qilij Arslan learned that his son Suleiman was contesting the succession of Kai-Khusraw I (1192–1196) to the sultanate of Konya. Kai-Khusraw eventually was overthrown and forced to seek refuge in Constantinople, notwithstanding the fact that he had recently defeated the forces of the Byzantine emperor Alexius III Angelus. After more than a decade of internecine struggle, Suleiman II (1196–1204) succeeded in reuniting the Seljukid domains only several days before he died. This permitted the return of Kai-Khusraw I (1204–1210) to the throne from his exile at a moment of great turbulence on the Byzantine-Seljukid frontier.

In August 1198, shortly after Innocent III mounted the papal throne, he issued a call for a fourth crusade. However, by the time that the crusader armies were organized and ready to sail for Egypt, and from there to fight their way to Jerusalem, the complex politics of medieval Europe intervened to bring about a radical change in those plans. For reasons that need not detain us here, the Fourth Crusade was diverted to Byzantium; that is, instead of Jerusalem, its goal became the conquest of Constantinople, which fell on April 13, 1204. The Byzantine Empire collapsed and was replaced by a Latin empire that remained centered in Constantinople.

Although the Latins planned to extend their control to Anatolia, they soon became fully preoccupied with events in the Balkans, and paid little attention to developments in Asia. As a result, a group of Byzantine refugees under the leadership of Theodore I Lascaris (1204–1222), and with the support of the local Byzantine population, were able to establish the Empire of Nicaea, which was to last until 1261.

Simultaneously, but for reasons unconnected with the fall of Constantinople, another independent Byzantine state was established in April 1204 at Trebizond, on the Anatolian Black Sea coast. In this case, Alexius and David, the grandsons of the deposed Byzantine emperor Andronicus Comnenus (1183–1185), captured the ancient city with the support of the queen Thamar (1184–1212) of Georgia, with whom they had taken refuge. From their base at Trebizond, David marched into and occupied Sinope, then brought the territories of Paphlagonia and Pontine Heraclea under his control, and next advanced westward along the coast until he reached the frontiers of Theodore's new kingdom of Nicaea.

Relations between the Seljukid sultan Kai-Khusraw and Theodore were reasonably tolerable at first, but soon began to sour as their interests in Anatolia collided. In 1207, Kai-Khusraw attacked and seized the Mediterranean port of Antalya, an acquisition that had the effect of significantly improving the Seljukid economy by providing it with a maritime outlet, something that the Lascarids were not at all pleased with, since it diverted trade away from Nicaea. Their relations deteriorated further after Theodore refused to turn over Nicaea to his father-in-law, the recently deposed Byzantine emperor Alexius III Angelus (1195–1203), who now made claim to the kingdom. Alexius appealed to Kai-Khusraw, who had earlier been accorded refuge at his court in Constantinople, for his assistance in compelling Theodore to step down in his favor. Grateful for the considerate treatment he had received at the emperor's hands at a time of great need, Kai-Khusraw became Alexius' host and an ardent supporter of his claim to Nicaea.

This was not an entirely selfless act on the sultan's part, however, since Kai-Khusraw was quite perturbed by the alliance that Theodore had entered into with Leo II of Armenia, a pact that had serious security implications for the Seljukids. War between them and the Lascarids broke out in 1210, and quickly turned into a debacle for the Seljukids. Although the Lascarids were actually defeated on the battlefield, Kai-Khusraw was killed accidentally and, in the confusion that followed, Theodore was able to snatch the victory away from his adversary. Alexius was taken captive, and Theodore disposed of his claims by imprisoning him for life in a Nicaean monastery. Theodore then proceeded to expand his realm eastward along the Black Sea coast, while Leo II retook Eregli and Karaman. To make matters worse for the Seljukids, the Franks retook the port of Antalya, once again denying them direct access to a maritime outlet.

The state of Seljukid affairs took a turn for the better under Kai-Khusraw's successor, Kai-Kaus (1210–1219). Although the first years of his reign were spent in dealing with a number of internal challenges to his succession, by 1214 he managed to take significant steps toward restoring the earlier Seljukid position in Anatolia. He retook Antalya and launched a northern offensive designed to break through to the Black Sea coast.

Achieving the latter goal was essential if he was to reap any benefits from the lucrative transit trade between China, India, Persia, and Europe. In late 1214, Kai-Kaus conquered Sinope, giving him the outlet on the Black Sea that he needed. In the process, he also captured Alexius I Comnenus, the ruler of Trebizond, whom he made his vassal and then released. He then turned eastward and drove Leo II out of Anatolia, forcing him to withdraw to Lesser Armenia in 1216.

Within a few years, Kai-Kaus had managed to restore the lustre of the sultanate of Konya and introduce a hitherto unknown sense of stability within the territories under his control. The trade routes through Seljukid lands had been made secure, bringing new prosperity to the country. Potential enemies, such as the Lascarids of Nicaea, were preoccupied with their wars with the Franks and the Turkish emirs of the Anatolian peninsula, and were not strong enough to pose a security threat of any great significance. However, this relatively comfortable situation was to be violently disturbed within just a few years as a consequence of events taking place far to the east, which will be described shortly.

Since, as noted earlier, the Fourth Crusade had been diverted from its original purpose of conquering the Holy Land, Pope Innocent III proclaimed yet another crusade in 1215 to achieve that goal. Before long, a large number of volunteers, including as many as two thousand knights and perhaps ten times as many foot soldiers, began arriving at Acre. Crusader military operations started in November 1217 with an incursion into the Galilee. It soon became apparent, however, that a campaign in northern Palestine would accomplish little. The number of troops that the Ayyubids were capable of mobilizing to oppose them seemed to be virtually unlimited. If the crusaders had persisted in the campaign, it would have turned into a war of attrition that they could not possibly have sustained for any length of time.

Under the leadership of Jean de Brienne (1210–1225), ruler of the truncated Frankish Kingdom of Jerusalem, the crusaders adopted an alternate and rather novel strategy. Instead of attempting to break through the Muslim defensive lines that blocked their way to the re-conquest of Jerusalem, their new plan was to invade Egypt and seize the strategically important port of Damietta in the Nile Delta. They would then offer to return it to the Ayyubid sultan Adil in exchange for Jerusalem. The plan was put into effect in May 1218, when the crusader forces embarked for Egypt, and received unexpected help from the coincidental death of the sultan in August 1218. His sudden demise caused a great deal of confusion among the Ayyubids, who failed to adequately organize the defense of Damietta, which subsequently fell to the crusaders on November 5, 1219.

The crusader successes, coupled with the internal problems arising out of the question of the Ayyubid succession, had a devastating effect on Ayyubid morale. As Ibn al-Athir observed, "All the rest of Egypt and Syria was on the point of collapse and everyone was terrified of the invaders and went in anticipation of disaster night and day. The population of Egypt was even ready to evacuate the country for fear of the enemy."[1] Under the circumstances, it is perhaps not surprising that the new Ayyubid sultan Kamil (1218–1238) agreed to the exchange of Jerusalem for the captured city of Damietta; he might not have been able to prevent the loss of Jerusalem to the crusader army in any case. His appeals to his brothers Muazzam (1218–1227) in Damascus and Ashraf (1210–1229) in the Jazira for reinforcements produced some early relief from the former. While Ashraf would willingly have come to Kamil's aid, he was faced by a revolt of his own vassals at the moment and could not reach Egypt for some time.

As fate would have it, the papal legate, Cardinal Pelagius, arrived at Damietta in the interim and assumed command of the crusade. Pelagius ignored Kamil's readiness to exchange Jerusalem for Damietta, since he had already set his heart on the conquest of Egypt. Nonetheless, he delayed the campaign to take Cairo for a year and a half while he awaited the arrival of the supporting army of Frederick II Hohenstaufen (1220–1250), emperor of Germany and king of Sicily. Unknown to Pelagius, Frederick had only sent a small force of some 500 knights. The relief army was expected to arrive in Egypt by the spring of 1221. When July came, and there were still no German reinforcements, Pelagius decided to wait no longer and directed the crusader forces southward into the delta, heading for the Egyptian capital. By this time, of course, Kamil's army had been significantly reinforced. Furthermore, the season for the annual rise of the Nile had arrived, and by August the mud in the delta was such that the crusader army could advance no farther. Then, as they began their retreat, the Egyptians opened the dikes, leaving the crusaders to be engulfed by the swirling waters and mired in a sea of mud. Pelagius, now desperate to save his army from annihilation, sued for peace. According to the Ayyubid historian Ibn Wasil, Kamil rejected the suggestion of his advisers that he insist on unconditional surrender by the crusader forces. The sultan argued: "There are other Franks; even if we destroy them too it will take us a long time and a hard fight to win Damietta. The Franks beyond the sea will hear what has befallen them and will arrive in more than double the numbers of these here, and we shall have to face a siege."[2] Kamil accepted Pelagius' petition on the sole condition that the crusaders peacefully evacuate Egypt by sea and agree to an eight-year truce.

Following the collapse of the Fifth Crusade, Kamil sought to establish a relationship with Frederick II that might be exploited in the complex politics of the Ayyubid Empire. By 1225, an exchange of correspondence between the two monarchs had developed and Kamil invited Frederick to come to the Middle East, adding that he would be pleased to see the German king in possession of Jerusalem. For Kamil, this was a strategic move designed to enhance Egypt's security posture. As Ibn Wasil relates: "The idea of the approaches made to the Emperor, the King of the Franks, and of his invitation, was to create difficulties for al-Malik al-Mu'azzam and prevent his availing himself of the help offered to him by the Sultan Jalal ad-Din ibn Ala ad-Din Khwarizmshah and Muzaffar ad-Din of Arbela, in his quarrel with al-Kamil and al-Malik al-Ashraf."[3]

The Ayyubid Empire in the east was in turmoil and Kamil was concerned about the possible threat to Egypt from the Khwarizmians, who were pushing westward under the pressure of the unrelenting Mongol push into the region. From Kamil's perspective, the occupation of Palestine by the powerful Frederick would create a friendly buffer state in the land bridge between Egypt and the volatile Muslim states of Asia. Furthermore, offering Jerusalem to Frederick cost Kamil nothing since it was not under his control at the time; it was ruled by Muazzam, with whom, as already indicated, Kamil was not on very good terms.

For his part, Frederick was entranced by the idea, since the acquisition of Jerusalem for Christianity once again would strengthen his position in his own struggle with the pope who had just excommunicated him as punishment for having delayed his expedition to the Holy Land. After a period of preparation, Frederick took up Kamil's offer and sailed for Palestine. He arrived at Acre in September 1228, expecting to enter Jerusalem in triumph shortly thereafter. However, by the time of his arrival, the regional situation had changed significantly. Muazzam had died in November 1227 and left Damascus to his inexperienced son Nasir (1227–1229). Kamil, who now looked forward to the possibility of adding both Damascus and Palestine to his domains, was no longer interested in establishing a buffer state that would isolate Egypt from Asia.

Frederick, not expecting to have to fight for Jerusalem and Palestine, came with only a force of some 3,000 men and was in no position to demand that Kamil make good on his promise. He wrote to Kamil: "It was you who urged me to make this trip. The pope and all the kings of the West now know of my mission. If I return empty-handed, I will lose much prestige. For pity's sake, give me Jerusalem, that I may hold my head high." Kamil, who considered himself a man of honor, was embarrassed by his need to renege on his commitment. He replied: "I too must take account of opinion. If I deliver Jerusalem to you, it could lead not only to a condemnation of my actions by the caliph, but also to a religious insurrection that would threaten my throne."[4]

Toward the end of 1228, the internal squabbling among the Ayyubids finally produced a new partition of the empire in the Treaty of Tel-Ajul. Ashraf (1229–1237), Kamil's brother and governor of the Jazira, was to receive Syria and Damascus at the expense of their nephew Nasir. Kamil was to receive Palestine and remain nominal sultan of the Ayyubids. However, as it stood, the partition agreement was a mere scrap of paper. Nasir would resist its implementation strenuously, and he therefore would have to be defeated in battle before Kamil would realize any practical benefits from the partition accord. Kamil now faced the prospect of the two-front war that he had sought to avoid at all costs. He now needed to keep Frederick pacified while he dealt with his nephew. As stated by Ibn Wasil, "he was in favour of satisfying the Franks with a disarmed Jerusalem and making a temporary truce with them. He could seize the concessions back from them later, when he chose to."[5]

Kamil's ambassador, Fakhr ad-Din, suggested a solution that would save face for both rulers without significantly affecting Kamil's strategic interests. He suggested to Frederick that it was impossible for Kamil simply to give up Jerusalem, which had been conquered by Saladin at heavy cost. On the other hand, if an agreement regarding Jerusalem were to avoid a major struggle for the city that would be very costly in terms of blood, honor would be satisfied. Frederick quickly grasped the subtlety of the ploy being suggested and ordered his small force to prepare for war. At the end of 1228, as Frederick marched toward Jaffa with much display, Kamil spread the word that it was necessary to prepare for a major protracted war with the powerful king of Germany and Sicily. A few weeks later, without swords ever having been crossed, a peace treaty was signed between Frederick and Fakhr ad-Din, acting on behalf of the sultan. Kamil was now able to claim that he reluctantly yielded Jerusalem only to save his people from a devastating but avoidable war. The treaty of February 18, 1229, awarded the city of Jerusalem, along with a transit corridor to the coast, to Frederick. The Muslim population was evacuated from the city, although a Muslim presence was preserved in the Haram ash-Sharif sector (the Temple Mount), which contained the great mosques. Frederick also received Bethlehem and Nazareth as part of the deal.

News of the treaty and the cession of Jerusalem to the Franks provoked a violent reaction in Damascus, where Nasir declared war on Kamil. This gave Kamil the excuse he had been looking for to carry out his expansionist ambitions in Syria and Palestine. He quickly imposed a blockade of Damascus with his far superior Egyptian army, and in June 1229 forced Nasir to abandon his capital and flee for safety to Kerak in Trans-Jordan.

No sooner had the conflict between Kamil and Nasir been resolved than a new struggle broke out between Kamil and his brother Ashraf that lasted until the latter died in 1237. Kamil himself died in 1238 and the Ayyubid Empire collapsed in the wake of the civil war that broke out between his sons Salih Ayyub in Damascus and Adil II (1238–1240) in Egypt. Salih Ayyub (1240–1249) prevailed in the conflict and took over in Egypt in 1240.

In the meanwhile, another crusader army under Richard of Cornwall arrived in Palestine. Salih Ayyub, with Damascus now in revolt against him, was faced with the need to re-conquer his own former territories. To enable him to pursue this objective, he had to first make sure that he would not come under attack from the new crusader army. This led Salih Ayyub to conclude a treaty with Richard in 1241 under which he not only confirmed the concessions made by Kamil to Frederick II in 1229, but also conceded the hinterland of Sidon, Tiberias, the eastern Galilee, and the areas around Jaffa and Ashkelon. Only the districts of Samaria and Hebron remained in Ayyubid hands in Palestine. Soon thereafter, to offset the advantage gained by Salih Ayyub, his opponents in Damascus made their own rapprochement with the Frankish Kingdom of Jerusalem, effectively renewing the alliance that had existed a century earlier.

Full-scale war between the Ayyubid rulers of Egypt and Damascus broke out in 1244. However, in anticipation of this conflict, Salih Ayyub had made an alliance with the displaced Khwarizmian troops that were roaming the region ever since the destruction of Khwarizm by the Mongols, to be discussed in the next chapter. The Khwarizmians swept through Palestine from the north and occupied Jerusalem without encountering any significant resistance. This time, Jerusalem was lost to the Franks permanently. The Khwarizmians then joined forces with the Egyptians and inflicted a crushing defeat on the combined Frankish-Damascene forces at Gaza in October 1244. Salih Ayyub retook Damascus and, at least for the moment, reunified the Ayyubid Empire once more. He then turned to deal with those Franks who had aligned themselves with the Damascene rebels. As a result of the ensuing campaign, by 1250 the Frankish Kingdom of Jerusalem was again reduced to a small and rather inconsequential strip along the Mediterranean coast.

THE BRIEF ASCENDANCY OF KHWARIZM

The death of Saladin in 1193, followed by the dynastic struggles of the Ayyubids, which virtually coincided with the death of the last of the Seljukid sultans of Persia, Tugrul III, in 1194, created a power vacuum in Iraq that the newly resurgent Abbasids tried to fill. No sooner had the shah of Khwarizm, Takash, become occupied in Afghanistan once again, than he suffered a reversal in the west at the hands of the Abbasid caliph Nasir (1180–1225). Pushing out beyond the long-standing confines of the Abbasids in the region of ancient Babylonia, Nasir conquered Khuzistan and the bordering Persian provinces. However, Takash retook the territories as far as Khuzistan in 1196, once he was able to redirect his attention to the west. The Khwarizmian Empire was then expanded further by Takash's son and successor Ala ad-Din Muhammad II (1200–1220), who brought the empire to its zenith, making it for a few short years the dominant state in the eastern Middle East. His first major task upon ascending the throne was to deal with the Ghorids in Afghanistan.

During the same period that Ala ad-Din Muhammad's predecessors were building the Khwarizmian state on the lower Oxus, another significant power had emerged in Afghanistan. About 1150, a clan of Suri Afghans rebelled against the Ghaznavids in the Ghor Mountains between Herat and Bamyan. That year, the chief of the Ghorids, Jahan Soz, raided and plundered the capital, Ghazni. His successor, Ghiyath ad-Din, occupied the city permanently in 1173, forcing the Ghaznavids to take refuge in Lahore, in the Punjab. Then, during the reign of Shihab ad-Din Muhammad (1173–1206), the Ghorids undertook a major expansion eastward against the Ghaznavids in India. It was at this point that Ala ad-Din Muhammad attacked the Ghorids in Afghanistan.

The Khwarizmians suffered a setback in their first encounter with the Ghorids at the Oxus in 1204, when the latter were able to march into Khwarizm and plunder the territory. Ala ad-Din Muhammad appealed to his nominal suzerain Chih-lu-ku, the overlord of the Qara-Khitai horde, for help. The latter responded by dispatching an army to assist him. With Qara-Khitai help, Ala ad-Din Muhammad was able to defeat the Ghorids at Hazarasp and drive them out of Khwarizm. The Qara-Khitai then pursued the Ghorid ruler Shihab ad-Din Muhammad, decisively defeating him at Andkhoi west of Balkh in the early fall of 1204. It took another two years before Ala ad-Din Muhammad was able to conquer and annex Herat and Ghor (Ghazni itself was not taken until 1215).

Although he was indebted to the Qara-Khitai for the salvation of Khwarizm and the defeat of the Ghorids, Ala ad-Din Muhammad, who had now assumed the title of sultan, felt it was improper for him as a Muslim to remain the vassal of Buddhists. The Qara-Khanid ruler of Samarkand, Uthman ibn Ibrahim (1200–1212), who was also a vassal of the Qara-Khitai, shared this sentiment. After the two Muslim princes came to an agreement in 1207, Ala ad-Din Muhammad occupied Bukhara and Samarkand, substituting Khwarizmian suzerainty for that of the Qara-Khitai. Then, in 1210, with Uthman's help, he repulsed and defeated the Qara-Khitai, further extending the Khwarizmian frontier to the Jaxartes and bringing all of Transoxiana under his control. Two years later Uthman rebelled and Ala ad-Din Muhammad attacked and pillaged Samarkand. Uthman was killed, and with his death the Qara-Khanid line came to an end after more than two centuries.

In 1214, a Turk named Mengli seized power in Jibal (Media). Uzbeg, the Pahlavanid ruler of Azerbaijan and a kinsman of the previous ruler of Jibal, challenged his ascendancy. The Abbasid caliph, Nasir, threw his support behind Uzbeg and marched into the region from Baghdad. Uzbeg succeeded in gaining control of Jibal with the caliph's help and installed the Turkish chieftain Oglumish as its governor. However, when the latter attempted to establish an alliance with Khwarizm, Nasir had him assassinated. This intervention from Baghdad infuriated Ala ad-Din Muhammad, whose empire now encompassed almost all of Persia, Afghanistan, and Transoxiana. He became determined to rid himself of the increasingly troublesome Abbasids by undermining the fundamental source of their power, the caliphate.

Ala ad-Din Muhammad summoned an ecclesiastical council in 1217 for the purpose of determining whether it was not more appropriate for the caliphate to be occupied by the descendants of Ali. By raising this ancient controversy, Ala ad-Din Muhammad hoped to rally behind him all the Shiites who were spread throughout Persia and Iraq. He then proceeded to set up Ala al-Mulk as a rival Alid caliph and began organizing and equipping an army that was expected to place him on the throne in Baghdad. However, winter set in very early that year and the plans for a campaign against the Abbasids had to be delayed till the following spring. By that time, temporary salvation for the Abbasid caliphate had already emerged from an unanticipated source.

NOTES

1. *Arab Historians of the Crusades*, p. 260.
2. Ibid., p. 264.
3. Ibid., p. 268.
4. Amin Maalouf, *The Crusades through Arab Eyes*, p. 228.
5. *Arab Historians of the Crusades*, p. 270.

10

The Mongol Onslaught

In 1206, a Mongol chieftain named Temujin, who became known subsequently as Genghis Khan (1206–1227), emerged as the victor in a struggle for supremacy that had been raging for some years among the Mongol-Turkic tribes of Inner Asia. That spring Genghis Khan convened a gathering of the tribes of Outer Mongolia near Lake Baikal, where he had himself acknowledged as their paramount khan or khagan. He devoted most of the next decade to the consolidation of his power and the conquest of the greater part of northern China. Then in 1219, he set his sights westward and began a relentless drive in that direction.

One immediate consequence of Genghis Khan's ascendancy was the displacement of the Nestorian Christian Naiman, one of the principal Mongol-Turkic tribal groups. The ruler of the Naiman, Kuchlug, was a major opponent of Genghis Khan and was forced to seek refuge among the Qara-Khitai in Turkestan, where he married the daughter of their gurkhan, Chih-lu-ku (1178–1211). Kuchlug then conspired with Ala ad-Din Muhammad of Khwarizm to overthrow the gurkhan of the Qara-Khitai and to divide his lands between them. As noted earlier, Ala ad-Din Muhammad rebelled against his Qara-Khitai suzerain Chih-lu-ku in 1207 by seizing Bukhara and Samarkand, which he followed with the complete defeat of the Qara-Khitai in Transoxiana in 1210. The following year, Kuchlug took the gurkhan, his father-in-law, prisoner, thereby gaining de facto control of the Qara-Khitai Empire beyond the Jaxartes, which he ruled until 1218.

During his tumultuous reign, Kuchlug had made the serious mistake of making himself extremely unpopular with the Muslim emirs of Kashgaria, who were therefore ready to assist anyone who would attempt to overthrow him. He then compounded his folly by attacking Buzar, the king of

Almaligh (Kuldja), who had already rendered his homage to Genghis Khan. The latter was not prepared to allow his long-standing enemy to remain ruler of the Qara-Khitai realm, and certainly not to poach on the vassals of the khagan of the Mongols.

In 1218, Genghis Khan dispatched an army of some 20,000 men under one of his ablest commanders, Jebe, to defend Almaligh and to secure the inheritance of Buzar's family. By the time Jebe arrived at Almaligh, Kuchlug had already withdrawn back into Kashgaria. Nonetheless, Jebe followed him there and was welcomed by the Muslims as a savior. Kuchlug was caught and killed soon afterward. As a consequence, all of eastern Turkestan was annexed to the rapidly expanding Mongol Empire, which now shared a common frontier with Khwarizm.

Although the extent of Genghis Khan's imperial ambitions cannot be known with any assurance, it seems to be the case that Khwarizm precipitated the conflict with the Mongols, who appeared ready for correct political and commercial relations with their new neighbor. In 1218, a Mongolian commercial caravan was stopped at the Khwarizmian frontier town of Utrar on the Jaxartes. The Khwarizmian governor, Qadir-khan, convinced that the primary purpose of the caravan was espionage, seized the goods it was carrying and executed about 100 of its members. Properly outraged at the hostile act, Genghis Khan demanded the payment of an appropriate indemnity. When Ala ad-Din Muhammad flatly refused to pay any compensation, the Mongols made ready for war.

In the fall of 1219, Genghis Khan and his Mongol horde crossed the Jaxartes and swept into Transoxiana. Although the Khwarizmian forces significantly outnumbered the Mongols, Ala ad-Din Muhammad was unable to take advantage of his superior troop strength. The Khwarizmian army consisted largely of mercenaries whose loyalties under heavy stress were questionable. Accordingly, Ala ad-Din was reluctant to risk any pitched battles with the hard-fighting Mongols. Instead, he dispersed his forces in garrisons in the principal cities, assuming that the Mongols were unskilled in siege warfare. While there was some truth in this, it proved to be insufficient to have justified the sacrifice of the advantage of superior numbers. As it turned out, the Mongol forces quickly overran Bukhara and Samarkand, which fell in February and March 1220 respectively. Ala ad-Din Muhammad was quite simply overwhelmed by the ferocity of the attacks and, unable to mobilize an effective defense against them, he fled westward to regroup his forces.

Although Ala ad-Din Muhammad had been effectively defeated by any measure, it appears that Genghis Khan had sufficient respect for him as an enemy to continue to consider him as a viable threat. According to the Persian historian Juvaini, the Mongol leader exclaimed: "It is necessary to make an end of him and be well rid of him before men gather around him and nobles join him from every side."[1] Genghis Khan dispatched a force of some 30,000 men under his two best generals, Jebe and Subotai, to pursue Ala ad-Din Muhammad across northern Persia, much of which was laid waste in the process. Ala ad-Din Muhammad finally made it safely to an islet off the shore of the Caspian Sea, where he died toward the end of the year.

Having disposed of the sultan of Khwarizm and whatever threat he represented, Genghis Khan then crossed the Oxus with the main Mongol army in the spring of 1221 and began the conquest of Afghanistan and Khorasan from the remaining Khwarizmian forces. For the next several years, with only a few exceptions, the Mongols systematically reduced most of eastern Persia to a shambles, virtually eliminating all evidence of the flourishing civilizations that had developed in Transoxiana, Afghanistan, and Khorasan over a period of more than 1,000 years. Everything was transformed into ashes and rubble. Genghis Khan did not occupy—he simply destroyed and slaughtered and moved on.

Before his death on August 18, 1227, Genghis Khan divided his vast empire among his four sons or their heirs. The sons of the eldest, Juji, who died in February 1227, were to have the country north of the Caspian; Jagatai, the territory east of the Jaxartes; Tului, the Mongol homeland around Lake Baikal; and Ogotai, the Imil valley. The two most prized of the possessions, China and Persia, were to be reserved for the supreme khan, and Genghis Khan designated Ogotai (1229–1241) to be the overlord, the khagan of the Mongols. The grand council of the Mongols that convened in September 1229 subsequently confirmed Ogotai's nomination, and he established his capital at Karakorum.

Ogotai had a radically different temperament and outlook than his father. He was fundamentally more interested in enjoying the fruits of the Mongol conquest than in further expansion of the empire. Nonetheless, he was caught up in the legacy of Genghis Khan and was unable politically to discard the latter's goals and ambitions. The Mongol leadership, for the most part, held strongly to their shamanist beliefs, which demanded that the nations of the world be brought to submit to the khagan, the living representative of the sky-god Tengri. Refusal to acknowledge his supremacy was tantamount to blasphemy and sacrilege. In their view, the Mongol Empire was not merely one state among others. It had a transcendent importance as the universal monarchy to which all other states were inferior and were to be made subservient. The powerful Mongol army was committed to these propositions and could not return to its tents until they were realized. Accordingly, Ogotai had little choice, if he were to keep his throne, but to work to bring Genghis Khan's dreams of empire to fruition.

Ogotai sought to expand the frontiers of the Mongol Empire in three directions. First, and foremost, he went to war against the Chin Empire in China, which had taken full advantage of the respite granted to them, as a consequence of the withdrawal of the Mongol army under Genghis Khan for the purpose of his war against Khwarizm, to recoup their losses. Second, he launched a campaign for control of the Eurasian steppe that ultimately brought the Mongols as far to the west as Hungary. Finally, he would direct his attention to Persia and southwestern Asia.

Jalal ad-Din (1220–1231), Ala ad-Din Muhammad's son and successor, had taken refuge in India during the Mongol onslaught in Khwarizm. Once Genghis Khan returned to Mongolia from his western campaign, Jalal ad-Din felt it was safe to return and in 1224 he began the reconstruction of the Khwarizmian state. He was welcomed by the Turkish atabegs of Kerman and Fars, which had escaped destruction during the initial Mongol invasion, and seized Isfahan and the Jibal from his brother Ghiyath ad-Din, who had established a principality for himself in those territories. However, instead of building defensive alliances with the other states of the region against a possible return of the Mongol hordes, Jalal ad-Din sought to bring them under his control. He attacked the Christian kingdoms of Transcaucasia and quarreled with the caliph in Baghdad, the Ayyubid sultan in Damascus, and the Seljukid sultan of Konya. Jalal ad-Din conquered Azerbaijan, whose ruler Uzbeg had survived by paying tribute to the Mongols, taking Tabriz in 1225. In only two years, he had made himself master of virtually all of Persia.

The following year Jalal ad-Din struck at Georgia, which was still recovering under Queen Rusudan (1223–1247) from the destruction wreaked by Jebe and Subotai during their earlier sweep through the region. He pillaged Tiflis in 1226, and returned there again in 1228. He then made a thrust through the highlands of Armenia, colliding with the Ayyubids of Syria on the western shore of Lake Van. This precipitated the formation of a defensive alliance between the Ayyubids and Seljukids that was designed to block any further Khwarizmian advance. Undeterred, Jalal ad-Din crossed the Seljukid frontier into Anatolia, but he was sharply defeated in August 1230 by the coalition of the Seljukid Ala ad-Din Kaikubad and the Ayyubid Ashraf at Erzincan along the upper western Euphrates. It was at this juncture that Ogotai decided to intervene in Persia once again, to prevent the resurgence of a Khwarizmian empire.

In 1231, a Mongol army of some 30,000 men under the command of Chormaqan (Chormaghun) invaded western Persia. Its first objective was the headquarters of Jalal ad-Din at Tabriz in Azerbaijan. Jalal ad-Din fled in panic to Diyarbekir, where a Kurdish peasant murdered him on August 15, 1231. This brought the Khwarizmian resurgence to an end.

From the strategic crossroads of Azerbaijan, the Mongol army was in a position to strike westward at Iraq, Syria, and Anatolia, as well as northward against the Christian kingdoms of the Caucasus. And, during the period 1235–1239, Chormaqan undertook a highly destructive campaign that ravaged Armenia and Georgia, presumably to ensure control of the lines of communication with the northern steppes from which an invasion of Europe was soon to be initiated.

Farther west, Hethum I (1226–1269), the king of Lesser Armenia, had managed to avoid destruction by voluntarily submitting to Mongol suzerainty in 1244. Hethum evidently perceived the advent of the Mongols as a heaven-sent opportunity to be rid of his hostile Muslim neighbors. The Nestorian clergy at the court of the khagan were reported to be very influential, and Hethum apparently believed that the Mongol Empire as a whole might be converted to Christianity. Sempad, the emissary of Hethum to the khagan, wrote in February 1248: "The Christians of the East have placed themselves under the protection of the khan, who has received them with much honor, granted them immunity, and publicly forbidden anyone to molest them."[2] Accordingly, he wanted to forge an alliance between the Eastern Christians and the Mongols against Islam. This seemed to be a real possibility when Baiju replaced Chormaqan in 1241. The former came to his position determined to extend Mongol rule into Anatolia.

The great fortress of Erzerum fell to the Mongols in 1242, and in June 1243 Kai-Khusraw II (1237–1245), the Seljukid sultan of Konya, was defeated decisively at Kusadagh. However, Baiju made no attempt to continue his conquest of Anatolia farther westward toward the Aegean. The Mongol lines of communication were simply stretched too thin and prudence demanded a halt to their further extension. Moreover, there was some uncertainty over developments in Karakorum, where Ogotai had died and the empire had come under the regency of his wife Toragana (1242–1246) pending the outcome of the struggle for the succession that was taking place. Under the circumstances, Baiju was prepared to accept Kai-Khusraw's less than enthusiastic acknowledgment of Mongol suzerainty, and the remaining Seljukid lands were left untouched for the most part.

Hethum's dreams of a Mongol-Christian alliance were dispelled for a time as the Mongol drive against the lands of Islam was suddenly stopped, and a new and major offensive was launched against Christian Europe. Indeed, in 1246, in response to a letter from Pope Innocent IV criticizing the Mongol massacre of Christians in Poland and Hungary, Guyuk Khan (1246–1249) responded with apparently honest bewilderment: "I do not understand these words of yours. The Eternal Heaven (Tengri) has slain and annihilated these peoples, because they have adhered neither to Chinghis Khan nor to the Khagan, both of whom have been sent to make known God's command."[3] It was clear that Genghis Khan's conception of the Mongol's divine geopolitical mission had not undergone any modification in the years since his death.

At the grand council of Mongol chiefs that was held in 1251, the new khagan Mongka (1251–1259) assigned the viceroyalty of Persia to his younger brother Hulagu (1251–1265). Mongka charged Hulagu with two immediate tasks: the suppression of the principality ruled by the imams of the Ismailis (Assassins) in Mazanderan, and the elimination of the Abbasid caliphate of Baghdad. Mongka was concerned about ensuring the unity of the empire, and would no longer tolerate the existence of independent power centers to which men directed loyalties that were to be rendered to the khagan alone. The Assassins and the Abbasid caliphate were two such centers that had to be eliminated; the Assassins because of their anarchy, and the caliphate because its claim of authority over all Muslims was considered an affront to Tengri and his representative on earth, the khagan. After achieving these objectives, Hulagu was to proceed with the conquest of Syria. Since Mongol imperialism was suffused with ideological content, Hulagu was also instructed to "Establish the usages, customs, and laws of Jenghiz Khan from the banks of the Amu Darya to the ends of the land of Egypt. Treat with kindness and good will every man who submits and is obedient to your orders. Whoever resists you, plunge him into humiliation."[4]

Hulagu went about fulfilling his assignments systematically. First, he moved against the Assassins in their mountain redoubts of Maimun-Diz and Alamut in Mazanderan. The grand master of the Assassins, Rukn ad-Din Kurshah, was besieged in the fortress of Maimun-Diz and forced to capitulate on November 19, 1256. By late December the defenders of Alamut, the last of the Assassin's "eagles' nests," surrendered. After disposing of the Assassins who had plagued Persia for more than a century, Hulagu moved on to Hamadan in March 1257, from where he now directed his attention to the matter of disposing of the Abbasids.

Since the tenth century, the caliphate had managed to survive largely as a result of the readiness of the caliphs to come to terms with the dominant regional power. Now, the reigning caliph Mustasim (1242–1258) seemed convinced that he had eternity on his side, and arrogantly failed to recognize the danger that confronted him from the Mongols. According to a contemporary writer, Rashid ad-Din, Hulagu demanded that the temporal power earlier conceded by the caliphs to the Buwayhids and the Seljukids now be transferred to the Mongols. He warned: "You have learned the fate brought upon the world since Jenghiz Khan by the Mongol armies. What humiliation, by the grace of Eternal heaven, has overtaken the dynasties of the shahs of Khwarizm, of the Seljuks, of the kings of Daylam, and of the different atabegs! Yet the gates of Baghdad were never closed to any of these races, which all established their dominion there. How then should entry into this city be refused to us, who possess such strength and such power? Beware of taking arms against the Standard."

Mustasim, however, was not prepared to seriously consider granting anyone temporal power over Baghdad, which had finally been wrested away from the Seljukids by his recent predecessors. He had no intention of handing it over to Hulagu and the Mongols. In response to Hulagu's barely veiled ultimatum, Mustasim had the temerity to compare the theoretical universal sovereignty of the caliphate to the power of the Mongol Empire. "O young man," he answered, "who have barely entered upon your career and who, drunk with a ten-day success, believe yourself superior to the whole world, do you not know that from the East to the Maghreb, all the worshippers of Allah, whether kings or beggars, are slaves to this court of mine, and that I can command them to muster?"[5]

This vain posturing was to cost the Abbasids and the people of Baghdad dearly. The Ayyubid sultan of Syria, who had no inclination whatever to challenge the Mongols, quickly abandoned Mustasim. Three Mongol armies converged on Baghdad in January 1258, and the assault on the city began the following month. The caliph was forced to surrender on February 13, and the city was put to the sack for seven days. The entire garrison and some 90,000 residents are thought to have been massacred, while most of the city was burned to the ground. Only the Christians were spared, primarily as a consequence of the intervention of Hulagu's Nestorian wife, Doquz-Khatun. Out of respect for his dignity as a religious leader, Mustasim's blood was not shed visibly. The last of the Abbasid caliphs was rolled up in a carpet and trampled to death, the method of execution employed by the Mongols on their own dignitaries.

After the destruction of the caliphate, Hulagu returned to Azerbaijan, where he established his capital at Tabriz, and began to prepare for the fulfillment of the third task assigned to him by the khagan. The fall of Baghdad sent shock waves throughout those parts of the Middle East where Mongol power had not yet been felt. Now it was the turn of Syria and Egypt to face the fury of Hulagu's onslaught.

At the time, the prospects for a Christian-Mongol alliance seemed brighter than ever. Northwestern Syria, encompassing the combined principality of Antioch and county of Tripoli, was ruled by Bohemond VI (1252–1275), the son-in-law of Hethum of Lesser Armenia. Bohemond, however, resided exclusively in Tripoli and, as a practical matter, Hethum, whose realm was contiguous with it, ruled Antioch. Accordingly, Antioch was drawn into the Mongolian-Armenian alliance. The Ayyubid sultan Nasir Yusuf (1250–1260) tried to forestall the Mongol invasion of Muslim Syria by a prior voluntary submission to vassalage in 1258. However, it was to prove of no avail. Hulagu was determined to conquer the Jazira and Syria from the Ayyubids.

The Mongol offensive began with an assault against the Ayyubid emir Kamil II (1244–1260) of Diyarbekir. The immediate justification for the attack was that Kamil, a fanatical Muslim, had crucified a Jacobite priest who was travelling through his territory carrying a Mongol passport. A small Mongol detachment, supported by a much larger force of Georgians and Armenians who saw themselves as participating in a crusade against the Muslims under the command of the Georgian leader Hasan Brosh, moved against Diyarbekir, which fell after a long siege. While the siege was under way, Hulagu, together with a Christian army from Lesser Armenia, prepared to conquer Muslim Syria. According to the Armenian historian Hayton: "The khan had asked Hethum to join him with the whole Armenian army at Edessa, for he desired to go to Jerusalem to deliver the Holy Land from the Mussulmans and restore it to the Christians. King Hethum, joyful at this news, gathered together a great army and marched to join Hulagu."[6] There is no good reason to believe that Hulagu was particularly well disposed toward Christianity and antipathetic to Islam. His apparent partiality was primarily tactical and was without religious motivation. Had Syria and Iraq been under Christian rule at the time, Hulagu would have undoubtedly contrived a relationship with the Muslims. He himself was a follower of traditional shamanism and, if anything, leaned toward Buddhism.

The Mongol army departed Azerbaijan for the campaign against Syria in September 1259, with the advance force under the command of Ket-Buqa, a Nestorian Naiman. Marching through Kurdistan to the Jazira, Hulagu took Nisibis and received the voluntary submission of Harran and Edessa. He then crossed the Euphrates and laid siege to Aleppo on January 18, 1260, with the support of Hethum's Armenians and the Frankish troops supplied by Bohemond VI from Antioch. The city fell on January 24, although the citadel managed to hold out for another month. Hulagu rewarded his Christian allies by restoring their control over those territories that had been wrested from them, and had been in Muslim hands since the days of Saladin.

Operating under the Mongol security umbrella, Bohemond also seized the Muslim coastal enclave at Latakia, thereby reestablishing Frankish control of all the land between Tripoli and Antioch for the first time since 1187. The sultan Nasir Yusuf, who had made no attempt to defend Aleppo, now abandoned Damascus as well and fled to Egypt, where he was denied entry. As will be seen later, there had been a coup d'etat staged by the Mamluks against the Ayyubids in Cairo and the Ayyubid Nasir Yusuf was simply not welcome. He then sought refuge in Trans-Jordan but was eventually seized by the Mongols near Amman and put to death. Damascus was occupied on March 1, 1260. The Muslims saw the entry of the Mongols into the ancient city as a tragedy comparable to the destruction of the caliphate, whereas for many beleaguered Christians it seemed that the Mongols served as a divine instrument of deliverance.

During the next several weeks, Ket-Buqa completed the conquest of Syria and marched into Palestine, penetrating as far Samaria before meeting with some resistance at Nablus. After annihilating the garrison there he proceeded south to Gaza unopposed. Once the situation in Syria and Palestine seemed to be under control, Hulagu made ready to march on Egypt. He issued the usual summons to surrender, warning that there was no escape from the fate that awaited them if they resisted and assuring them that their prayers would prove of little avail in preventing their destruction.

However, it was just at this juncture that an event that had occurred at the other end of Asia the previous year precipitated dramatic changes in the current situation in the Middle East. On August 11, 1259, the khagan Mongka died in China, and a struggle for the succession broke out between his brothers Kublai and Ariq-boga. Hulagu had as much as he could wish for in Persia and the Middle East and harbored no aspirations to become khagan of the Mongols, which would have required that he return to Central Asia. However, he favored Kublai for the throne and stood prepared to lend his active support of Kublai's claim if he were to be called upon. At the same time, a challenge to Hulagu himself emerged on the Caucasian frontier because his cousin Berke, the khan of the so-called Golden Horde, had become favorably disposed to Islam and threatened to take retribution on Hulagu for the massacre he had perpetrated in Baghdad. In view of the circumstances, Hulagu was forced to abandon his plans for an invasion of Egypt and, to be in a better position physically to respond to either situation, he took his main force and returned to Azerbaijan. Ket-Buqa was left behind to control Syria and Palestine with an occupation force of no more than 20,000 men.

Although both Ket-Buqa and Bohemond VI fully appreciated the mutual advantages of the Frank-Mongol alliance, the Frankish barons of Acre did not share this positive assessment. The latter preferred to reach an accommodation with the Muslims rather than align themselves with the Mongols, whom they considered to be nothing more than contemptible barbarians. As Pope Urban IV put it: "This cruel race of Tartars, doomed to damnation, oppress the land they have enslaved with intolerable exactions; they torture and afflict the inhabitants so inhumanely that those who dwell under such tyranny prefer to die rather than endure such torments."[7]

Matters soon got out of hand when one of the Frankish barons, Count Julien of Sidon, attacked a Mongol patrol and killed a nephew of Ket-Buqa. Suitably provoked, the Mongols responded by pillaging Sidon, thereby bringing an effective end to the Frank-Mongol alliance. The split between them created a new situation that once again gave hope to the Egyptians that all was not totally lost. Without the support of the Franks, it did not seem likely that the Mongols were any longer in a position to threaten Egypt. Indeed, it did not even seem possible for Ket-Buqa to hold on in Syria and Palestine with the limited forces at his disposal without the help of the Franks. This raised the prospect of Egypt being able to mount a serious challenge to Ket-Buqa, something that was not long in coming.

NOTES

1. Juvaini, *The History of the World-Conqueror*, vol. 1, p. 143.
2. Rene Grousset, *The Empire of the Steppes*, p. 271.
3. C. Dawson, ed., *Mission to Asia*, p. 85.
4. Grousset, *The Empire of the Steppes*, p. 353.
5. Ibid., p. 355.
6. Ibid., p. 361.
7. Jean Richard, *The Latin Kingdom of Jerusalem*, vol. 2, p. 388.

11

Between Mamluks and Mongols

The Ayyubid Empire, stretching from Egypt to the Jazira, which had been reunified by Salih Ayyub in 1245, was not destined to last for very long. In 1247, the Ayyubid princes of Aleppo and Hama revolted and Salih Ayyub had to return to Syria in an effort to prevent his domain from disintegrating. However, when he learned that a new crusade under Louis IX (1226–1270) of France was about to land in Egypt, he was forced to conclude a truce with the rebels early in 1249 and return to there.

It is not clear what impelled Louis IX to launch yet another crusade. It may well have been inspired by the loss of Jerusalem to the Ayyubids once again in 1244, although that event seems to have had rather little impact on a Europe that was becoming increasingly preoccupied with its own internal wars. In any case, one thing was evident. Louis approached the matter from a strategic perspective that differed considerably from that which characterized the preceding efforts to gain control over the Holy Land. He understood that the security of Palestine was inextricably linked to that of Egypt, and that the viability of the Frankish position in Palestine was contingent upon a satisfactory security arrangement with the latter. As a practical matter, this meant either that Egypt had to be conquered or, at the least, that a strong and secure foothold had to be obtained on its northeastern frontier, one that would facilitate control of the invasion routes across the Sinai from the Nile Delta. Accordingly, Louis' crusade, emulating the earlier campaign led by Jean de Brienne, headed not for Acre but for Damietta.

Louis and his army of some 20,000 men spent the winter of 1248–1249 in Cyprus, watching events unfold in Syria where Salih Ayyub was engaged in suppressing the revolt in Aleppo. It was Louis' presence in the nearby island that sent Salih Ayyub scurrying back to Egypt to organize its defense.

The crusaders embarked from Cyprus at the end of May 1249, but only part of the army managed to land near Damietta on June 5. A raging storm forced those ships carrying the remainder of Louis' troops to seek temporary shelter along the Syrian coast.

The French king had prepared for this campaign most carefully, even to the extent of employing flat-bottomed landing craft that enabled his troops to sail almost up to the beach before disembarking. This permitted them to charge and overwhelm the unsuspecting Egyptian forces. The latter were expecting to be able to cut the crusaders down as they waded some distance to the shore from their transports. The change in tactics caught them wholly unprepared. Unable to prevent the crusaders from establishing a beachhead, the Egyptians decided, for reasons that remain unclear, to withdraw up the Nile rather than defend Damietta. Perhaps they had hoped to lure the crusaders after them and thereby set the stage for a repetition of the fiasco that occurred in the same place in 1221 when a crusader army was trapped in the Nile mud and forced to capitulate. In any case, Louis decided not to pursue the Egyptians and spent the summer and autumn of 1249 in Damietta, awaiting the arrival of the rest of his forces from Syria.

The French army began its march south toward Cairo along the east bank of the Nile on November 20, 1249, two days before Salih Ayyub died of natural causes. With the help of the palace guard, his wife was able to hold the regime together until the heir Turan Shah (1249–1250) could return to Egypt from the Jazira. Louis reached as far as Mansurah before the Egyptian army engaged him in February 1250. In the meantime, Turan Shah sent a number of dismantled ships on camelback some distance down the Nile behind the French forces, where they were reassembled and floated. With this improvised fleet he was able to cut off the French supply line from Damietta, making the position of the stranded French army extremely precarious. In addition, the crusader army was being afflicted by an epidemic of dysentery, which had a serious demoralizing effect on the troops. Louis felt compelled to surrender along with his entire army early in April 1250. The crusade, begun with such promise, had turned into an embarrassing debacle. Louis was subsequently released from captivity in May 1250 in exchange for a complete withdrawal of his forces from Damietta and the payment of a substantial ransom.

As final arrangements for the release of Louis were being completed, a coup d'etat took place in Cairo that had far-reaching consequences. The Mamluks—the corps of Turkish youngsters who had been sold into perpetual military service—had always constituted an important elite force in the sultan's service. They traditionally served as the Middle Eastern equivalent of the Roman praetorian guards. In Egypt, as long as most of the Ayyubid army was composed of Kurds, the Mamluks posed no internal threat to the regime. However, during the reign of Salih Ayyub the Ayyubid Empire was continually in a state of disarray, with Kurd aligned against Kurd. In this situation, Salih Ayyub came to rely increasingly on his elite Mamluk (mostly Kipchak) force as the instrument with which he would reassert his control over the disintegrating empire. To finance the purchase of additional mamluks and military equipment, Salih Ayyub diverted much of the revenues that Egypt was deriving from its important role in the oriental spice trade with Europe. But, as had happened so many times before in the region, the mercenary guards developed vested political interests in the persistence of the existing regime and were prepared to act independently to prevent any unfavorable changes in circumstances. Thus, when Turan Shah was perceived by them to be on the verge of saturating the regime with retainers who had followed him to Cairo from the Jazira, the Mamluks intervened to prevent their own loss of status and perquisites. Turan Shah was murdered on May 2, 1250, and the Mamluk chief al-Muizz Aibek (1250–1257) became sultan of Egypt in his place. The Kurdish regime originally put in place by Saladin was now replaced by an autonomous Turkish military oligarchy.

With the death of Turan Shah his cousin Nasir Yusuf became the sultan of Ayyubid Syria. War soon broke out between Syria and Egypt as Nasir Yusuf marched on Cairo with his own mamluk troops in January 1251. The battle between the opposing mamluk armies at Abbasa near Cairo the following month proved inconclusive. However, after some of his mamluks, who became fascinated by the idea of an all-Mamluk regime, went over to the Egyptian side, Nasir Yusuf turned and fled back to Syria. Ultimately, the two sides reached an accommodation in 1253 that left the Ayyubids in control of Syria and northern Palestine, and the Mamluks in control of Egypt and southern Palestine. The small remaining Frankish kingdom along the Palestinian coast served as a buffer zone between them and was ruled by Louis IX until 1254, when he returned to Europe. The following year, a ten-year truce was concluded between the Franks and the Mamluks.

While still in Palestine, Louis tried to negotiate an alliance with the Mongols that would have served as an offset to both Mamluks and Ayyubids, but the khagan Mongka was only willing to consider it if Louis would acknowledge him as his suzerain. For Louis this was a categorically unacceptable proposition and the negotiations were terminated without result.

The Mamluks watched the progress of the Mongol conquest with intense concern. Notwithstanding their own competence as a fighting force, they fully expected to be overwhelmed by Hulagu's army. Thus, the latter's sudden withdrawal from Palestine and Syria in 1260 came as a godsend for them. The Mamluks were quite confident that they could deal with the relatively small occupation force that Hulagu had left behind with Ket-Buqa. Saif ad-Din Qutuz (1259–1260), who had served as regent for the teenage Ali (1257–1259) who had succeeded his murdered father Aibek, took the throne for himself on the basis of the need to provide a strong central leadership to deal with the Mongol threat. The general sentiment of the Mamluk emirs was that they were prepared to fight to defend Egypt, but had no interest in attempting to engage the Mongols in Syria. Qutuz, on the other hand, was anxious to seize the opportunity presented to defeat the Mongol force under Ket-Buqa while Hulagu and the main horde were occupied in the east. The sultan contrived to get the emirs to follow him and he set out to meet Ket-Buqa, with Rukn ad-Din Baibars commanding the advance force.

The Mamluks proceeded up the coast of Palestine toward Acre, capital of the Kingdom of Jerusalem. With the collapse of the Frank-Mongol alliance, the Franks became divided internally over the question of which side to align with, the Mamluks or the Mongols. Tripoli and Antioch had already submitted to Hulagu and had become his vassals, while Acre was under pressure from the Mamluks to ally with them. Ultimately, the Franks of Palestine opted for neutrality, although they considered it necessary to accommodate Qutuz to the extent of allowing free passage for the Mamluk army through their territory. They refused, however, to provide him with any direct military support.

In the meantime, Ket-Buqa advanced south from Damascus to confront Qutuz. He then crossed the Jordan and advanced up the Plain of Esdraelon past Beisan. The armies clashed at Ain Jalud, where the width of the plain narrows to about three miles, on September 3, 1260. Despite the ferocity of the Mongol attack, the Mamluks were able to hold the line, and before long their far superior numbers prevailed. The Mongols were defeated, and those who survived the battle withdrew toward the Euphrates with Baibars coming after them in hot pursuit. Qutuz occupied Damascus on September 10, and the new Mamluk Empire now stretched from Egypt to the Euphrates. A few weeks later, on October 24, 1260, Baibars, commander in chief of the army, murdered Qutuz and became sultan (1260–1277) in his place.

Baibars understood that the defeat of Ket-Buqa and a relatively small Mongol army was not quite the same as a defeat of Hulagu and his horde, a formidable force that remained a serious threat to the security of the now enlarged Mamluk Empire. Hulagu, who was given the title of Il-Khan, had been reconfirmed as ruler of Persia by his brother Kublai, who was to become the khagan of the Mongols once the struggle over the succession was concluded. He soon took steps to expand the territory of the Il-Khanid Empire and consolidate his control over its frontier regions. Hulagu annexed Mosul and extended his rule over southern Persia and Cilicia. The remaining Seljukids of Anatolia all became his vassals, thereby extending his sphere of control from the Oxus to within 150 miles of Constantinople.

In the summer of 1262, Baibars induced Izz ad-Din, the Seljukid sultan of western Anatolia, to repudiate his vassalage to Hulagu. In a swift campaign, Izz ad-Din drove the Mongols out of his territory and then advanced eastward, seizing Konya from his brother Rukn ad-Din. Hulagu, who was about to attack Syria, had to divert his forces northward to deal with this unanticipated development. He invaded Anatolia and soon defeated Izz ad-Din, forcing him to take refuge in Constantinople. Hulagu reasserted Mongol suzerainty over all of Seljukid Anatolia, which was subsequently placed under the rule of his faithful vassal Rukn ad-Din.

For his part, Baibars continued to pursue a twofold approach to strengthening the Mamluk position. He undertook the consolidation of his control over Syria and Palestine. To assure the security of his lines of communication between Egypt and the eastern Syrian frontier, he forced the Franks of Antioch, who had aligned with the Mongols, to sue for peace in 1262. Toward the end of the year he launched a major punitive raid against Lesser Armenia, which had earlier also aligned itself with Hulagu. At the same time, Baibars also sought to exploit the potent animosities that existed between the Mongol khans for the purpose of weakening Hulagu's position in the western reaches of his empire.

One of the reasons why Hulagu had originally withdrawn from Syria and Palestine to Azerbaijan was to be in a better strategic position to deal with a threat from his cousin Berke. The descendants of Juji, the eldest son of Genghis Khan who predeceased him, had become the khans of the Golden and White hordes which controlled the territories north of the Caucasus from the Volga River northward as far as Moscow and westward as far as Hungary. The Kipchaks, the Turkic tribe from which Baibars originated, were now included within the realm of the Golden Horde, whose ruler, Berke Khan (1256–1266), had become a convert to Islam. In 1262 Baibars appealed to him as a fellow Muslim to attack Hulagu who, in Muslim eyes, was the archenemy of Islam. According to a contemporary biographer, Muhi ad-Din:

He sent a letter to Bereke, the great Mongol king, which I myself wrote, inciting him against Hulagu and sowing enmity and hatred between them; showing that he ought to fight a holy war against the Mongols, because the news had spread about his embracing Islam, and as a consequence of that he ought to wage a holy war against the infidels, though they might be his own people; for the Prophet . . . fought against his nearest kin and waged a holy war against the Qoraish . . . and in view of the following fact [that] "News is continually arriving that Hulagu has established the religion of the Cross on account of his wife who is a Christian, placing the interests of the religion of his wife above those of your religion, and has established an infidel archbishop in the land of the caliphs, preferring his wife before you." In this letter there were many exhortations, and a description of the holy war in which the sultan was engaged.[1]

Berke is also reported to have said of Hulagu: "He has sacked all the cities of the Muslims and, without consulting his kinsmen, has brought about the death of the caliph. With the help of Allah I will call him to account for so much innocent blood."[2] In 1262, perhaps in response to Baibars' instigation, Berke declared war on Hulagu. The Il-Khan took to the offensive against Berke in the early winter of that year, crossing the Derbent pass, which marked the frontier between the Il-Khanid Empire and the domains of the Golden Horde. Hulagu advanced into Kipchak territory but was repulsed in a battle at the Terek River and forced to withdraw back to Azerbaijan. Berke pursued him across the Caucasus but was unable to defeat Hulagu decisively before he was forced to break off the engagement and withdraw back across the Derbent pass at the approach of spring. Although this meant foregoing an opportunity to crush Hulagu's forces, it was a practical necessity. Berke was afraid of getting stranded in Persia, where he would be cut off from his bases and at the mercy of Hulagu, if he did not withdraw across the Caucasus before the winter snows began to melt making the route impassable.

In addition to his troubles with Berke and the Golden Horde on his Caucasian frontier, Hulagu was also on poor terms with the khans of the Jagatai branch of his extended family. They controlled Transoxiana and were conducting raids across his eastern frontiers. The prospect of an alliance between Baibars and Berke effectively eliminated the threat of a full-scale invasion of Syria by Hulagu. Were Hulagu to attempt such an assault on Syria, he would run the risk of a counterattack from the Caucasus that could split his empire in half and leave his forces in Syria caught in the middle between the Mamluks to the west and the Golden Horde to the east. Furthermore, Hulagu ran the risk of his antagonists mounting a coordinated attack on Persia from both the Caucasus and Transoxiana. As a practical matter, the continual struggles between the Mongol khans brought Hulagu's expansionism to an end, thereby providing Baibars with the respite from war that he needed to build a powerful army that might be able to withstand a full-force attack by the Il-Khanid Mongols.

Hulagu's concerns about the security of his western flank became more intense during the summer of 1263, when a delegation from Berke arrived in Cairo to inform Baibars that the entire Golden Horde had been converted to Islam. This signal event was followed shortly by the arrival of a contingent of more than 1,000 Mongols from the Golden Horde, followed by other such groups later, who came to serve in Baibars' army. That same autumn, Baibars wrote to the ruler of Shiraz and urged him to rebel against Hulagu, hoping thereby to force the Il-Khan to deploy his forces as far from Egypt and Syria as possible. Baibars similarly appealed to the Khafaja, a Bedouin tribe of the region west of the Euphrates, to harass the Mongols at every opportunity.

Baibars also sought to build an alliance with the Byzantines, who had regained control of Constantinople from the Latins in 1261, to complete the encirclement of Hulagu. Moreover, since the only reliable communications link between Baibars and Berke was by sea through the Dardanelles and the Bosphorus, Byzantium's cooperation was essential. However, the emperor Michael VIII Paleologus (1261–1282), who had been favorably disposed toward both Berke and Baibars, ultimately decided to cast his lot with Hulagu as the more pragmatic option. His principal reason was that Kublai Khan, once he became khagan at the end of 1263, had sent substantial reinforcements to Hulagu to assist him in his struggles with Berke, whom the khagan considered to be a rebel against his legitimate authority. These reinforcements arrived in the spring of 1264 and caused Michael to reconsider his relationship with Berke. From the Byzantine perspective, as long as Hulagu was capable of holding his own against the Golden Horde, an alliance with him was strategically more advantageous. By challenging Berke on his southern flank in the Caucasus, Hulagu would effectively mitigate the immediate threat to Constantinople's hinterland by diverting the Golden Horde and its Bulgarian allies away from Thrace.

Berke, however, was not prepared to accept Michael's alignment with Hulagu and launched a devastating attack on the Byzantine Empire in 1264, which was carried out in conjunction with a simultaneous assault by the Bulgarians. Thrace was devastated and Michael nearly lost his life in the conflict. As a result, Michael was forced to be far more accommodating to the Mamluk-Golden Horde alliance. According to Muhi ad-Din, he sent a letter to Baibars that promised: "When the kingdom of al-Malik al-Zahir needs help, I will help with all the resources of my country."[3] Michael took no further steps to actively support Hulagu, who made one last halfhearted attempt to invade Syria at the end of 1264, but it came to nothing and the Mongol forces withdrew before even engaging the Mamluks.

The effective mitigation of the Mongol threat left Baibars free to direct his attention to dealing once and for all time with the remaining Frankish enclaves in Syria and Palestine. While Baibars was determined to eliminate the Frankish presence—his avowed aim was to drive them into the sea—he wanted to do so in a way that would not precipitate another crusade. This he was not able to accomplish as long as he failed to appreciate the significance of maritime power in the regional military balance. Baibars never quite fully grasped that the reason the Franks were able to hold out for so long was the virtual Italian monopoly of control of the eastern Mediterranean, and the sea lines of communication between the Syrian and Palestinian coasts and Europe, which permitted their constant resupply and reinforcement. Nonetheless, he was the only Mamluk to try to build an Egyptian fleet, although it is not clear that he intended to use it for anything more than an invasion of Cyprus, which he attempted unsuccessfully in 1270. Muhi ad-Din tells us:

When God gave the kingdom to the sultan, he found that those who preceded him had neglected the matter of galleys, though these were the horses of the sea and the walls of the frontiers. The kings [the Ayyubids] had always paid attention to this matter and given fiefs to their crews. He found that the amirs had taken some of the crews from the galleys away to fireships and other vessels. The sultan brought things back to the level they had been in the days of al-Kamil and as-Salih. He pro-

tected the wooded valleys and prohibited the sale of timber used for the construction of galleys. He ordered the construction of galleys at the two ports [Damietta
and Alexandria]; coming in person to the dockyard, he set in order the arrangements which were necessary as regards the galleys.[4]

Baibars moved against the Frankish enclaves methodically, one at a
time. His strategy was to drive a wedge through the Frankish kingdom and
to destroy the ports in order to prevent the landing of new reinforcements.
Caesarea was taken in March 1265, cutting off Jaffa from the rest of the kingdom. Within a matter of days Baibars seized Haifa and struck at Toron and
Arsuf, which soon fell as well. Although he was temporarily prevented
from mounting an effective assault on Acre, Baibars began attacking the inland positions of the Franks in the spring of 1266, taking Safed after a long
siege. In 1267, he invaded Cilicia as far to the west as Tarsus, and annexed
the frontier region that abutted Syria. Jaffa was taken the following March
and Antioch in May. All that remained to the Franks was the strip of coast
from Athlit, south of Mount Carmel, north to Latakia. The fall of Antioch
placed Hethum of Lesser Armenia in an untenable position as an ally of the
Il-Khan. He was forced to come to terms with Baibars and return all the territory that the Armenians had occupied in Syria as a consequence of their
alliance with the Mongols. Hethum abdicated soon afterward in favor of
his son Leo III (1269–1289).

Notwithstanding Baibars' determined efforts to rid himself of the
Franks without precipitating another crusade, Louis IX of France began organizing yet another campaign in 1267. However, Baibars had also become
active on the European diplomatic front in an attempt to find other means
of foiling Louis' plans. In 1264, Baibars entered into a profitable commercial
treaty with Charles of Anjou, one that the latter was not anxious to place in
jeopardy. Accordingly, Charles served as an advocate of a pro-Egyptian
policy in the councils of Europe. Baibars also bought off the Venetians by
promising them special trade privileges in Egypt and Syria. They not only
refused to participate in the new crusade—they also placed such high
prices on their ships that Louis could not afford to lease them. As a consequence of these and other considerations, when the crusade was finally
launched in 1270, it was directed not at Egypt and Palestine but against Tunis. Charles of Anjou convinced Louis that the sultan of Tunis was prepared
to adopt Christianity if the crusaders would be diverted to his country. He
was also led to believe that Baibars was heavily dependent on Tunis for
men and materiel, and that an assault on Tunis would seriously weaken the
Mamluk regime.

In the spring of 1271, as Baibars was about to attack the Frankish enclave
at Tripoli, he learned that Prince Edward of Cornwall, who had arrived at
Tunis well after Louis, had decided to sail on to Palestine and had landed at
Acre with a small force. Although Edward had only some 300 knights with
him, his contingent was soon augmented by reinforcements from Cyprus

sent by Hugh III, who was ruler of both Cyprus and the Kingdom of Jerusalem (1268–1284). Correctly assuming that the Il-Khanids were implacable foes of the Mamluks, Edward had also previously arranged for additional support from Hulagu's successor, Abaqa (1265–1282). The long-standing conflict between the Golden Horde and the Il-Khanids had come to an end in 1266 with the death of Berke, at last leaving Abaqa free to deal with Baibars without fear of his forces being cut off by a flank attack from the Caucasus. Abaqa now decided to send some 10,000 Mongol troops to join Edward's crusader army.

The Il-Khanid force arrived in Aleppo in October 1271 and began to lay waste to a good part of northern Syria. Baibars immediately concluded a ten-year truce with the Franks of Tripoli and prepared to meet the Mongol onslaught. While Baibars was thus distracted by developments on his eastern frontiers, Edward seized the opportunity to carry out raids in Palestine at Ramle and Lydda as well as in some other Mamluk strongholds. The immediate crisis facing the Mamluks passed, however, as a consequence of the coincidental invasion of Khorasan by Baraq, the Jagatai khan of Transoxiana, who occupied Merv and Nishapur. Abaqa was forced to terminate his campaign in the west and withdraw from Syria to deal with this serious threat to Persia. He subsequently defeated Baraq and then sent a force to ravage Khwarizm and Transoxiana as a means of pacifying and securing his eastern frontier.

Edward's campaign in Palestine was effectively put on hold with the onset of winter. By the following spring, given the earlier withdrawal of the Mongol forces from the combined operation, he decided that it would be prudent to reach an accommodation with the Mamluks rather than continue a war he had little chance of winning without Abaqa's help. On April 22, 1272, Edward concluded a ten-year truce with Baibars that granted the Franks the right of pilgrimage to Jerusalem, Bethlehem, and Nazareth, a provision that represented only a gain in principle for the Franks since it was not enforceable. Nonetheless, the lesson of this last campaign was not lost on Baibars. He now recognized that the idea of an alliance against him between the Christians of Europe and the Mongols was a real possibility and a potentially serious threat to the security of the Mamluk Empire.

Toward the end of 1272, Abaqa returned to the Euphrates once again and began making incursions into Mamluk Syria while he strengthened his defensive positions along the river's banks. This time, however, with his rear secure as a result of the truces that he had negotiated with Tripoli and the Kingdom of Jerusalem, Baibars was able to commit himself fully to meeting the Il-Khanid challenge. With superior generalship, he managed to outflank the Mongol army on the eastern bank of the Euphrates, effectively trapping it against the river. Abaqa was forced to abandon his fortified positions in December 1273 in the hope of preventing the systematic decimation of his army. He subsequently appealed to Pope Gregory X for a general

Mongol-European alliance against the Mamluks. This appeal was well received and seemed to be on the verge of success when Gregory called for another crusade at the Council of Lyons in 1274, with the apparent support of the Byzantine emperor Michael Paleologus. The effort collapsed, however, with the imminent death of Gregory. After this episode, Baibars became less concerned about the likelihood of a combined Mongol-European threat to him and less constrained in pursuing his own expansionist aims.

Baibars invaded Armenian Cilicia once again in March 1275, occupying the capital at Sis and, more importantly, destroying the port at Ayas (Lajazzo). The latter port, in addition to Tripoli and Acre, was essential to the transshipment of goods from the East to Europe. By eliminating these ports, Baibars hoped to rechannel most of the oriental trade from its overland routes to the Mediterranean to the southern maritime route up the Red Sea and then overland across Egypt to Alexandria, which would again become the central entrepôt for the region.

In the meantime, farther north in Anatolia, Muin ad-Din Suleiman, the vizier of the Seljukid sultan Qilij Arslan IV (1257–1265), contrived to have the sultan eliminated by the Mongols. He then took over as regent for the three-year-old heir to the throne, Kai-Khusraw III (1265–1282). In response to this act of usurpation, a group of disgruntled Seljukid emirs appealed to Baibars to intervene and take control of the country. Baibars responded favorably to the petition and departed Cairo in February 1277, accompanied by the Seljukid emirs, to invade Anatolia. On April 16, he engaged and defeated a joint Seljukid-Mongol army at Abulistan on the upper Jihun River at the entrance to Cappadocia. He then crossed the Taurus Mountains and marched into the Seljukid capital at Kayseri (Caesarea) a week later, warmly welcomed by the mostly Turkish and Muslim population, and mounted the newly vacant Seljukid throne.

Baibars' moment of glory was to be short-lived. He soon learned that Abaqa was advancing toward him with the main body of the Il-Khanid army. Baibars could not afford to run the risk of being cut off from Syria and trapped behind the Taurus; he was therefore forced to withdraw from Anatolia back to Antioch. As a result, the entire Anatolian campaign turned out to be counterproductive except from the standpoint of Baibars' vanity. He clearly was never in a position to leave a force behind in control of Anatolia that would have been sufficiently strong to withstand an attack from the main body of the Mongol army. Consequently, the net outcome of the campaign was the complete elimination of the last vestige of Seljukid independence as Abaqa avenged himself for the defeat suffered by his forces at Abulistan by destroying the city of Kayseri and slaughtering its Muslim population. Baibars himself died a few weeks later in Damascus.

THE END OF MONGOL ASCENDANCY

Following the death of Baibars on June 27, 1277, a succession crisis developed that soon threatened the secession of Syria from the Mamluk Empire. In Cairo, the commander in chief of the army Qalawun al-Elfi (1279–1290) enthroned and dethroned Baibars' minor successors and won the support of the other emirs to the proclamation of himself as sultan on December 4, 1279. In Damascus, the viceroy Sonkor al-Ashqar saw this as an opportunity to take full control of Syria and proclaimed himself as its sultan on May 3, 1280, triggering a war with Egypt. Qalawun promptly invaded Syria and defeated Sonkor near Damascus on June 21, forcing the latter to seek refuge at the castle of Rahba on the Euphrates. From there he wrote to the Il-Khan Abaqa, urging him to intervene in Syria on his behalf.

Abaqa saw this open rift among the Mamluks as a golden opportunity for punishing them, and sent an army under his brother Mangu Timur to invade Syria. The Mongols reached Aleppo toward the end of October 1280, but withdrew across the Euphrates again after looting and destroying the city. Their withdrawal did not end the threat of future invasions, however, and Qalawun, like Baibars before him, sought to prevent an alliance between the Franks and the Mongols that could force him to fight a two-front war. He too signed a ten-year truce with the Knights of St. John (the Hospitallers), followed by a similar agreement with Bohemond VII (1275–1287), count of Tripoli.

Qalawun anticipated a new major attack by Mangu Timur, which was expected to occur about October 1281. He believed it necessary to come to terms with Sonkor, who had established himself in Lebanon, where he was gathering behind him a growing force of Mamluks that were disenchanted or out of favor with Qalawun. Accordingly, Qalawun issued a decree awarding Sonkor a small principality reaching from Latakia to Antioch, hoping that this would be sufficient to dissuade him from joining forces with the Mongols. The Mamluk and Mongol armies, more than a third of the latter consisting of Georgian and Armenian troops under King Leo III, clashed at Homs on October 31, 1281. The Mamluks emerged victorious, and Mangu Timur retired across the Euphrates to Jazira ibn Umar north of Mosul. Abaqa subsequently abandoned the campaign in the west and returned to Persia, where he died on April 1, 1282. He was succeeded by his brother Tequdar (1282–1284), who informed Qalawun in December 1282 that he had converted to Islam, adopting the title of Sultan Ahmed, and that although he would pursue the traditional Mongol goal of world conquest he would no longer make war against fellow Muslims.

Tequdar's attempt to reorient the Il-Khanids toward Islam aroused the ire of the Buddhists and Nestorians in his horde. They appealed directly to the khagan, Kublai Khan, to intervene in order to prevent the civil strife that seemed inevitable if Tequdar persisted in his efforts to convert the horde to Islam. Before a response was received from the court in Beijing, Tequdar's opponents rallied behind Arghun, another of Abaqa's sons and governor of Khorasan, triggering a civil war in August 1283. At stake in the struggle was the political balance of the Middle East. Tequdar's earlier overture to Qalawun in Cairo seemed to suggest a potential realignment of forces in the broader region. It would bring Il-Khanid Persia to abandon its long-standing cooperation with the Georgians and Armenians, as well as its special relationship with the Franks of Syria and Palestine, in favor of an alliance with the Mamluks.

The forces of Arghun and Tequdar clashed near Qazvin on May 4, 1284, with the latter emerging victorious, ostensibly putting an end to the civil war. However, Tequdar was soon overthrown in a palace revolution that placed Arghun (1284–1291) on the throne on August 10, returning the Il-Khanid regime to its traditional Buddhist-Nestorian orientation and relentless hostility toward the Mamluks.

Arghun actively sought a European-Mongol alliance against the Mamluks. He wrote to Pope Honorius IV in 1285 proposing a joint attack on the common enemy. He asked that a Christian army be landed while he invaded Syria. In this way, "As the land of the Saracens will lie between yourselves and us, together we will surround and strangle it. . . . We will drive out the Saracens with the help of God, the Pope, and the Grand Khan."[5] Arghun then dispatched the Nestorian ecclesiastic Rabban Sauma to Europe as his emissary who, during 1287–1288, brought his proposal to Constantinople, Rome, Paris, and Bordeaux. However, he received nothing concrete by way of answer beyond the vague reported response of Philip IV of France: "If the armies of the Ilkhan go to war against Egypt, we too shall set out from here to go to war and to attack in a common operation."[6] In 1289 Arghun sent another emissary to Pope Nicholas IV, Philip, and Edward I of England, in an attempt to obtain a clear commitment for a joint campaign. He wrote that, with regard to Philip's offer:

We decided after reporting to heaven, to mount our horses in the last month of winter in the Year of the Tiger [1290] and to dismount outside Damascus on the 15th of the first month in spring [1291]. Now, We make it known to you, that in accordance with Our honest word, We shall send Our armies [to arrive] at the [time and place] agreed, and, if by the authority of heaven, We conquer those people, We shall give you Jerusalem. If [however], you should fail to meet the appropriate day, and thus lead our armies into an abortive action, would that be fitting? Even if you should later regret it, what use would that be to you? [You would have reason to regret it later][7]

All this was to no avail. The European states were too preoccupied with their own tumultuous affairs to give much serious attention to Middle Eastern problems. Arghun himself soon had to divert his attention away from Syria and Palestine as well to deal with the new threats that had arisen on his northern frontiers. A revolt had broken out in Khorasan that had to be suppressed, and in 1290, the khan of the Kipchaks of the Golden Horde came in force across the Derbent pass into Persia. The invasion was repulsed in May 1290, and the Kipchak vanguard was subsequently defeated on the banks of the Kara-Su in Circassia.

No longer concerned about a possible Frank-Mongol alliance against him, in April 1285 Qalawun violated the ten-year truce that he had earlier sought and concluded with the Hospitallers before the battle at Homs. Adherence to the agreement no longer served his interest and he simply discarded it. Qalawun proceeded to attack and take the Hospitaller fortress at Marqab, formerly thought to be impregnable, after more than a month-long struggle. This was followed by the fall of Latakia to the Mamluks in 1287. At the same time, Qalawun was able to reap advantage from the succession crisis that arose in Tripoli upon the death of the Bohemond VII, who was without an heir, on October 19, 1287. Genoa threw its weight behind the candidacy of Bohemond's sister Lucia to become the ruling countess of Tripoli, in exchange for her recognition of Genoa's special position there. This enhancement of the Genoese position was considered unacceptable to Genoa's principal maritime rival, Venice. In 1289, the Venetians turned to Qalawun and encouraged him to attack Tripoli. He did not need too much encouragement from them and soon assaulted and captured the city.

While these events were taking place in Syria, Qalawun also made a concerted effort to expand the Mamluk Empire southward. In January 1288, he sent an army up the Nile into Nubia, capturing the capital at Dongola. However, Qalawun was not able to leave anything more than a small garrison there, and as soon as the main force withdrew, the Nubian king Semamoun drove out the garrison and reoccupied the city. This same scenario was repeated in the spring of 1289. Qalawun then reached an accommodation with Semamoun whereby the latter promised to pay an annual tribute in return for a Mamluk policy of benign neglect toward Nubia. Qalawun's experience in Nubia confirmed the experience of the rulers of Egypt for some three millennia that the preferred direction of Egyptian expansion was toward Asia rather than into Africa.

In 1290, Qalawun marched against Acre, but he died before he achieved his goal of completing what Baibars had started, that is, the complete elimination of the Franks from Syria and Palestine. The city fell to his son and successor, al-Ashraf Khalil (1290–1293), on May 28, 1291. With the loss of Acre, the rest of Frankish Palestine surrendered without a struggle. Farther north, Tyre capitulated on May 19, Sidon the following month, and Beirut on July 31. The two fortresses of Tortosa (Tartus) and the Castle of the Pilgrims surrendered in August. To ensure that there would be no return of the Franks to Syria and Palestine, the Mamluks systematically destroyed everything along the entire length of the coastal region. The Templars, who continued to dream of a return to the Holy Land, finally acknowledged that the Frankish era in the region was at an end in 1303. They abandoned their last base on the small island of Ruad near Tartus, from which they had hoped to stage a comeback.

Within a few days of the fall of Acre, Arghun died and a succession crisis developed that was ultimately resolved by the assumption of power by Ghazan (1295–1304). The latter, the governor of Khorasan and a son of Arghun, had originally been passed over for the succession by the Mongol generals in favor of his dissolute uncle Kaikhatu (1291–1295).

A fundamental change had overtaken the Mongols in Persia over the mere thirty years since the death of Hulagu. A whole generation had grown up in Persia, far from the traditions of the steppe, and had become susceptible to Persian culture, now including the religion of most Persians—Islam. The death of Kublai Khan in 1294 severed the last links between the Il-Khanid Empire and China. Persia became a completely independent Mongol state, the majority of whose inhabitants were Muslims. Ghazan, who was a Buddhist, was advised that if he truly wished to succeed to the Il-Khanid throne, it would be wise to abandon Buddhism, which was far more abhorrent to Persia's Muslims than the Christianity professed by his rival for the throne, and accept Islam. Ghazan eventually took this advice and in 1295 assumed the name of Mahmud, converting to Islam along with many of his officers. Overnight the imams embraced his cause against his competitors, and he soon received the homage of the nation as its legitimate ruler in November 1295.

Ghazan's acceptance of Islam evidently had no effect on the traditional hostility that prevailed between Mamluks and Mongols. In 1299, he crossed the Euphrates and captured Aleppo on December 12 and defeated the Mamluk army at Homs ten days later. He then marched into Damascus on January 6, 1300, where he was acknowledged in the central mosque as the legitimate ruler of Syria. However, Ghazan was unable to defeat the Mamluks decisively. He was forced to return to Persia the following month to deal with the challenge posed by Qutlugh-Khoja, the son of the Jagatai khan of Turkestan, who had taken control of Ghazni and Ghor in Afghanistan and conducted raids into the Persian provinces of Kerman and Fars during Ghazan's absence. Shortly after Ghazan's departure from Syria, the Mamluks reoccupied Damascus.

A last major Mongol incursion into Syria was made in the spring of 1303 under Ghazan's general Qutlugh-Shah, who was decisively beaten by the Mamluks at Marj as-Suffar near Damascus on April 21. This defeat effectively ended the long-standing Mongol threat to Syria and left Lesser Armenia, an Il-Khanid vassal state, fully exposed to Mamluk vengeance.

Ghazan's brother Oljeitu (1304–1316) succeeded him and followed the same foreign policy as his predecessors. Hit-and-run border warfare with the Mamluks broke out once again. Oljeitu also sought an alliance with the European powers, but he met with no greater success in this than did

Ghazan. As a practical matter, Ghazan's death in 1304 spelled the effective end of the era of Mongol ascendancy in the Middle East.

NOTES

1. Muhi ad-Din, *Sirat al-Malik al-Zahir*, translated by Syedah Fatima Sadeque in *Baybars I of Egypt*, p. 113.
2. Rene Grousset, *The Empire of the Steppes*, p. 366.
3. Muhi ad-Din, *Sirat al-Malik al-Zahir*, p. 112.
4. Ibid., pp. 116–117.
5. Grousset, *The Empire of the Steppes*, p. 374.
6. Berthold Spuler, *History of the Mongols*, p. 142.
7. Ibid.

12

The Rise of the
Ottomans

Coincidental with the decline of Il-Khanid power there appeared a new star in the Middle East political constellation, the Osmanlis or Ottomans. The Mongol invasion of Persia had precipitated a new wave of Turkish migration westward from Khorasan that overran a good part of Anatolia. This took place as the Byzantines were preoccupied with their wars in the Balkans, and the Seljukids were mired in the process of political disintegration. Among these Turkish migrants was a clan of the Oghuz led by Ertoghrul (c. 1240–1280), who was granted control of a district in the northwestern part of the Anatolian peninsula as a reward for his exceptional military services on behalf of the Seljukid sultan of Konya, Kai-Qubadh II (1249–1257).

The sultan's generosity was not entirely selfless, since it also served an important strategic interest. The territory assigned to Ertoghrul was located on the increasingly unstable frontiers of the Byzantine province of Bithynia. Kai-Qubadh, whose patrimony was shrinking under the continual pressures from both the Mongols and the Byzantines, saw in Ertoghrul and his followers an instrument with which to prevent further deterioration in the territorial configuration of the sultanate. And, in fact, Ertoghrul soon proved to be a potent force for securing Konya's northwestern frontier and received the strategically important district of Eskisehir (Dorylaeum) as additional compensation for his services to the Seljukid sultanate.

Throughout his lifetime, Ertoghrul remained a loyal vassal of the sultan of Konya. At the same time, he systematically imposed and consolidated his control over the local chiefs within his domain, which constituted only about one-seventeenth of the territory of the Seljukid sultanate. Ertoghrul's son and successor Osman or Othman (1281–1324) generally followed in his footsteps until about 1300. At that point, with the Seljukid sultanate of Konya increasingly coming under direct Il-Khanid control, Othman considered himself free of further obligations to the sultan.

From his base in northwestern Anatolia, which was beyond the effective reach of the Mongols, Othman assumed the posture of an independent potentate. He began to compete with the emirs of the Qaramanids, who had settled in ancient Lycaonia and Isauria, with regard to who would become the successors to the Seljukids in the peninsula. The Qaramanids claimed this right as a result of the marriage of the founder of the dynasty to the daughter of the Seljukid sultan.

However, Othman's prestige among the Turks soared after his defeat of a major Byzantine force at Baphaeon in 1301. A large number of the Turkish beys came over to his standard with their followers, an allegiance that was made all the more attractive since Othman's emirate straddled the lucrative caravan route between Konya and Constantinople, and thereby presented significant opportunities for both legitimate revenue and booty.

Between 1308 and 1314, the Qaramanid emir Badr ad-Din Mahmud (1278–1319) made himself de facto ruler of Konya, provoking the Il-Khan Oljeitu to send an army against him and to reassert Mongol dominion in the area. During the same period, Othman advanced against the Byzantine territories along his western frontiers, seizing control of Bithynia and Phrygia and blockading the well-fortified strongholds of Brusa (Bursa), Nicaea (Iznik), and Nicomedia (Izmid). The Ottoman drive was relentless and carefully designed. As one historian of the period remarked:

The method employed by the Ottomans to gain possession of the large, populous, and well-fortified cities, inhabited by the wealthy but unwarlike Greeks, was not unlike that employed by the Dorians in the early ages of Greece. Indeed it is almost the only way by which the courage and perseverance of a small force can conquer art and numbers. Instead of attempting to form a regular blockade of the city against which they directed their operations, and thereby compelling the inhabitants to exert all their unbroken power to deliver themselves from the attack, the Ottoman Turks established strong posts in the vicinity of the city, ravaged the fields, carried off cattle and slaves, and interrupted the commercial communications of the inhabitants. The devastation of the country and the insecurity of the roads gradually raised the price of provisions and caused emigration and famine. In this way Nicaea, the cradle of the Greek Church, and which had been for two generations the capital of the Greek Empire, was closely blockaded.[1]

This situation caused the Byzantine emperor, Andronicus II Palaeologus (1282–1328), to seek an offsetting alliance with Oljeitu, offering him his sister Maria in marriage in order to seal the bargain. Although this Byzantine-Mongol alliance brought an invasion of the Ottoman district of Eskisehir by an Il-Khanid force, which was subsequently expelled, it was already too late to reverse the Ottoman drive for empire.

The Il-Khanid Empire itself was under growing pressure in the east, and it was there that Oljeitu had to direct the focus of his attention. The Jagataite khans of Transoxiana were encroaching on the frontier of the empire, and the Afghans, under the domination of the Kert ruler Fakhr ad-Din of Herat, were striving to break loose of Il-Khanid control and assert their autonomy. In 1306, Oljeitu had to send a force to lay seige to Herat for the purpose of squelching these aspirations.

In an effort to restore some lustre to the fading Il-Khanid image and thereby help deflect Jagataite expansionism in another direction, Oljeitu undertook the conquest of the Caspian province of Gilan in May 1307. Nestled behind the Elburz Mountains and covered by dense forests that made access difficult, Gilan had escaped conquest by the Il-Khanids for half a century. Oljeitu, evidently intending to use its conquest to demonstrate that he was still in command of awesome power, launched a major invasion of the province, deploying four different armies that struck at different points along the frontier. The campaign went well at first, as the Gilaki forces succumbed to the Il-Khanid drive. Then, one of the Mongol armies was lured into a battle that took place on ground favorable to the Gilakis and met with disaster, turning the tide of the campaign. Within a few weeks, after trying unsuccessfully to inflict a decisive defeat on the Gilakis, Oljeitu decided to terminate the campaign and withdraw from Gilan.

Struggling to maintain his grip in the east, Oljeitu succeeded in seizing the territories of the Nigudari, allies of the Jagataites, in southern Afghanistan in 1313. This precipitated an invasion of Khorasan the following year by an army led by Kebek, brother of the Jagataite khan Esen-Buqa (1309–1318). The Jagataite forces, however, were soon recalled by Esen-Buqa who had need of them to cope with an assault on his own eastern flank by the armies of the Great Khan of China, giving the Il-Khanids a much needed breather.

Oljeitu, who died in 1317, was formally succeeded by his twelve-year-old son and heir Abu Said (1317–1335). As a practical matter, however, the Il-Khanid Empire was actually administered by a Mongol emir, Choban, who appeared to be succeeding in keeping it intact. In 1319 and again in 1325 Choban succeeded in turning back attempted invasions of the Il-Khanid realm by Ozbeg, leader of the Golden Horde, and managed to mount a counterattack that took the conflict into the enemy's own territory. However, in 1327, Abu Said broke with Choban over a palace intrigue involving the latter's married daughter. This soon escalated into a civil war that effectively drained the state of its remaining vigor. By the time of the death of Abu Said a few years later it was no longer possible to keep the Il-Khanid Empire together.

In Anatolia, the decline of Il-Khanid authority created a major power vacuum. The Seljukid sultanate of Konya had virtually ceased to exist after the death of the sultan Masud II (1282–1304), the country being ruled for all practical purposes by Mongol viceroys appointed by the Il-Khan in Persia. They increasingly acted as independent sovereigns. Without a strong leader to keep them in check, they were free to pursue their individual ambitions. Moreover, with the collapse of any central Mongol authority in the region, Anatolia quickly came under the control of the Turkish houses of Qaraman in the southeast and Othman in the northwest. These two competed against each other for hegemony, a struggle that had significant consequences for the future history of the region as the Ottomans emerged victorious from the conflict. As one modern historian put it, it is not without irony that "the rise of the Ottoman Empire resulted indirectly from the conflicts at the Mongol court of Persia during the crucial years 1327–35."[2]

The political disintegration that took place in Anatolia also occurred in Persia itself, where it was fueled by a series of crises that developed over the succession to the khanate. In 1338, a grandson of Choban, Hasan-i Kuchak, captured Tabriz and established an independent kingdom that included Azerbaijan and the Jazira. Two years later, Hasan-i Buzurg proclaimed an independent Jalayir kingdom in Iraq with its capital at Baghdad. At the same time, the Kert rulers of eastern Khorasan and Herat took advantage of the prevailing political disarray to assert their complete independence of the Mongols and to establish a new and relatively powerful state under Muizz ad-Din Husain (1332–1370). In western Khorasan, an independent principality of the Sarbadarids was established during 1337–1338, with its capital at Nishapur.

The Kerts, who were Sunnite Afghans, and the Sarbadarids, who were Shiite Persians, waged a savage war against each other, their competing territorial ambitions inflamed by religious differences, adding significantly to the political turmoil in the region. In Kerman and Fars, an independent Arab-Iranian dynasty, the Muzaffarid, was founded by Mubariz ad-Din Muhammad (1314–1358), who had earlier been appointed as governor in Yazd by Abu Said, and had extended his rule to Shiraz in 1353 and Isfahan in 1357.

The collapse of the Il-Khanid Empire also freed the Mamluks completely from their only serious competitor for power in Syria, even though it also left the frontier region in a state of anarchy. With the Mongol protective umbrella removed from Cilicia, the kingdom of Lesser Armenia became virtually defenseless. Although the Mamluk sultan Nasir Muhammad (1298–1341) generally preferred to have his enemies assassinated rather than confront them on the battlefield, he made an exception in the case of Christian Lesser Armenia. In late 1336, he launched another expedition against Cilicia and again destroyed the port of Ayas and occupied most of the fortresses along the Syrian frontier. Cilicia was invaded again in 1359, at which time Adana, Tarsus, and Massissa were annexed to the Mamluk Empire.

Compounding the problem further, Byzantium had been seriously weakened as a consequence of the Mongol onslaught of the mid-thirteenth century that pushed many Turkish tribes against its permeable frontiers in both Europe and Asia. It was also being drawn into the conflict between the maritime states of Venice and Genoa for control of the eastern Mediterranean. The defenses erected earlier along the Byzantine-Seljukid frontiers in Anatolia were in a state of decay and highly vulnerable to attack.

At the time of the rise of the Ottomans, the focal point of Byzantine imperial policy had shifted from Asia to the Balkans and Europe, further weakening Constantinople's ability to withstand the new challenge emerging in Anatolia. Troops usually assigned to frontier defense in Asia were reassigned to Europe, leaving Byzantine Anatolia virtually defenseless. As a contemporary wrote, "In this way, the defences of the eastern territory were weakened, whilst the Persians (Turks) were emboldened to invade lands which had no means of driving them off."[3]

By the time Othman's successor Orkhan (1324–1360) became sultan, most of Anatolia was already in the hands of a variety of Turkish chieftains, with the exception of a few Byzantine fortresses that had managed to hold out against them. However, once regular maritime communications between these remnants of Byzantine power in Asia Minor and Constantinople were interrupted, it was only a matter of time before they succumbed to the relentless Ottoman pressure, the major center at Bursa falling to the Turks in 1326. As Orkhan continued his drive toward the Sea of Marmara, the new Byzantine emperor Andronicus III Palaeologus (1328–1341) attempted to put a stop to the Ottoman advance with a major expedition into Anatolia. However, this effort soon turned into a debacle as the Byzantine forces were routed at Maltepe (Pelecanon) in 1328. Andronicus fled back to Constantinople, effectively abandoning the remaining Byzantine strongholds in Anatolia to their collective fate. After Orkhan seized most of the Nicaean peninsula and the coasts of the Gulf of Nicomedia, Nicaea (Iznik) capitulated in 1331.

Orkhan was able to expand his realm further in 1336 when he took advantage of a succession struggle to annex the adjacent emirate of Karesi, including its capital Bergama (Pergamon), which extended Ottoman dominion to the Aegean coast. This was an especially significant strategic acquisition since it gave the Ottomans control of Canakkale, directly opposite the Gallipoli Peninsula on the other side of the Dardanelles, a position from which it became relatively easy for them to intervene at will in the Byzantine mainland. Nicomedia (Izmid) fell in 1337, after a six-year siege, and Uskudar (Scutari) the following year. Although there remained some Byzantine footholds such as Trebizond in northeastern Anatolia and Amastris in Paphlagonia, they were too isolated and geographically scattered to represent any significant political or military challenge to the Ottomans, who now controlled most of western Anatolia.

Orkhan devoted the next two decades of his reign to the further consolidation of his empire rather than to its continuing expansion. As remarked by a historian of the Ottomans:

It is indeed a remarkable trait in the characters of the first princes of the Ottoman dynasty, that, unlike the generality of conquerors, especially of Asiatic conquerors, they did not hurry on from one war to another in ceaseless avidity for fresh victories and new dominions; but, on the contrary, they were not more eager to seize, than they were cautious and earnest to consolidate. They paused over each subdued province, till, by assimilation of civil and military institutions, it was fully blended into the general nationality of their empire. They thus gradually molded, in Asia Minor, an homogeneous and a stable power, instead of precipitately heaping together a motley mass of ill-arranged provinces and discordant populations. To this policy the long endurance of the Ottoman Empire, compared with other Oriental empires of both ancient and modern times, is greatly to be ascribed.[4]

The capture of Bursa, which became the Ottoman capital, signaled the beginning of the transition of the Ottoman realm from an ill-defined nomadic principality into a substantial state with delimited borders and a settled population. Orkhan's older brother Ala ad-Din, the first Ottoman vizier, astutely recognized that building a stable state in the highly volatile region required the establishment of a different type of military organization than that which had brought the Ottomans to power in the first place. They could no longer rely on the occasional mobilization of their Oghuz clansmen for a particular campaign, which would be followed by their being permitted to continue to plunder the region according to their fancy. Moreover, since they were now ruling over a mixed population, Ottoman interests necessarily transcended those of their tribal kinsmen, whose free-booting ways needed to be restrained and who also had to be made subservient to the state.

Ala ad-Din concluded that it would be necessary to build a powerful, well-trained and well-paid standing army, something that not one of the Balkan states possessed, thereby giving the Ottomans a significant advantage both from the standpoint of readiness and military efficiency. In addition, the army, which was no longer to be based almost exclusively on Oghuz warriors, was to have an elite force in its vanguard that was to be similar to the mamluks that had been used so effectively in the past history of the region. Accordingly, in 1326 Ala ad-Din initiated the annual practice of inducting specially selected young Christian boys for lifetime service in the Ottoman military. They were designated as Yeni Tscheri (Janissaries), that is, "new troops," a force that was to play a major part in the growth and politics of the Ottoman Empire. These youngsters were raised as Muslims and were trained exclusively to become dedicated and disciplined soldiers. According to the rules prescribed later by the sultan Murad, "No Janissary should be allowed to learn a trade, or to work as an artisan. His exclusive occupation ought to be exercise in the art of war."[5]

In the process of consolidating his grip on the country, Orkhan sought to bring the remaining Seljukid territories within the growing Ottoman domain, although he was not prepared to expend any significant effort in this enterprise. He was far more interested in Byzantium, which promised great spoil, than in imposing his control over the fiercely independent, but mostly impoverished, emirs of Anatolia. Indeed, some Seljukid rulers such as Omur-Beg of Izmir entered into alliances with the Byzantines in an effort to contain the increasing Ottoman threat, a project that proved infeasible. Accordingly, it was not long before the Byzantine emperor Andronicus found it necessary to seek to reach an accommodation with Orkhan that resulted in at least a temporary normalization of relations. He also began the practice of using Ottoman mercenaries for his wars in the Balkans and with the western European powers, something that could be exploited politically by the sultan under the right circumstances.

With the death of Andronicus in 1341, a domestic crisis developed in Constantinople that soon provided the occasion for an Ottoman advance into Europe. The heir to the throne, John V Palaeologus (1341–1391), was only nine years old and a struggle began over the regency that was to govern on his behalf until he came of age. The Grand Domestic John Cantacuzenus, who had served as de facto head of government during Andronicus' reign, was precluded from assuming the position by a coup d'etat engineered by his opponents in collaboration with the dowager empress Anne of Savoy. Cantacuzenus refused to accept the coup as a *fait accompli* and had himself proclaimed emperor at Didymotichus on October 26, 1341. This triggered a civil war that he prosecuted for the ostensible purpose of securing the throne for the young Palaeologian. In 1342, as Cantcuzenus appeared to be gaining the upper hand in the conflict, the ruler of Serbia, Stephen Dushan (1331–1355), switched alliances from Cantacuzenus to the regency in Constantinople. This was an effort on his part to prevent either party from changing the existing regional balance of power that was favorable to Serbian interests. This forced Cantacuzenus to look to Anatolia for allies to offset the unfavorable realignment of forces in the Balkans.

Omur of Aydin came to Cantacuzenus' aid toward the end of 1342, and with his help, Cantacuzenus undertook the conquest of Thrace. It was not long, however, before Omur was forced to return to Anatolia to deal with the threat to his territory from the confederacy of Venice, Cyprus, and the Knights of St. John that occupied Smyrna in 1344 and seized control of the coastal regions of ancient Lycia and Pamphylia. Omur recommended that Cantacuzenus turn to the Ottomans for help in his stead. The regency in Constantinople had entertained the same thought and sought unsuccessfully to bring the Ottomans over to its side to forestall an alliance between them and Cantacuzenus. For his part, Orkhan was only too pleased to be invited to intervene in Byzantium and agreed to an alliance with Cantacuzenus later that year, presumably because it fit better with his plans for the future expansion of his realm. To help assure the stability of the political relationship, Cantacuzenus gave his daughter Theodora in marriage to the aging Ottoman sultan in 1346.

Now confident of victory, with Orkhan's assistance, Cantacuzenus had himself crowned emperor in Adrianople on May 21, 1344, by the patriarch of Jerusalem. The dowager empress Anne continued to seek help against him from the Turks and finally succeeded in arranging for some 6,000 Seljukids from the emirate of Sarukhan in ancient Magnesia to attack Cantacuzenus in Thrace. However, the Seljukids had little interest in war-torn Thrace and preferred to seek booty in Bulgaria, which they invaded instead. When the Seljukid forces subsequently withdrew back to Anatolia, they first exploited the opportunity to ravage the region around Constantinople. After this debacle, Anne was forced to concede defeat and John VI Cantacuzenus (1347–1354) entered Constantinople in triumph in February 1347. The civil war had been brought to an end, at least for the moment.

No sooner had Cantacuzenus established himself in Constantinople than he found himself in a devastating war with the Genoese who controlled Galata, a suburb of the capital, over the issue of who had the right to the customs revenues derived from the maritime traffic in the Bosphorus. Then, in 1349, the Serbian Stephen Dushan seized Salonika from the Byzantines, causing Cantacuzenus to appeal to Orkhan once more for help in retrieving the territory. Orkhan welcomed the invitation to intervene in Byzantine affairs again and dispatched his son Suleiman with a force of 20,000 men, which, in cooperation with the Byzantine fleet, retook Salonika for Cantacuzenus. When the affair was concluded, Suleiman returned to Anatolia with his troops.

A few months later, in 1350, a new war between Venice and Genoa broke out over control of the Black Sea trade. This conflict was to have particularly significant long-term consequences for the region. Presumably motivated by a desire to avenge himself on the Genoese for the defeat he suffered at their hands during their earlier confrontation, Cantacuzenus entered the fray by joining the pro-Venetian alliance led by Peter IV of Aragon. Orkhan, however, was at odds with the Venetians whose interests and ambitions in the Aegean region conflicted with his own. As a result, he found greater common cause with the Genoese, which pitted him against his Byzantine father-in-law.

Orkhan sent a small force under Suleiman across the strait to Galata once again. However, this time it was to support his new ally against the Byzantines. Although the major battle fought between the two antagonists on the Bosphorus in February 1352 was indecisive, Suleiman exploited the opportunity to seize and occupy the fortress of Tzympe on the isthmus of Callipolis (Gallipoli).

With the subsequent withdrawal of the Venetian and Aragonese fleets from the Bosphorus, Cantacuzenus felt that he had little choice but to come to terms with the Genoese. However, as a consequence of this reversal of alliances by Cantacuzenus, the Venetians similarly switched allies and reached an understanding with John Palaeologus, who, as he matured, had begun to rebel against the constraints placed on him by Cantacuzenus. In the fall of 1352, with the financial support of Venice, which had placed some 20,000 ducats at his disposal, John Palaeologus invaded the district of Adrianople, which had been given by Cantacuzenus to his nephew Matthew to govern as an autonomous principality.

Cantacuzenus promptly intervened to restore the situation to its previous condition. This prompted John Palaeologus to appeal for help from the Serbs and Bulgarians in preserving his gains. The former responded to his plea by sending a force of some 4,000 men. Faced by this new external threat, Cantacuzenus dropped his demands that Orkhan remove his forces from Tzympe, and instead turned to the Ottomans for additional assistance in the growing conflict with John Palaeologus. Orkhan, who had a vested interest in defeating Venice's policy in the region, sent an army of some 10,000 men under Suleiman to Cantacuzenus' aid in the new Byzantine civil war that was otherwise of little consequence to him. As a result, it seemed that the dispute between the two emperors of Byzantium was to be settled on the battlefield between the Ottoman and Serbian armies, the Bulgarians having withdrawn from the conflict at Suleiman's approach. Cantacuzenus carried the day as the superior Turkish forces overwhelmed those of the Serbs and John Palaeologus.

Having achieved his purpose with their help, Cantacuzenus now sought to arrange for the removal of the Ottoman forces from Thrace. He offered Orkhan 10,000 ducats in exchange for his withdrawal from the toehold that Suleiman had established in Europe. Orkhan accepted the offer, but before the arrangement could be put into effect, in March 1354 nature intervened. A major earthquake shook Thrace and caused a great deal of damage and chaos. Suleiman seized the moment and occupied Gallipoli, which was virtually abandoned by its inhabitants. With his original toehold in Europe now enlarged to a foothold that provided a solid base for further expansion, Orkhan refused to budge and Cantacuzenus was in no position to compel his withdrawal from Europe.

Constantinople was in panic over the new Turkish threat, and Cantacuzenus was forced to repudiate his relationship with Orkhan and to appeal to the tsars of Serbia and Bulgaria for aid in driving the Ottomans out of Europe. The appeal was rejected, the Bulgarian ruler responding: "Three years ago I remonstrated with you for your unholy alliance with the Turks. Now that the storm has burst, let the Byzantines weather it. If the Turks come against me we shall know how to defend ourselves."[6] This was soon to prove a rather naive and unfortunate stance, given the realities of the prevailing regional military balance, which was not yet tilted in favor of the Ottomans. An alliance between the three states at this juncture might well have changed the course of history by successfully forcing the Turks out of Europe.

When the full implications of what Cantacuzenus' foreign policy had wrought were recognized by the power structure in Constantinople, he was forced to abdicate the Byzantine throne in November 1354 in favor of the sole rule of John Palaeologus. The latter, however, was unable to bring about any improvement in the situation. He was compelled to acknowledge Orkhan's conquests in Europe in 1356, in exchange for an Ottoman commitment to allow an undisturbed flow of food and other supplies to the beleaguered Byzantine capital, which now appeared to be at the mercy of the Ottoman sultan.

With the death of Stephen Dushan in December 1355, the situation became highly favorable for further Ottoman expansion into Europe. At this point in time, it was Serbia rather than Byzantium, or the budding Ottoman Empire for that matter, that was the major power in the Balkans. Stephen Dushan, however, had no real successor and his Serbian Empire quickly disintegrated once he was no longer there to rein in its unruly components. This created a power vacuum in the region that only the Ottomans were in a position to fill, and fill it they did.

The Ottoman foothold in Thrace expanded rapidly as the people of the area fled in anticipation of the Turkish advance. A steady stream of troops and settlers from overcrowded regions of Anatolia poured across the strait to fill the vacuum as Orkhan's armies began driving inland. The rapid Turkish expansion throughout the Balkan region may be attributed perhaps as much to geopolitical factors as to the considerable strength of the Ottomans as a military power.

The Balkans themselves were never a significant natural defensive barrier. By gaining control of several riverways, an invading force could gain ready access to the valley of the Danube leading to Hungary and central Europe. An invading army also had the option of marching into Moldavia and Wallachia, and then proceeding eastward along the Black Sea littoral. The defense of this vast region required political coherence and an integrated defense system that could allocate men and resources to meet the threat anywhere along a wide front. During the latter part of the fourteenth century, however, the Balkan states were in a state of almost complete disarray. Both Byzantium and Bulgaria were in unremitting decay while the Serbian Empire of Stephen Dushan had been disintegrating in the wake of his death. They simply were unable to mobilize a competent defense against the powerful Ottoman juggernaut that was building momentum as their own power waned.

NOTES

1. George Finlay, *A History of Greece*, vol. 3, pp. 423–424.

2. Rene Grousset, *The Empire of the Steppes*, p. 389.

3. George Ostrogorsky, *History of the Byzantine State*, p. 438.

4. Edward S. Creasy, *History of the Ottoman Turks: From the Beginning of Their Empire to the Present Time*, p. 17.

5. Ahmed Djevad Bey, *Etat militaire Ottoman depuis la fondation de l'empire jusqu'a nos jours*, p. 66.

6. Lord Eversley, *The Turkish Empire: From 1288 to 1914*, p. 28.

13

The Era of Murad and Bayezid

Murad I (1362–1389), who pursued territorial expansion even more vigorously than his father Orkhan, and was an outstanding strategist, had decided to bypass Constantinople for the time being. The main arm of the Ottoman army was still the Turkish cavalry, and it made little military sense to commit it to the storming of the walled and heavily defended city. Instead, he made his primary initial objective Adrianople (Edirne), the strongest point between Constantinople and the Danube, which commanded the Maritsa river gap between the Balkan and Rhodope Mountains.

From Adrianople, which was taken in 1361, Murad launched a three-pronged offensive through the region. One army marched across the western Balkan passes toward Serres in Serbia and the road leading from the important port of Salonika to Belgrade. In the center, another army headed north for Philippolis, which gave Murad control of the entire Maritsa valley—the source of much of Constantinople's grain and rice supply—which was occupied in 1363, and Sofia, which commanded the watershed between the valleys of the Nisava and the Maritsa Rivers. This forced John Palaeologus to reach an accommodation with Murad in 1363 that committed the Byzantine ruler to refrain from hatching any plots with the Balkan rulers, in exchange for an Ottoman commitment not to attack Constantinople and to allow food to reach the city. Control of the Maritsa valley also enabled Murad to prevent the Greeks who were resisting his advance along the Aegean coast from linking up with the Bulgarians. At the same time, another Ottoman detachment under Murad's personal command seized control of the Thracian Black Sea coast that had come under the rule of the Bulgarian prince John Alexander (1355–1365) after the death of Stephen

Dushan. This cut off the Byzantines from direct land contact with Europe; they now had to rely entirely on maritime communications. To facilitate the consolidation of his conquests, Murad moved the Ottoman capital from Bursa to Adrianople in 1365.

In the meanwhile, John Palaeologus began a desperate search for allies against the Ottomans. To make matters worse, the Bulgarians attempted to deflect the Ottoman advance by joining forces with them in 1364, thereby precipitating a war with Latin Catholic Hungary, which mounted a crusade of it own against the Greek Orthodox "heretics." Byzantium's search for support in Europe was a failure for all practical purposes, even though the pope tried to influence Hungary and a number of the Italian city-states to rally to its aid. Pope Urban V, who had proclaimed a new crusade to regain the Holy Land, tried to get it redirected against the Ottoman Turks in April 1365, but only Count Amadeus II of Savoy responded favorably. He led a fleet eastward that managed to dislodge the Turks from Gallipoli in August 1366. Amadeus also marched against the Bulgarians, forcing them to cede the territories of Mesembria and Sozopolis to John, thereby giving the Byzantines a temporary foothold on the western coast of the Black Sea. At best, this gave Byzantium a brief respite from the Ottoman onslaught. These apparent setbacks, however, had little effect on the overall Turkish position in Thrace, which Murad now further consolidated by a program of mass immigration of Turks from Anatolia. Amadeus soon abandoned Gallipoli to the Byzantines after he was unable to reach agreement with John on the future course of their relations.

At the same time, the crusader army that was being assembled at Rhodes was aimed at Egypt rather than at providing relief for the Byzantines. A force of some eighty ships, half from Cyprus and the remainder from Venice, Genoa, France, and the Knights of St. John of Rhodes, under the leadership of Peter I Lusignan, king of Cyprus, had managed to seize Alexandria on October 10, 1365. Peter's plan was essentially a replication of what had been attempted two centuries earlier with respect to Damietta; that is, he intended to take Alexandria and offer to return it to the Mamluks in exchange for Jerusalem. However, it soon changed from an ill-conceived and somewhat quixotic attempt to regain control of the Holy Land into a blatant act of simple piracy as the "crusaders" looted the city for several days and then sailed away. This senseless act had very significant unanticipated consequences for all concerned. Alexandria had held a virtual monopoly as the principal entrepôt for the lucrative oriental trade, which was now disrupted and effectively lost with severe consequences for the Egyptian economy. It also did great harm to the economic interests of the great maritime cities of Europe—Genoa, Venice, and Marseilles—and ultimately brought about the destruction of the independent kingdom of Cyprus.

The political viability of John Palaeologus in Constantinople was becoming increasingly tenuous and, in a desperate but ultimately futile bid to gain papal support, he went to Rome in October 1369 and converted to Roman Catholicism, an act that was repudiated by the Orthodox Church of Byzantium. Returning home empty-handed, he had little choice but to reach an accommodation with Murad, and under the circumstances that could only be one that would transform Byzantium into an Ottoman vassal state. As a practical matter, this led to John's active participation in Murad's campaigns in Anatolia.

At the same time, the Ottoman drive into Europe continued relentlessly. Between 1371 and 1375, western Thrace and Macedonia were invaded and occupied, raising serious doubts as to the continued viability of Byzantium as an independent state. By 1376, only some two decades after the first Ottoman toehold was established in Europe, Bulgaria was also forced to acknowledge Ottoman suzerainty, with Murad marrying the daughter of the Bulgarian king, Ivan Shishman (1371–1393). The new Byzantine emperor Andronicus IV Palaeologus (1376–1379) was forced to return Gallipoli, which had been seized from the Ottomans by Amadeus of Savoy a decade earlier, to Murad as well as to reaffirm Byzantium's acknowledgment of Ottoman suzerainty. Although this formal act of humiliation eliminated the immediate threat to Constantinople, given the pattern of Ottoman conquest there was little reason for complacency about Byzantium's future.

The Ottoman approach to empire building that already emerged at the time of Othman's absorption of most of western Anatolia reflected a two-phase process. Initially, the Ottomans attempted to maximize their sphere of control by entering into a variety of arrangements with the territories brought within their orbit, usually involving their transformation into vassal states and dependencies. In the second phase, that of consolidation, all independent or autonomous power centers were eliminated and the dependent territories annexed. As one student of the period observed: "The Turks gave proof of their great astuteness, at this early stage of their history, by their using chiefly Christian money and Christian arms to subdue, and afterwards to destroy, the Christian states of the Balkan. It was a general rule of their policy not to occupy at once the country of the defeated Christian Prince, but to impose a heavy tribute in money, and to exact that a contingent of his best soldiers should be regularly provided to fight against the Sultan's enemies, even if the latter were friendly Christian neighbours of the vassal Prince."[1]

The Ottoman drive into Europe was still in its first deceptive phase, which proved very useful to Murad as he reaped the benefits of tribute paid into his coffers by his vassal states. This phase lasted for about a decade, during which Murad's forces spread throughout the Balkans, marching into Serbia in 1386 and forcing Prince Lazar (1371–1389) to accept Ottoman suzerainty.

It seems clear that the rapidity of the Ottoman advance cannot be attributed solely to Murad's strategic brilliance or the military excellence of the

Turkish forces. Murad understood quite well that a real defensive alliance between the Balkan states, and particularly between the Balkan states and those of western Europe, could well spell the end for Ottoman expansionist aims. A primary aim of Ottoman foreign policy thus became that of preventing such alliances from coming into being. And the Turks were prepared to employ any means available to achieve this purpose, although they clearly preferred successful diplomacy to war. Accordingly, on his deathbed, John Palaeologus gave the following policy advice to his sons: "Whenever the Turks begin to be troublesome, send embassies to the West at once, offer to accept union, and protract negotiations to great length; the Turks so greatly fear such union that they will become reasonable; and still the union will not be accomplished because of the vanity of the Latin nations."[2] On the other hand, where prospects for diplomatic success were poor, the Ottomans had no reluctance to employ more forceful and direct means of carrying out their policy. Thus, when Murad discovered that Shishman of Bulgaria was negotiating for a military alliance with Lazar of Serbia and Sigismund of Hungary, the Ottomans staged an unanticipated invasion of Bulgaria, capturing Shishman along with his entire family at Nicopolis in 1386.

Another factor of considerable importance that facilitated Ottoman expansionism was the chronic political instability of the Balkan region, which undermined the national sentiments and loyalties of many of its peoples and provided the Ottomans with the means and opportunity to exploit the situation to their advantage. As argued by a Serbian historian:

The presence of Christian malcontents, refugees, pretenders, and adventurers in the Turkish camp and at the Sultan's "Porte," materially aided Turkish policy and Turkish arms to progress from victory to victory. Without them the Turkish Viziers and generals could hardly have obtained that minute and exact knowledge of men and circumstances in Christian countries, which so often astonished their contemporaries. Thus the Porte became promptly informed of the plans of the Christian kings, and was enabled to counteract them. Indeed, the leadership of the new Empire speedily passed into the hands of Christian renegades, and almost all the great statesmen and generals of the Sultans at this period were of Greek, Bulgarian, or Serbian origin.[3]

As the Ottoman sphere of control continued to grow, the Balkan vassal rulers began to grasp that they might soon be eliminated entirely by Murad and resolved to organize a unified resistance. Under the leadership of Lazar of Serbia, they formed a Balkan Union to challenge the Turks, and, in order to deflect Murad from concentrating his full strength against them, they encouraged the Qaramanids of Konya to attack the Ottomans in their rear in Anatolia.

It is ironic that the Ottoman pattern of conquest was particularly problematic not in Europe but in Anatolia. Since Islamic law generally prohibits war against fellow Muslims, the Ottomans were hard-pressed to justify their wars of annexation against the remaining Seljukid emirs, especially the Qaramanids of Konya. The latter undertook an extensive propaganda campaign that characterized the Ottomans as disloyal Muslims because of their attacks. In return, the Ottomans accused them of treachery to Islam because of their attacks on the Ottoman rear in Anatolia while they attempted to carry out their sacred mission of perennial war against the infidels in Europe.

The situation in Anatolia was extremely complicated, if not confused. There were basically three main Turkish emirates in the peninsula that had thus far evaded vassalage or direct incorporation by the Ottomans. These were the Eretna Turks at Sivas, the Aq-Qoyunlu Turks in the southeast who were busy extending their own realm from Diyarbekir and Erzincan into Azerbaijan, and the Qaramanids who controlled the south including Cilicia and Lesser Armenia. Murad had followed the expansionist pattern set by Orkhan, who had attempted to extend the Ottoman domains in Anatolia by primarily peaceful means to avoid the charge that he was warring against fellow Muslims without just cause. Through diplomacy and the marriage of his son Bayezid to the daughter of the ruler of Germiyan, Murad succeeded in gaining control over those portions of the territories of Germiyan and Hamid that brought the Ottomans to the Taurus Mountains and the borders of Qaraman. With the encouragement of the members of the Balkan Union, the Qaramanids exploited the opportunity presented by Murad's preoccupation with the Balkans to seize those parts of Hamid that had been purchased by the Ottoman sultan. This forced Murad to freeze his operations in Europe and return to Anatolia to settle matters there. However, aware that his Turkish troops might be reluctant to fight against another Turkish Muslim emirate, he brought a force of Bulgarian troops supplied by his vassals to spearhead the assault that recaptured Hamid and reestablished the predominant Ottoman position in Anatolia.

With matters under control in the peninsula, Murad returned to Europe to deal with the challenge being offered by the Balkan Union. In a major battle at Kossovo in southern Serbia that took place in 1389, the Balkan Union was defeated decisively. This brought Serbia firmly under Ottoman control, which now covered most of southeastern Europe.

In Anatolia, the death of Murad during the battle at Kossovo was greeted by the widespread rebellion of his vassals, who attempted to seize the opportunity presented by the Ottoman preoccupation in the Balkans to rid themselves of its imperial yoke. The new sultan Bayezid (1389–1402), however, exploited these revolts to justify the liquidation of their vassal status and the imposition of direct Ottoman control of these Muslim lands. Again using Serbian and Byzantine vassal troops, for fear that his Turkish forces might rebel against the idea of warring against fellow Muslim Turks, Bayezid systematically reduced the smaller principalities that had aligned with the Qaramanids during the summer and autumn of 1390. This campaign forced the Qaramanids to sue for peace the following year.

Ever cautious about alienating his own Turkish troops and causing them to defect to his enemies, Bayezid accepted the Qaramanid peace proposals and established the Carasanba Suyu River as the boundary between the two states. This permitted Bayezid to redirect his attention to northern Anatolia where he soon took Sinope and Kastamonu. By 1394, only the principalities of the Qaramanids and that of Burhan ad-Din in Sivas remained as centers of opposition to Ottoman rule. Although Bayezid was now enabled to direct his attention to Europe once again, he was not free to do so without reservation. His rear was not reliably secured, particularly in view of the new threat posed by the appearance of another powerful Central Asian horde under the leadership of Tamerlane (discussed later on) on the eastern frontiers of Anatolia. Exploiting the opportunity afforded by Bayezid's renewed involvement in Europe, one that did not permit him to react to developments in Anatolia for some time, the Qaramanids again extended their own sphere of control into areas that had already been incorporated within the Ottoman Empire.

Bayezid imposed a blockade of Constantinople in 1394 and, in the following year, took steps to deal with the threat against him that was developing in Hungary. Sigismund of Hungary (1387–1437), whose domain extended as far south as Dalmatia and Belgrade, and who was also suzerain over Wallachia and Moldavia, now came in direct contact with the advancing Ottomans. While Bayezid was engaged in imposing his control over Anatolia, Sigismund seized Nicopolis and marched into Bulgaria. This forced Bayezid to terminate his campaign in Anatolia, at least temporarily, and return to Europe where he retook Nicopolis toward the end of the year.

Sigismund was an adversary that fell into a rather different category than the other Christian monarchs against whom the Ottomans had warred in Europe. Hungary, as noted, was Latin Catholic, not Greek Orthodox. Accordingly, while the Latin Church could sit back and watch with some relish the onslaught of the Turks against the "heretics" of the East, it was another matter when it was the Hungarian king that was calling upon the pope for help. Pope Boniface IX felt compelled to take up Hungary's cause and he called for a crusade against the Turks in 1394. A crusader army consisting primarily of Franks, Germans, and Hungarians, supported by Vlachs and Bulgarians, was duly assembled and marched across southern Europe to Serbia. Bayezid, however, was able to deter the Serbs from rebelling against their Ottoman overlord and joining the European alliance. He expressly warned the Serbian ruler Stefan Lazarevich (1389–1427) against getting carried away and joining forces with the Hungarians, "because no good can come to those who lean that way; think what became of King Shishman and the other princes who sought alliances with Hungary!"[4]

Ostensibly, the plan for the crusade was to drive the Turks out of Europe, cross the Bosphorus and fight its way across Anatolia, and then march through Syria and liberate the Holy Land from the Mamluks. It would be an understatement to characterize such a scheme as hopelessly naive. It seems quite clear that the leaders of the crusade entertained no such unrealistic expectations. Indeed, they would have been more than gratified were they able to force the Turks out of Thrace. As it was, even this more limited objective was far beyond their grasp.

The crusader army confronted the forces of Bayezid at the fortress of Nicopolis on September 25, 1396, and for a moment seemed to be on the verge of inflicting a serious defeat on the Ottomans. However, when "the French knights, aided by the Polish and Hungarian cavalry, routed the Janissaries of Bayazed Ildirim, the Sultan's reserve, consisting of several thousands of Serbian Cuirassiers, under the command of Prince Stephan Lazarevich, came rushing down to snatch the victory from the Christians."[5] Sigismund's crusade, like so many of its predecessors, had turned into a debacle.

Once again, while Bayezid was preoccupied in Europe, the Qaramanid Ala ad-Din Ali seized Ankara and began driving toward the old Ottoman capital of Bursa. However, with the Hungarian threat eliminated, Bayezid was able to return to Anatolia in force and counterattack. He disposed of the Qaramanid challenge by decisively defeating Ala ad-Din Ali at Akcay in 1397, subsequently incorporating the Qaramanid lands into the growing Ottoman Empire. With the death of Burhan ad-Din the following year, Bayezid had little difficulty in absorbing the Sivas region as well. Finally, with the conquest of Cilicia from the Mamluks in 1399, Bayezid brought all of Anatolia under Ottoman rule for the first time.

The Ottoman-Qaramanid conflict points up one of the key problems that plagued the Ottoman Empire, as it did many earlier imperial states in the Middle East. As one historian has observed, "the Ottomans were militarily a two-front state with but a one-front army."[6] The Ottomans were simply unable to carry on a two-front war. If challenged on his Anatolian frontier while engaged in a conflict in the Balkans, the sultan would have to cease offensive operations in Europe to eliminate the threat to his rear in Asia. As a result, it became an imperative of Ottoman foreign policy and diplomacy to prevent a simultaneous challenge on both its Asian and European frontiers. However, this was not always possible. Thus, as Bayezid prepared to press his siege of Constantinople to a conclusion, a new threat arose on his eastern flank that could not be ignored. He was again forced to break off his campaign against the last stronghold of the Byzantines, giving Constantinople a reprieve that was to last for another half century.

NOTES

1. Chedomil Mijatovich, *Constantine: The Last Emperor of the Greeks or the Conquest of Constantinople by the Turks*, p. 13.

2. Ibid., pp. 24–25.

3. Ibid., p. 12.

4. Ibid., p. 24.

5. Ibid., p. 13.

6. Norman Itzkowitz, *Ottoman Empire and Islamic Tradition*, p. 16.

14

Tamerlane

The decline of the Il-Khanid state during the first half of the fourteenth century resulted in the emergence of a number of indigenous dynasties in Afghanistan and Khorasan. Transoxiana also experienced a comparable pattern of developments. The Jagataite khan Kazan (1343–1346) was the last real Mongol ruler of the latter region. He ultimately met his end at the hands of the Turkish nobility of the country, which was headed by the emir Qazghan (1347–1357) who became the dominant political leader of the territory. The Jagataite khans who followed Kazan were nothing more than mere figureheads who were maintained in office only because of the aura of legitimacy that descent from the line of the revered Genghis Khan bestowed upon them.

Once firmly established in power, Qazghan soon began to encroach on the countries south of the Oxus. In 1351 he crossed the Afghan frontier and laid siege to Herat, forcing the Kert ruler Muizz ad-Din Husain to acknowledge his suzerainty. Thus, just when there appeared to be an indigenous Iranian political resurgence in eastern Persia and Afghanistan, the nobility of Transoxiana intervened to impose Turkish hegemony over the region. However, this situation did not prevail for very long. As it turned out, Qazghan was assassinated in 1357, and the other Turkish nobles were unable to maintain control over the territory. Anarchy ensued, creating an opportunity for the reassertion of Mongol control. In March 1360, the Jagataite khan of the Ili, Tughlugh Timur (1359–1370), invaded and subjugated Transoxiana, and appointed his son Ilyas-Khoja to rule the territory as his viceroy.

Timur *lenk* (the Lame), or Tamerlane (1370–1405), who came from the area of Kesh (Shahr-i Sebz), south of Samarkand in Transoxiana, was a member of the Barlas, a Turkish-speaking tribe of Mongol origin that had adopted Islam as its religion. Although Tamerlane shrewdly had made his peace with the dominant Jagataite Mongols, and with their help became leader of the Barlas in 1361, he was dissatisfied with the prevailing state of affairs. He soon defected to join his brother-in-law, Mir Husain, the ruler of Balkh, Kunduz, and Kabul in Afghanistan. From there he helped mobilize the Turkish clans for a campaign to liberate their traditional homeland in Transoxiana from the Mongols.

After engaging and defeating the forces of Ilyas-Khoja near Samarkand in 1363, Mir Husain and Tamerlane took over effective control of Transoxiana. The Turkish clan leaders were aware, however, that the Jagataites would not accept this defeat as anything more than a temporary setback. Accordingly, they decided that it would be prudent to place a Mongol, one with connections to the line of Genghis Khan, on the throne of Transoxiana to give the government of the country a facade of legitimacy. They found a descendant of the great khan named Kabul-Shah (1363–1370) to whom they made formal obeisance and then subsequently ignored, while Tamerlane and Mir Husain actually ruled the country.

Although Kabul-Shah's presence on the throne in both Bukhara and Samarkand was supposed to be sufficient to give the kingdom of Transoxiana legitimacy in Mongol eyes, Ilyas-Khoja, who had now succeeded to the khanate of the Ili, saw the matter differently. He returned to Transoxiana with a new army in 1364 and in the following year defeated Tamerlane and Mir Husain, driving them as far as the Oxus. However, when Ilyas-Khoja laid siege to Samarkand, he ran into unanticipated resistance from the populace. By 1365, as his forces were being thinned out by an epidemic, he was forced to evacuate Transoxiana, allowing Mir Husain and Tamerlane to reassume control of the country.

Mir Husain and Tamerlane soon fell out with each other. Initially, Mir Husain gained the upper hand. However, by April 1370, Tamerlane had contrived to eliminate his rival and proclaimed himself ruler of Balkh. Since Kabul-Shah had sided with Mir Husain in the conflict, Tamerlane soon eliminated him as well and replaced him as ruler of Transoxiana with another descendant of the great khan, Soyurghatmish (1370–1388). The latter proved to be more constant in his loyalty to Tamerlane, as did his son and successor Mahmud (1388–1402).

It was Tamerlane's aspiration to be accepted as the legitimate heir of the great Genghis Khan. This ambition, however, was to remain beyond his reach. Tamerlane was popularly perceived as a Turk and, in accordance with the prevailing political traditions in the region, only the direct Mongol descendants of Genghis could bear the title of khan. Accordingly, he found it necessary to adopt the lesser title of emir and to formally reconstitute the Mongol Empire under nominal khans who were in fact his subjects.

Tamerlane's ascendancy came at a moment in history when major changes were taking place in the power structure of Southwest Asia. For some 200 years, the mixed Turko-Mongol horde of the Jagatai had effectively been shut up in Turkestan and Transoxiana. To the east, the hordes under the rule of Kublai Khan and his descendants held sway. To the northwest, the Golden Horde had driven across Eurasia as far as Hungary. To the southwest, the Il-Khanids had controlled the region from the frontiers of Transoxiana as far as the approaches to Egypt. Now the Mongol hordes that had hemmed in the Jagataites on all sides were themselves in a state of decline. They no longer barred the way to Jagataite expansion.

From his base in Transoxiana, Tamerlane launched offensives in all three directions simultaneously. However, without a clear set of political goals, and with his forces split in three, there was little prospect that Tamerlane's efforts would produce anything by way of empire comparable to that of the Turko-Mongol conquerors who preceded him. Nonetheless, the fury of the Timurid onslaught was such that it would leave scars on the region for generations to come.

In Persia, Tamerlane found a country ripe for conquest. The collapse of the Il-Khanid state had left the country divided among a number of competing power centers. Following in the footsteps of the emir Qazghan three decades earlier, Tamerlane was determined to subdue the Kerts of Herat once again. In 1380, he demanded the submission of Ghiyath ad-Din II Pir Ali (1370–1381) to vassalage. Although the latter generally complied with that demand, he hesitated to obey Tamerlane's summons to appear at his court, not quite trusting his overlord's intentions. Tamerlane would brook no such indication of opposition to him and marched on Herat the following spring. Ghiyath ad-Din soon capitulated and was forced to take up permanent residence at Samarkand. However, when some bands of Afghans from Ghor, with the help of the populace of Herat, seized control of the city in 1382, Tamerlane's son Miranshah suppressed the revolt with great brutality and Ghiyath ad-Din and his family were executed, bringing the Afghan dynasty of the Kerts to an end.

As soon as Herat was subdued in 1381, the Timurids marched into eastern Khorasan whose control was, at the time, the object of a struggle between Ali Muayyad (1364–1381) of the Sarbadarids and Emir Wali (1360–1384) who had made himself ruler of Mazanderan. Ali Muayyad, coming under heavy pressure from his adversary, appealed to Tamerlane for assistance. The price Ali Muayyad had to pay was acknowledgment of Timurid suzerainty over the Sarbadarids, which took place in 1381.

It was to take some time for the significance of the Sarbadarid vassalage to Tamerlane to be realized, since for several years he was preoccupied farther east. In 1383, Tamerlane suppressed a revolt in Sistan with exceptional brutality and at the same time demolished the irrigation system of the country, transforming it into a barren desert. He then was able to turn to the task of dealing with Emir Wali, who had become a thorn in his side. Emir Wali proved to be a worthy opponent who forced Tamerlane to fight hard for every foot of his territory. Finally, in 1384, Tamerlane took the capital of Mazanderan at Astarabad, forcing Emir Wali to flee for safety to Azerbaijan. In his signature style, Tamerlane slaughtered the entire population of the city.

Tamerlane undertook the conquest of western Persia in 1386, always careful to cloak his aggression against another Muslim country with a religious fig leaf. In this case, he initially justified his invasion on the basis of the necessity to punish the mountain tribesmen of Luristan for attacking and plundering the caravans passing through the area en route to Mecca. He then marched into Azerbaijan, setting up court at Tabriz before detouring north through Nakhichevan to invade Georgia. Since the latter was a Christian kingdom, Tamerlane sanctimoniously characterized his campaign of aggression as a holy war against the infidel. He captured Tiflis in the winter of 1386, also snaring the Georgian king Bagrat V (1360–1393) who soon gained his release by means of a pretended conversion to Islam. Next, Tamerlane undertook the conquest of Armenia, which at the time was divided among a number of Turkish emirs, all of whom were Muslims. Once again, he charged them with having attacked the caravans to Mecca and declared a holy war against them. After taking Van in 1387, he headed for the Muzaffarid states of Fars (Shiraz), Isfahan, and Kerman. The Muzaffarid ruler, Shah Shuja (1364–1384), promptly acknowledged Tamerlane's suzerainty, hoping thereby to forestall an invasion. However, Tamerlane invaded anyway and marched on Isfahan in the fall of 1387, deposing Zayn al-Abidin Ali (1384–1387), who had promptly capitulated. After making a triumphal entry into the city, the Timurid forces subsequently set up camp outside. Unfortunately, some of the inhabitants rebelled against the Timurid tax collectors and killed them. Tamerlane retaliated with a wholesale massacre of the population, indiscriminately killing as many as 70,000 people. Following this, Shiraz submitted without a murmur.

What remained of Persia was granted a reprieve at this point because Tamerlane was forced to return to Transoxiana to confront an invasion of the country by the khan of the Kipchaks. No sooner had he left Persia than Shah Mansur (1387–1393), a Muzaffarid prince, subjugated the other indigenous chiefs, repudiated Tamerlane's suzerainty, and reorganized the Muzaffarid territories for defense in anticipation of Tamerlane's return, which did not occur until 1392, when he invaded and subjugated Mazanderan once again. Then, after a bitterly fought campaign, the Timurids succeeded in defeating the Muzaffarids at Shiraz in May 1393. Shortly thereafter, determined to stamp out any vestige of current or future resistance to his rule, Tamerlane executed the remaining Muzaffarid rulers of Kerman and Yazd, Imad ad-Din Ahmad (1384–1393) and Nusrat ad-Din

Yahya (1387–1393) respectively, along with their families, notwithstanding their voluntary submission to his authority.

In June 1393, Tamerlane began his assault on Iraq, appearing before the walls of Baghdad in October. The Mongol Jalayirid chief, Ghiyath ad-Din Ahmad (1382–1410), who had been driven out of Persia earlier by the Timurids and had settled in Baghdad, abandoned the city and fled to Egypt, where he was received by the Mamluk sultan Barquq (1382–1399). From Baghdad, Tamerlane marched north through Kurdistan to Diyarbekir, which he took in 1394. He then pushed into Armenia once again, driving out Qara-Yusuf (1389–1420), chief of the Qara-Qoyunlu horde, before heading into Georgia once again.

As already observed, Tamerlane operated without political goals. He built no system for controlling the territories he conquered, and consequently his power only extended as far and was effective only for as long as his armies were actually present in a particular place. As a result, no sooner had he left Iraq than Ghiyath ad-Din Ahmad, with the assistance of Barquq as well as of Qara-Yusuf, reestablished himself in Baghdad. The sequence of these events created the false impression that Barquq had in effect forced Tamerlane to retreat from Syria and Iraq without even engaging him in battle. The reality was that Tamerlane had to cut short his campaign in Iraq in order to deal with a higher priority problem on his northern frontier.

In 1395, as Tamerlane marched through the Caucasus to challenge the Kipchak khan in southern Russia, the Georgians defeated and killed his son Miranshah in a battle near Nakhichevan. Tamerlane took his revenge when he returned in 1399 and devastated eastern Georgia, and again in 1400 when he took Tiflis, wreaking havoc throughout the countryside and driving the Georgian king Giorgi VI to seek refuge in the mountains. Then, quite unexpectedly, Tamerlane aborted his campaign in Georgia and reached an agreement with Giorgi under which the latter was granted clemency in exchange for the payment of tribute. However, this did not happen because Tamerlane had undergone a change of heart or purpose. It was just that he was being distracted by more serious problems on his western flanks, and he wished to effectively freeze the currently prevailing situation in Georgia until he could return to deal with it more decisively later on.

The only force in the Middle East that posed a significant challenge to Timurid power was the emerging Ottoman Empire. Sultan Bayezid had expanded the empire substantially over the brief period since his accession to the throne in 1389. During the first dozen years of his reign he had subjugated the few remaining independent Turkish emirates of Anatolia, and had expanded his domain in Europe to include Thrace (except for Constantinople), Macedonia (except for Salonika), Bulgaria, and Serbia, the last being transformed into a protectorate. In Asia, his empire reached the Taurus, which served as the frontier with Mamluk Cilicia; the Armenian massif, which was the frontier of Tamerlane's dominions; and the Pontic range, which served as the boundary with the Byzantine kingdom of Trebizond, the last such Greek foothold in Asia Minor.

Since its founding two centuries earlier, Trebizond had managed to survive in an alien and politically hostile environment by finding and making friends among its enemies. Alexius III, who died in 1390, had bought a measure of security for Trebizond by marrying off his four daughters to the Turkish emirs who controlled much of the mountainous hinterland to the south and east. One of these was Taherten, the emir of Erzincan, who sought to avoid subjugation by Bayezid through the device of voluntarily becoming a vassal of Tamerlane. This turned the emirate into a buffer zone that effectively secured the Timurid flank in Anatolia, and into a major point of friction between the Ottomans and the Timurids, one that was soon to ignite into a major conflagration.

Tamerlane and Bayezid both approached each other cautiously. There was a good deal at stake for each in the event of a defeat by the other. It was doubtful that Bayezid could maintain his empire in Europe if he lost his base in Anatolia. On the other hand, a serious defeat could also have cost Tamerlane everything, since he would have had to fight his way back across all of southwestern Asia to reach the steppes of Turkestan without having adequate forces available for that purpose. As matters unfolded, it was Bayezid who triggered the initiation of hostilities. Not only had he welcomed Qara-Yusuf of the Qara-Qoyunlu horde, an implacable foe of Tamerlane, into his territory, but also he had attempted to impose Ottoman suzerainty on Taherten, Tamerlane's vassal, in 1399. Tamerlane retaliated by crossing into Anatolia in August 1400, and a few weeks later he laid siege to Sivas, which capitulated after holding out for about three weeks.

Determined to teach the Timurids a lesson they would not forget, Bayezid now proposed to the Mamluks that they form an alliance against Tamerlane. However, the advisers of the Mamluk sultan Nasir ad-Din Faraj (1399–1412), who was only ten at the time, were preoccupied with internal political machinations and the sulton rejected the Ottoman overture. At that point, Tamerlane was uncertain as to whether the Ottomans and Mamluks would actually form an alliance against him. Accordingly, he proceeded no farther into Anatolia since he was vulnerable to attack in his rear from the Mamluks as well as from Ghiyath ad-Din Ahmad, who was still in control of Baghdad and Iraq. It seemed clear that he had to eliminate these latter threats before he could continue his campaign against the Ottomans. Once again, it was a case of being incapable of fighting a two-front war. Tamerlane decided to deal with the Mamluks in Syria first, since they posed the greater danger to his exposed flank.

Tamerlane marched on Aleppo in late October 1400, and defeated a Mamluk army near the city, which he pillaged for three days before destroying it completely. Hama, Homs, and Baalbek then fell in rapid order as

Tamerlane moved his forces south toward Damascus. In the meanwhile, the young Mamluk sultan Faraj arrived in the city to inspire its defense by his presence. A significant but indecisive battle between the opposing armies took place on December 25, 1400, and it appeared that the Timurids would have to conduct a long siege of Damascus before it would be forced to submit. However, on January 8, 1401, a rumor fortuitously swept through the Mamluk camp suggesting that a rival group of emirs was planning to carry out a coup d'etat in Cairo in the absence of the sultan, who was away in Syria. In reaction to this rumor, and notwithstanding the presence of the powerful Timurid army that was preparing to assault the city, the sultan and the senior Mamluk officers left the field of battle and raced back to Egypt. By their departure they effectively abandoned Damascus and a good part of the army to its fate at the hands of Tamerlane.

Although Damascus capitulated to avoid the rigors of a protracted siege, it was sacked anyway, much of it being destroyed by an uncontrollable fire that had broken out. Having ruined Syria, Tamerlane withdrew from it in March 1401 and marched in the direction of Baghdad to deal with Ghiyath ad-Din Ahmad. Once again, as soon as he withdrew, the Mamluks promptly returned to take control of the country, although they were now far less likely to contemplate an attack on the Timurid flank.

As Tamerlane approached Baghdad, Ghiyath ad-Din Ahmad fled to Egypt once again, where Faraj welcomed him. Nonetheless, his officers decided to defend the city, but were no match for the Turko-Mongol forces and the city fell on July 10, 1401. Tamerlane ordered the entire population of some 90,000 people slaughtered. He also demolished all the structures in the city except for the mosques. In terms of wanton destruction, by fusing Turko-Mongol brutality with religious fanaticism, Tamerlane outdid even Genghis Khan, which may well have been his deliberate intent.

While Tamerlane was preoccupied in Syria and Iraq, Bayezid seized Erzincan from Taherten, setting the stage for the next phase of the Ottoman-Timurid conflict. For his part, Tamerlane did not rush to confront Bayezid. Instead, he took almost a year to rest and rebuild his armies for the forthcoming struggle. He also entered into a series of relationships with a number of European rulers who saw his fight with Bayezid as a qualified blessing. He urged the Genoese in Galata to ready their ships to prevent the Ottomans from escaping across the Bosphorus to Europe. Trebizond, which had voluntarily accepted Timurid suzerainty, was instructed to provide twenty ships for the same purpose. In August 1401, John VII Palaeologus, the regent of Byzantium during the absence of his uncle Manuel II Palaeologus (1391–1425) in the west, sent an envoy to Tamerlane with a further inducement for the latter to attack and defeat Bayezid. If Tamerlane were to defeat Bayezid, the Byzantines offered to pay him the same tribute they previously paid to the Ottomans.

Tamerlane struck in June 1402, focusing his initial attack on Erzincan, which he quickly restored to Taherten. He then marched on Ankara, through Kayseri, where he expected to confront Bayezid. A major battle was fought at Cubuk (Djibukabad), north of Ankara, on July 20, 1402. When it was over, the Ottoman army had been decisively defeated, with Bayezid himself taken prisoner. Although well treated, the sultan was a broken man and died in captivity on March 9, 1403. With the main Ottoman army destroyed and the sultan a prisoner, Anatolia lay helpless before the Timurids. The latter soon plundered Bayezid's Anatolian capital of Bursa and set the city ablaze. Tamerlane's grandson butchered and looted his way to Iznik, and Tamerlane himself crossed the length of Anatolia to lay siege to Smyrna, which was still in the hands of the Knights of Rhodes after the Ottomans had tried unsuccessfully to take it for seven years. It fell to Tamerlane in mid-December 1402 after a siege of two weeks.

One of the major unanticipated consequences of the Timurid invasion of Anatolia was the reprieve it provided for Byzantium, enabling it to survive for another half century. Bayezid had placed Constantinople under siege and it was only a matter of time before the city would have fallen. Now, the siege was lifted as Bayezid's heirs scrambled to piece together what they could of the remains of the shattered Ottoman Empire. The eldest, Suleiman, had managed to make his way to Gallipoli in August 1402, ahead of his brothers, and took control of the European portion of the empire, which had remained intact. Indeed, it was even strengthened by the new influx of Turkish soldiers from Anatolia who were fleeing the Timurids. The Ottoman realm in Asia was reduced to what it had been at the death of Murad; that is, it consisted only of northern Phrygia, Bithynia, and Mysia. The northeastern part of these territories came under the control of Bayezid's son Mehmed Celebi, who served as a vassal of Tamerlane, while the region around Bursa became a subject of dispute between two of Bayezid's other sons, Isa and Musa. As for the rest of Anatolia, Tamerlane restored the various independent Turkish emirs to their former lands, particularly the Qaramanids who once again became the primary Ottoman rivals in the peninsula. The Qaramanid chief Muhammad II (1403–1419, 1421–1424) was awarded control of all of eastern Anatolia.

Having thus disposed of those powers in the Middle East that were potentially capable of competing with him for regional hegemony, Tamerlane returned to his home base in Transoxiana. En route, he detoured once again to Georgia to complete the work he had left undone in 1400. Notwithstanding his agreement with Giorgi VI, Tamerlane ravaged the region in 1403, destroying some 700 towns and villages and demolishing all the Christian churches in Tiflis. He then returned to Samarkand in 1404, where he began to prepare for the conquest of China and its prospective conversion to Islam. That goal, however, was not to be realized. Tamerlane, who was already past seventy, soon became ill and died on January 19, 1405, to the great relief of most of Asia.

Tamerlane left behind a large family and, presumably to avoid a power struggle after his death, he awarded each of its members a fiefdom. He also designated Pir Muhammad, the eldest son of his own eldest son Jahangir who had died about 1375, to succeed him as head of the Timurid Empire. None of this was to prove of any avail, however, since Tamerlane's death precipitated a period of political chaos throughout the Timurid domains as his various sons and grandsons competed for the prize of power wherever they could.

Pir Muhammad was far away in Kandahar when his grandfather died, and he was therefore unable to act expeditiously to secure his legacy. Another grandson, Khalil (1405–1409), with the support of the army, marched on Samarkand and seized the throne of Transoxiana. Pir Muhammad (1405–1406) remained as ruler of Afghanistan for only half a year before he was assassinated by his own vizier. Khalil was to last in Transoxiana for several years until he was deposed by his emirs in favor of Tamerlane's highly competent son Shah Rukh (1405–1447), who had been ruler of Khorasan and Sistan since 1397 and who seized Mazanderan on the Caspian in 1406/1407. He continued to rule Persia from his capital at Herat, and made his son and successor Ulugh-Beg (1447–1449) governor in Samarkand after he took Transoxiana in 1409.

Shah Rukh ruled only eastern Persia directly, but imposed his suzerainty over Isfahan and Fars, which were under the immediate control of several of his quarrelsome nephews. Thus, while eastern Persia was stable, western Persia, as well as Azerbaijan and Iraq, was quite the opposite. Seemingly chronic instability made these regions highly vulnerable to assault by their former rulers who had been expelled by Tamerlane. Ghiyath ad-Din Ahmad returned and seized Baghdad once again in 1405, while Qara-Yusuf (1406–1419) of the Qara-Qoyunlu returned from exile in Egypt to Azerbaijan, where he defeated the Timurid ruler Abu Bakr and reoccupied Tabriz in 1406. Abu Bakr tried to retake Azerbaijan in 1408, but he was defeated decisively this time.

However, the two former allies soon fell out with one another and, in August 1410, Ghiyath ad-Din Ahmad tried to seize Azerbaijan. He was defeated and then killed, and Iraq and Baghdad passed into the hands of Qara-Yusuf, whose realm now stretched from Georgia to Iraq and who soon became a serious contender for domination of the entire region. In 1419, taking advantage of their effective immobilization because of internal conflicts among the Timurids, Qara-Yusuf was able to occupy Sultaniyeh and Qazvin in eastern Persia, further extending the reach of the rapidly expanding Qara-Qoyunlu Empire.

Shah Rukh soon became determined to reestablish Timurid control over western Persia and invaded Azerbaijan in 1421 (Qara-Yusuf having died in the meanwhile), easily routing the Qara-Qoyunlu under Iskandar (1420–1438). However, Shah Rukh took no effective steps to maintain Timurid control there and no sooner did he depart for Khorasan than Iskandar returned and reasserted his authority over the country. The identical scenario was repeated in 1429, except that Azerbaijan was taken over temporarily by Qara-Uthman (1403–1435) of the Aq-Qoyunlu who, as loyal Timurid vassals, came from Diyarbekir to assist Shah Rukh. In 1435, however, Qara-Uthman was defeated and killed by Iskandar, who again reassumed control of Azerbaijan. Another Timurid expedition against the Qara-Qoyunlu took place about 1437. In this instance, Shah Rukh made Iskandar's brother Jihan Shah (1438–1467) his viceroy in the troublesome region. This had the unintended effect of confirming the legitimacy of Qara-Qoyunlu rule in Azerbaijan and Iraq, thereby establishing the basis for the complete elimination of Timurid authority in western Persia that was to follow soon thereafter. Following the death of Shah Rukh in 1447, the Qara-Qoyunlu further extended their rule into Fars and Kerman to the east and as far south as Oman, bringing a substantial part of the region into their empire.

The campaigns of Shah Rukh against the Qara-Qoyunlu also had the unanticipated effect of eliminating the border fighting that had erupted between the Qara-Qoyunlu and the Mamluks. Instead of fighting each other, they now became natural allies against the recurrent Timurid advances into the unstable frontier region that were being supported by Shah Rukh's Aq-Qoyunlu vassals. Although these frontier wars were limited in both scope and scale, they reflected the broader and strategically more significant conflict between Shah Rukh and the Mamluk sultan al-Ashraf Barsbay (1422–1437). The two struggled over domination of Indian Ocean-Mediterranean trade through the Red Sea and control of the Holy Cities in the Hejaz, which conferred a good deal of political legitimacy in the Islamic world.

Nonetheless, the overall Timurid-Mamluk conflict was conducted at such a relatively low level that it had little effect on developments in Egypt. The net result was that the Mamluks found themselves without important active external enemies, and they were therefore able to give themselves up almost completely to the internal political machinations that sapped the vitality of the state. At the same time, the quality of the Mamluk army began to decline significantly because it found itself without much to do beyond getting involved in the innumerable plots and counterplots that occupied its leaders.

15

End of the Byzantine Empire

In the fall of 1402, no one could be sure of Tamerlane's intentions with respect to Europe, and prudence dictated that the Christian states and the Ottomans reach an accommodation in their mutual interest. Moreover, Bayezid had not left a true successor and it was evident that there was going to be a major power struggle among his heirs for control of the empire. As a consequence, Suleiman was prepared to make significant concessions to assure European support of his claims. A summit conference was convened at Gallipoli that lasted for some three months and culminated in a treaty that was signed early in 1403 by Suleiman, John VII of Byzantium, Stefan Lazarevich of Serbia, who had escaped from the defeat near Ankara, and the representatives of Venice, Genoa, and Rhodes.

The agreement that Suleiman consented to was quite favorable to the European states. The district of Thessalonica, a stretch of Black Sea coast between Constantinople and Mesembria, and several Aegean islands were returned to Byzantium. Furthermore, Byzantium was relieved of its obligations as an Ottoman vassal and no longer had to pay an annual tribute to the sultan. These concessions were considered so dramatic at the time that it was asserted by some that Suleiman had agreed, in effect, to become the vassal of the Byzantine emperor. According to the contemporary Byzantine historian Doukas, Suleiman is supposed to have fallen at the feet of the emperor and declared: "I will be as a son to you and you will be my father. Between us, henceforth, will grow no tares nor will there be scandals. Only proclaim me ruler of Thrace and of whatever other lands I have acquired from my parents."[1] The treaty with Byzantium and the Italian maritime states was reaffirmed in June 1403, when Manuel II finally returned from the West to reassume the imperial throne.

The intra-Ottoman struggle for supremacy took place initially in Anatolia. Musa was defeated by his brother Isa, and was forced to flee eastward where he subordinated himself to Mehmed Celebi. The latter soon drove Isa out of Anatolia and declared himself sultan at Bursa in 1403. Suleiman, with the support of the Byzantines who were only too pleased to do what they could to keep the Ottoman pot boiling, sent Isa back to Anatolia in 1404 with a large army in an attempt to defeat Mehmed. The effort failed and Isa disappeared entirely from the scene. Suleiman then invaded Anatolia himself in 1406 and took Ankara, splitting Mehmed's domain. It appeared likely that Suleiman would emerge victorious from the civil war and Mehmed was forced to form a defensive alliance with the Qaramanids to stop his brother from overrunning the peninsula. Then, in 1409, Mehmed attempted to force Suleiman's withdrawal from Anatolia by creating a threat to the latter's European possessions. In collusion with Wallachia and Serbia, both of which feared the expanding power of Suleiman, Mehmed sent Musa to Europe to attempt to undermine Suleiman's position there while he was preoccupied in Anatolia. Musa married the daughter of the ruler of Wallachia, built an army of Turks, Vlachs, Serbs, and Bulgars, and marched on Adrianople. As expected, Suleiman felt compelled to abandon his campaign in Anatolia and return to save the situation in Europe, permitting Mehmed to reoccupy the western part of the peninsula. Suleiman succeeded at first in pushing Musa back from Adrianople, but the military balance soon shifted in the latter's favor and Suleiman was defeated and killed in February 1411.

Once in control of Ottoman Europe, Musa renounced his allegiance to Mehmed and proclaimed himself sultan. He also repudiated the territorial and other concessions that Suleiman had made to the European states. He demanded that, in consonance with the geopolitical doctrine of dar al-Islam, all the lands that had at one time been under Muslim rule be returned; in addition, not only was the payment of tribute to be resumed, but payments previously withheld were to be paid as well. When Manuel rejected these demands, Musa placed Constantinople under siege once again and seized all the lands previously returned to Byzantium except Salonika.

In the meantime, Musa had taken the liberty of introducing a number of religious doctrines that were considered heretical by orthodox Muslims, and conservative religious leaders began to plot his overthrow and replacement by the more traditional Mehmed. Overtures were made to Manuel in this regard, promising him the restoration of the territories seized by Musa in exchange for Byzantine support of Mehmed. With Manuel's help, Mehmed landed in Europe with an army in 1412, but he was defeated by Musa and forced to return to Anatolia. Mehmed returned again the following year, this time landing on the Black Sea coast north of Constantinople, from where he marched on Adrianople. The two brothers met in a major clash near Philippolis (Plovdiv), and this time it was Musa who met with defeat.

He was subsequently captured and killed near Sofia in July 1413. The Ottoman Empire was now reunited under the rule of Mehmed (1413–1421).

Mehmed was grateful for the assistance rendered by Manuel in the recent struggle and rewarded him with a treaty confirming and restoring the
territorial concessions made by Suleiman a decade earlier. According to
Doukas, Mehmed instructed Manuel's ambassadors: "Go and tell my father, the Emperor of the Romans, that with God's help and the cooperation
of my father and emperor, I have girded on my paternal power. Henceforth,
I will be as obedient to him as a son to his father. I am not ungrateful nor
shall I ever prove to be thankless."[2]

Mehmed was as good as his word, even though the Byzantines soon violated his trust by becoming implicated in a rebellion against him by Duzme
Mustafa, a pretender who claimed to be the long-lost eldest son of Bayezid
and therefore the legitimate heir to the Ottoman throne. Manuel had even
become involved in a plot against Mehmed on the pretender's behalf along
with Stefan Lazarevich and the Qaramanid Muhammad II. After his defeat,
Duzme Mustafa took refuge with Manuel who refused to turn him over to
Mehmed, promising instead to keep him prisoner for life if the Ottomans
would pay for the service. Mehmed, who was not prepared to go to war
with Byzantium over the incident, agreed. As one historian of the period
has observed: "The affair illustrated the precarious nature of the relationship between Emperor and Sultan. They had a gentleman's agreement. But
neither was sufficiently confident of his own strength to wish that agreement broken by an outright act of war. Mehmed realized perfectly that the
Emperor now had in his hands a pretender who might one day prove very
useful. It was a clever stroke. But the two men understood each other, and
the incident did strangely little harm to their understanding."[3] The period
of Mehmed's reign was to be the last interval of peace that Byzantium was
to experience before its downfall.

Given his commitment of peace to Manuel and the other Balkan rulers
who assisted him in defeating Musa, a commitment he honored, Mehmed
treated Europe to a period of benign neglect. He devoted the rest of his life
to reestablishing Ottoman control over the territories in Anatolia that
Bayezid had originally brought within the empire. This was not to be an
easy task, since the Timurid irruption had created political chaos in the peninsula, and it was only completed under Mehmed's son and successor, Murad. In 1413, Ottoman rule extended only over northern Anatolia from the
Aegean to Erzincan. Most of the eastern Black Sea coastal region was under
the control of the Candaroglu, except for Trebizond, which still remained a
Byzantine enclave. The rest of eastern Anatolia was divided between the
Aq-Qoyunlu, with their center in Diyarbekir, and the Qara-Qoyunlu who
ranged over the area from their base in Azerbaijan. The southeast was under the control of the Dulgadir except for Malatya, which was held by the
Mamluks. The southwest was divided between Sarukhan, Germiyan, Ay-

din, and Menteshe, while most of the south-central and the remaining parts of eastern Anatolia were under the control of the Qaramanids, who continued to press their claims to all of the peninsula as the legitimate heirs of the Seljukids.

Murad II (1421–1451) spent the first three years of his reign contesting challenges to his succession, some of which were aided by the Byzantines who exploited every opportunity to weaken the Ottomans. It was at this time that Manuel released Duzme Mustafa from his imprisonment in the vain hope that he might succeed in toppling Murad. To punish the emperor for his support of the rebel, who posed one of the more serious challenges to Murad, the Ottomans mounted yet another siege of Constantinople in June 1422. The Byzantines responded to this by encouraging new challenges to Murad in Anatolia. They lent their support to an alliance of the Qaramanids with Germiyan and Murad's brother Mustafa, who was the governor of Hamid. The three formed a joint army that seized Nicaea and placed Bursa under siege in August 1422. This had the effect intended by Manuel; it forced Murad to abandon his siege of Constantinople and move to restore his authority in Anatolia.

Although Murad was soon able to re-impose his control over western Anatolia, he was forced to restrict his activity in the eastern part of the peninsula. He had good reason to be concerned that any attempt to annex Qaraman or Candar might provoke another Timurid invasion, since Tamerlane's successor Shah Rukh claimed suzerainty over all the territories once ruled by either the Seljukids or the Il-Khanids. Murad himself continued to acknowledge Timurid suzerainty over many of the Ottoman territories in Anatolia. Nonetheless, Murad did manage to obtain a promise of allegiance from the Qaramanids in exchange for guaranteeing the succession of Taj ad-Din Ibrahim (1424–1463) to the Qaramanid throne. This was a significant political gain for Murad since the Qaramanids had previously been aligned with the Mamluks on their southern frontier.

As a matter of practical politics, it was very difficult to draw a line between Ottoman affairs in Europe and in Asia. Murad's European adversaries repeatedly sought to exploit his difficulties in Anatolia as a means through which they might mitigate the threat he posed to them. Sigismund of Hungary formed an anti-Ottoman alliance with Wallachia and Qaraman for the purpose of forcing Murad into a two-front war. At the same time, Venice arranged for support of the Qaramanids from the Latins of Cyprus, and appealed to the Timurid ruler Shah Rukh to join in the campaign. To prevent the latter from intervening, Murad was compelled to cancel a full-scale assault on Qaraman, thereby convincing Shah Rukh of his continued loyalty as a Timurid vassal. Murad's approach worked, and Shah Rukh's concerns about Ottoman aims in Anatolia were successfully alleviated. By 1430, virtually all the region was either under direct Ottoman control or within its sphere of influence. Murad was now free to direct his full attention to Europe once again, where he became involved in a series of campaigns in Macedonia and the Balkans, finally taking Salonika from the Venetians on March 1, 1430.

Murad was drawn back to Anatolia in 1435 because of Shah Rukh's unanticipated intervention in the region. Although it is not clear as to what precipitated the Timurid incursion, it appears to have been directed primarily at the Mamluk and Qaramanid positions in Cilicia. Murad took advantage of the opportunity presented and attacked Qaraman from the north and west, seizing Hamid. However, he only annexed the western portion of the district, again leaving Qaraman intact. His restraint was motivated by a concern for Shah Rukh's sensitivity with regard to Ottoman expansion into Qaraman, as well as a desire to avoid precipitating a conflict at that time with the Mamluks. The latter might have reacted forcefully to an Ottoman occupation of Qaraman since it would have posed a serious threat to their position in Syria. Murad's limited move essentially preserved the regional balance of power and was deemed acceptable to both the Timurids and the Mamluks. With matters in Anatolia under control, Murad was able to return to his campaigns in Europe once again in 1437.

The Ottoman situation in Europe appeared to take a serious turn for the worse with the appointment of Janos Hunyadi as the new Hungarian governor of Transylvania. He inflicted a number of defeats on Murad's forces in 1441, thereby creating new interest in the call by Pope Eugenius IV for the organization of yet another crusade against the Turks. Although the Byzantine emperor John VIII Palaeologus (1425–1448) gave Murad his assurance in 1442 that he would not join in any such crusade, he simultaneously encouraged the Qaramanid ruler Ibrahim to attack the Ottomans in Anatolia. This again forced Murad to turn away from Europe in order to deal with the challenge in Asia.

While Murad was busy battling with the Qaramanids, the crusader army was being organized under the leadership of Hunyadi. The crusader force launched an offensive in July 1443 that soon netted it control of most of southern Serbia. It then struck into Bulgaria, taking Sofia, before Murad could return and try to head it off. Fortunately for the Ottomans, winter set in before the crusaders could cross the Balkan passes and gain access to the strategically important Maritsa valley. The campaign was stalled pending the arrival of spring.

Murad now found himself in an extremely precarious situation. The initial crusader victories brought thousands of new volunteers into Hungary, promising an even more devastating campaign once the weather improved. At the same time, the Qaramanids had renewed their attacks in Anatolia. Unable to prosecute a two-front war, it became imperative for Murad to make peace on one of his flanks, and he chose to do so in Europe where the danger of a decisive defeat was the greatest. To get the reprieve he needed, Murad had to offer concessionary terms in the truce agreement that was concluded at Adrianople on June 12, 1444. Murad conceded all the territory taken from Serbia since 1427, and agreed to recognize the autonomy of Serbia and Wallachia under Ottoman suzerainty. A ten-year truce between the Europeans and the Ottomans was instituted, and Murad consented to the stipulation that most of his troops be withdrawn to Anatolia. With Murad now able to bring overwhelming force to bear in Anatolia, the Qaramanids proved quite amenable to bringing the conflict in the peninsula to a close.

With the security of the empire ostensibly assured in both Europe and Asia, Murad abdicated in August 1444 in favor of his son Mehmed II (1444–1446 and 1451–1481). The crusaders, however, violated the treaty in the following month and Murad was quickly induced to reassume command of the Ottoman armies to meet the challenge; Mehmed was considered too young and inexperienced to maintain the confidence of the Turkish commanders. Murad led the Ottoman army back into Europe in October and decisively defeated the crusader forces at Varna on November 10, 1444, effectively sealing the fate of Byzantium and southeastern Europe for the next several centuries. To assure the successful pacification of the Ottoman domain in Europe, and to deal with a number of internal security problems, Murad became de facto ruler of the empire in 1446. His heir Mehmed, who continued to hold the title of sultan, was thoroughly groomed to assume his rightful place on the throne upon Murad's death in February 1451.

It was to fall to Mehmed II to complete the destruction of Byzantium by the conquest of Constantinople two years later, a task he devoted himself to from the day he became sole ruler of the Ottoman Empire. Neither diplomatic nor tactical maneuvers by the last of the Byzantine emperors, Constantine XI Palaeologus (1449–1453), could deter the Ottoman onslaught any longer.

The actual conquest of Constantinople was a substantial military feat by any measure. The city was built in a way that made it difficult to attack and easy to defend. Built in the shape of a rough triangle, it was bounded on two sides by water, the Sea of Marmara on the south and the Golden Horn to the north. On the western side, it was guarded by a series of three parallel walls separated by moats. The Ottoman forces placed the city under siege and mounted persistent artillery barrages at the walls, which became increasingly difficult for the defending forces to keep in good repair. Mehmed became convinced that it was necessary to mount a simultaneous attack from the Golden Horn, to which access was effectively blocked by an immense iron chain that stretched across the opening from shore to shore. With the aid of a corps of sophisticated military engineers, Mehmed ordered the construction of a greased ramp over a promontory located between the Bosphorus and the Golden Horn. A fleet of about seventy small boats were dragged by ox-driven pulleys across this ramp and allowed to slip into the

Golden Horn above the city. This compelled the Byzantines to split their already meager forces in order to block an amphibious attack on the city. The tactic proved fully successful. Constantinople fell on May 29, 1453, with Constantine XI dying in its defense. The millennium-old Byzantine Empire ceased to exist.

The conquest of Constantinople was not in itself of any great strategic significance for the victors, since the Ottomans had already succeeded in conquering much of southeastern Europe without it. Nonetheless, as pointed out by one writer:

Its capture deprived Europe of a base that, in the hands of an effective relief force, might have undermined the Ottoman defense system. Possession of the great commercial, administrative, and military center facilitated the assimilation, control, and defense of the sultan's conquests, while control of the waterways between the Black Sea and the Mediterranean established a stranglehold on European trade with the hinterlands to the north and east and provided considerable new revenue. The conquest made the Ottomans heirs to the imperial tradition as the conquered city once again became the capital of an extensive empire.[4]

The fall of Byzantium set the stage for a new phase of Ottoman imperialism that would dramatically affect the course of Middle Eastern history until the twentieth century.

NOTES

1. Doukas, *Decline and Fall of Byzantium to the Ottoman Turks*, p. 100.
2. Ibid., p. 111.
3. Donald M. Nicol, *The Last Centuries of Byzantium*, p. 345.
4. Stanford Shaw, *History of the Ottoman Empire and Modern Turkey*, vol. 1, p. 57.

16

Mehmed the Conqueror

The conquest of Constantinople in May 1453, aside from giving Mehmed II "the Conqueror" (1451–1481) enormous prestige in the Muslim world, also whetted his appetite for transforming the Ottoman domain into a worldwide empire. In other words, he no longer saw himself merely as the sultan of the Ottoman Turks but as an heir to the Roman emperors. This view was clearly articulated in the letter sent by the Byzantine scholar George Trapezuntios to Mehmed: "Let no one doubt that he [Mehmed] is by right the emperor of the Romans. For he is emperor who by right possesses the seat of the empire, but the seat of the Roman Empire is Constantinople: thus he who by right possesses this city is the emperor. But it is not from men but from God that you, thanks to your sword, have received this throne. Consequently, you are the legitimate emperor of the Romans. . . . And he who is and remains emperor of the Romans is also emperor of the entire earth."[1] According to another contemporary of the sultan, Giacomo de Languschi, "Today, he [Mehmed] says, the times have changed, and declares that he will advance from East to West as in former times the Westerners advanced into the Orient. There must, he says, be only one empire, one faith, and one sovereignty in the world."[2]

While the fall of Constantinople, and with it the final collapse of the Byzantine state, assured undisputed Ottoman control of Thrace and the strategic waterway linking the Aegean and Black Seas, the geopolitical situation on the European frontiers of the empire remained in flux. To the northwest, the effective power vacuum that existed in autonomous but weak Serbia made that country a poor buffer zone between ever-troublesome Hungary and the Ottoman Empire. Serbia, as it stood, could provide the avenue of approach for yet another crusade launched from central Europe. Farther south, in the Morea (Peloponnesus), the ruling Byzantine despots were susceptible to Venetian domination and could therefore also provide bases for a renewed attempt to push the Ottomans out of Europe. In the northeast, the Mongol Empire of the Golden Horde had finally disintegrated. This was brought about by the pressures deriving from the growing Polish-Lithuanian Empire of the Jagellonians who had seized the Ukraine in the previous century, and the Tatar khans of Kazan who had brought the southern Russian steppes under their control after 1445.

Along the northern coast of the Black Sea, in the Crimea, the Jagellonians had helped set up a dynasty of Tatar khans as a counterweight to the remnants of the Golden Horde who continued to aspire to regain control of the region. The Crimean Tatars then split with the Jagellonians at about the time of the final siege of Constantinople and entered into a new relationship with the Ottomans instead.

Although Mehmed made an initial effort to conquer the Black Sea coast of Moldavia in 1454, in order to strengthen his relationship with the Crimean Tatars by forming a contiguous link between their respective territories, he succeeded only in imposing his suzerainty there. At the time, his primary attention was drawn to the northwest and Serbia, from where the greatest threat to Ottoman interests was likely to emerge. To forestall a possible move against him from central Europe, Mehmed adopted the strategy of extending his defense perimeter to the Aegean Sea in the west and the Danube in the north. Beginning in 1454, Mehmed undertook a series of military campaigns designed to accomplish this purpose. By the following year, he had succeeded in destroying what remained of Serbian autonomy and had occupied the southern part of the country, thereby gaining control of the northern approaches to Macedonia for the first time. This also netted him control of the gold and silver mines of Novo Brdo, providing important monetary assets with which to finance further Ottoman economic expansion.

Mehmed returned to Serbia for the third time in 1456, when he attempted to seize Belgrade from the Hungarians and drive them northward across the Danube. The effort came to nothing at the time because of the timely arrival of Hungarian reinforcements under Janos Hunyadi, who forced Mehmed to withdraw from Belgrade after a six-week siege, giving Belgrade a reprieve from Ottoman occupation for another fifty years.

That same year, growing pirate activity in the Aegean, which originated from those islands in the area that were under the control of Genoa, precipitated the Ottoman conquest of the islands of Aynos, Imbros, Lemnos, and Thasos. At the same time, the incessant squabbling among the Byzantine despots of the Morea provided the opportunity for the subsequent Ottoman conquest of Attica and the Peloponnesus. The northern portion of the peninsula fell in the summer of 1458, followed by Athens in January 1459 and the southern part of the Morea in July 1460. This eliminated the last remnants of Byzantine rule in Europe, except for several ports that had been strongly fortified by the Venetians and which were able to hold out. All of Greece had effectively been brought under direct Ottoman rule. The Ottomans returned to Serbia once again in the summer of 1459, this time occupying all of the country except for Belgrade. Nominal Serbian independence was brought to an end and the entire country was incorporated within the still rapidly expanding Ottoman Empire.

After the conquest of Serbia and Greece, only Albania remained a lingering headache for Mehmed in the region. A tribal chieftain, George Castriotes, whom the Ottomans referred to as Iskander Beg, controlled the hill country of southern Albania and Epirus and led the resistance to the Ottoman advance. Encouraged by Alfonso V of Aragon (1416–1458), who was also hereditary king of Sicily and who had conquered Naples in 1442, the Albanian leader launched a guerrilla campaign to drive the Ottomans out of the country. Mehmed retaliated with a number of punitive expeditions that drove Iskander Beg into the southern hills of Albania for refuge. The situation in the country remained unsettled until after the death of Alfonso V in 1458. With his main source of external support eliminated, Iskander Beg became more amenable to reaching an accommodation with Mehmed. Under a truce that was concluded on June 22, 1461, he was permitted to retain control of southern Albania and the Epirus in exchange for his commitment to refrain from attacks on the Ottoman positions in the northern part of the country.

In the principalities of Moldavia and Wallachia, which lay to the north of Bulgaria, Mehmed's ambitions clashed with those of Stephen the Great (1457–1504) of Moldavia. Stephen had transformed Moldavia into a state of some regional consequence and was intervening in Wallachia as a first step in his drive for the conquest of the Black Sea littoral, including the Crimea. His ambitions placed him on a collision course with Mehmed, who harbored his own ambitions for establishing Ottoman hegemony in Wallachia. The sultan ultimately succeeded in pressuring the Vlachs (Wallachians) to acknowledge his suzerainty over the principality in 1460. However, this proved to be of little significance because the Vlach prince Vlad IV Tepesh (the Impaler) had also recognized Hungarian suzerainty, although Mehmed apparently was unaware of it at the time. Moreover, notwithstanding his nominal submission to Mehmed, Vlad refused to permit any further Ottoman advances through his domain in the direction of Moldavia for as long as Stephen did not attempt to extend his own control to Wallachia.

With the situation on the Ottoman frontiers in Europe reasonably stabilized, at least for the moment, Mehmed was at last free to direct his attention to Anatolia, where much remained to be settled. The Ottoman advances in Europe, which posed a serious threat to the interests of both Genoa and Venice, caused these maritime states to lend their direct support to the further destabilization of the Ottoman frontiers in Asia. They evidently hoped thereby to force Mehmed to reduce his pressures on the Balkan region. The situation in eastern and central Anatolia was particularly volatile, leaving Mehmed's flank in Asia seriously exposed.

THE GEOPOLITICAL SITUATION IN SOUTHWEST ASIA

The Timurid Empire of Tamerlane and his successors, which was centered in Persia, had maintained the balance of power in southwestern Asia for the preceding half century. However, with the death of Shah Rukh (1405–1447), the Timurid state began to disintegrate rapidly. His successor Ulugh-Beg (1447–1449) was overthrown and executed in October 1449 by his son Abd al-Latif, who was similarly assassinated only a short while later in May 1450. On the empire's Central Asian frontiers, one of Ulugh-Beg's nephews, Abdallah (1450–1452), made himself ruler of Samarkand and Transoxiana, while another nephew, Babur-Mirza (1452–1457), took control of Herat and Khorasan. Abdallah was overthrown and killed in 1452 by another Timurid, Abu Said, who seized control of Samarkand and Transoxiana with the aid of Abul Khair, khan of the Mongol Uzbeks.

Taking advantage of the instability resulting from the disintegration of the centralized Timurid state, Abul Khair seized control of the territory immediately beyond the Syr-Darya, a move that reflected a general resurgence of Mongol political and military activity in the region. At the same time, Esen-Buqa (1429–1462), ruler of the Jagataite Mongol khanate of Mogholistan, renewed the traditional Mongol practice of raiding along the frontiers of Transoxiana, ravaging Tashkent in 1451, and threatening Timurid control of the territory. To undermine Esen-Buqa's position, in 1456 Abu Said lent his support to Yunus-Khan, Esen-Buqa's older brother and rival claimant to the Jagataite throne. With Abu Said's help, Yunus-Khan managed to take control of western Mogholistan, splitting the Jagataite realm and thereby reducing the Mongol pressure on Timurid Transoxiana. Then, with the death of Babur-Mirza in 1457, Abu Said seized Khorasan and sought to use it as a base from which to attempt the restoration of the Timurid Empire as it stood under Shah Rukh.

At the same time these events were taking place on the eastern frontiers of the once powerful Timurid Empire, comparable developments were occurring farther to the west. The Qara-Qoyunlu Turks, who earlier had gained effective control of the area between Azerbaijan and the Persian Gulf, now sought to take advantage of the existing power vacuum in the region and began to expand eastward into the heart of Persia. Under Jihan Shah (1438–1467), the Qara-Qoyunlu seized western Persia (the Jibal or ancient Media) in 1452, and conquered Isfahan, Fars, and Kerman in 1458. Jihan Shah then marched on Khorasan and occupied Herat in July 1458. Abu Said, who was forced to withdraw to Balkh, returned in force at the end of the year and retook Khorasan, after inflicting a decisive defeat on the Qara-

Qoyunlu forces under Jihan Shah's son Pir Budaq. The border separating the Timurid dominions from those of the Qara-Qoyunlu was established at Samnan, east of Tehran, by the end of 1458.

While the Qara-Qoyunlu were preoccupied with their advances into Persia, their position in Azerbaijan came under challenge from the Aq-Qoyunlu Turks, who had long been established in Diyarbekir and had been the loyal vassals and allies of the Timurids since the days of Tamerlane. Under the leadership of Uzun Hasan (1453–1478), the Aq-Qoyunlu became increasingly expansionist and not only posed a significant threat to the Qara-Qoyunlu, but also emerged as a serious competitor with the Ottomans for control of eastern Anatolia and its strategically important Black Sea coast. Uzun Hasan, however, was not strong enough to take on the full might of the Ottomans alone; he recognized that his horde of undisciplined horsemen were unlikely to prevail in a major conflict with the comparatively well-organized and highly disciplined Ottoman army. Moreover, it made little strategic sense for the Aq-Qoyunlu to risk a two-front war with the Ottomans in the west and the Qara-Qoyunlu in the east. Since the latter had reached an accommodation with the Timurids on their own eastern flank in Khorasan, they would now be in a position to take advantage of Uzun Hasan's troubles with Mehmed to attack the Aq-Qoyunlu flank. Once it became clear that the Ottoman sultan had committed his highly proficient Janissary corps to the frontier pacification effort, Uzun Hasan had little choice but to split with his distant Venetian and Genoese backers and accept a separate peace. An agreement to that effect was concluded at Erzincan on August 14, 1461. With stability on their frontier with the Ottomans, the Aq-Qoyunlu were free to pursue the competition for empire with the Qara-Qoyunlu.

In Anatolia, the Qaramanid Turks still claimed to be the legitimate heirs of the Seljukids in Anatolia and transformed Konya into a buffer state separating the Mamluk and Ottoman empires. They also were busy stirring up rebellion against the Ottomans among the Turkish emirs that ruled the central part of the peninsula. However, the emirs had recently curtailed such activity out of fear of provoking harsh retaliation by the increasingly powerful Mehmed, and instead they focused their attention on expansion southward into the Mamluk territories of Adana and Tarsus in Cilicia.

The internal situation of the Mamluk Empire had deteriorated to the point where it appeared particularly vulnerable to external intervention and highly susceptible to disintegration. At the end of January 1453, in anticipation of his imminent death, the last of the great Mamluk sultans Jaqmaq (1438–1453) abdicated in favor of his eighteen-year-old son Othman in the hope of thereby securing his reign. The gesture proved of little avail; Othman was overthrown by a coup on April 9, 1453, and replaced as sultan by Ashraf Inal (1453–1461), a Circassian. Having inherited a virtually bankrupt treasury, by 1455 Inal was faced by repeated mutinies of even his own mamluks, who demanded increases in their pay to compensate for the raging inflation in the empire. The regime entered a period of unprecedented decay accompanied by virtual anarchy in the country. Inal managed to remain sultan only because it was not in the interest of his mamluks to see him overthrown, since this would undermine their own position among the several mamluk clans that competed for power in Cairo. It is of particular interest to note, as pointed out by a modern historian of the period: "The ordinary Egyptians took no part in the struggles for power between the ameers, or between the sultans and their mamluks. In the 267 years of the Mamluk Empire, there was never any question of a Syrian or Egyptian national rising. But the public suffered from the decline in administrative efficiency, the bankruptcy of the treasury, the neglect of the irrigation and public works, and the general insecurity paralysing trade."[3]

Given the problems confronting the Mamluk sultan, the Qaramanids saw relatively low risk in attempting to encroach on Mamluk territory in northern Syria and, as mentioned earlier, they began raiding Cilicia in the vicinity of Tarsus. Inal responded to these attacks by launching a punitive expedition against the Qaramanids in June 1457. By April 1458, reeling from the Mamluk onslaught, the Qaramanids considered it necessary to sue for peace. With quiet restored on his northern frontier, Inal was free to spend the next two years suppressing new internal mutinies and preparing to intervene in the succession crisis that erupted in Cyprus, a Mamluk vassal state, in the summer of 1458. Inal died early in 1461, leaving the empire to his son Ahmad, who managed to keep the throne for only four months before Dhahir Khushqadam (1461–1467) replaced him on June 28 of that year. Like his predecessors, Khushqadam was also faced by internal mutinies in Cairo and with potentially more serious rebellions by his provincial governors, especially in northern Syria. Some of the rebels sought support from the Aq-Qoyunlu that exploited the situation to encroach on Mamluk territory.

Political conditions along the Ottoman frontiers in Asia were such that Mehmed could hardly forego the opportunities presented for territorial expansion. However, no sooner had the sultan begun his campaign of conquest in Anatolia than he was confronted with raids into his territories in northern Bulgaria that were directed by Vlad IV, the ruler of Wallachia. Mehmed was forced once again to divert his attention away from Anatolia to deal with this problem, which he resolved by invading and annexing Wallachia in August 1462. However, this apparently created a new problem for Mehmed who could not afford both to garrison Wallachia and meet other pressing demands on his forces elsewhere in Europe and Asia. The sultan was learning that, with limited available resources, it was sometimes easier to conquer an empire than to maintain one. Accordingly, when the deposed Vlach ruler's brother Radu IV (1462–1479) agreed to become a loyal vassal of the Ottomans in exchange for the throne, Mehmed restored autonomy to Wallachia. This left him free to deal with a new challenge that had been stirred up by Venice.

Concerned about Ottoman expansion in the Adriatic, Venice contrived to get Iskander Beg to break his treaty with the sultan in February 1462 and to renew his attacks on the Ottoman positions in northern Albania. At the same time, the new king of Bosnia, Stephen Tomasevic (1461–1463), repudiated Ottoman suzerainty and accepted Hungarian occupation, turning Bosnia into a Hungarian protectorate. Mehmed marched from Wallachia to Albania where he soon forced Iskander Beg to agree to a new peace treaty on April 27, 1463, restoring the previous political arrangements in the country. He then invaded Bosnia, conquering almost all of the country by midsummer that same year, although the Hungarians still held on to two northern districts where they set up a puppet Bosnian government.

Venice, however, viewed the subsequent acceptance of Ottoman suzerainty by the principality of Herzegovina, and its eventual annexation, as an intolerable encroachment into its sphere of interest in the Adriatic region. The likelihood of a direct confrontation between Venice and the Ottoman Empire now became a virtual certainty, particularly after the intervention of Pope Pius II in the crisis. Under his auspices, an anti-Ottoman alliance between Venice and Hungary was concluded and yet another crusade was launched on September 12, 1463. The European states decided that if the crusade were to prove successful, the political map of southeastern Europe would be redrawn completely. Venice would get the Morea and the Greek territories along the Adriatic coast; Iskander Beg would get all of Albania and Macedonia; Hungary would become master of Bosnia, Serbia, Bulgaria, and Wallachia; and Constantinople and its environs would be restored to the remnants of the Byzantine imperial family.

As the pope was assembling a crusader army at Ancona, the Ottoman-Venetian war began with the seizure by Venice of several Aegean islands, in addition to much of the Morea. The Venetian fleet occupied Lemnos and Tenedos and effectively sealed the Dardanelles, thereby preventing the Ottomans from sending supplies to support their forces in the Morea. To counter the maritime threat, the Ottomans began the construction of a new fleet at Istanbul (Constantinople) and built two strong forts facing each other across the Dardanelles to prevent the Venetians from entering the Turkish Strait. A major expedition under the leadership of the grand vizir was then mounted against the Venetians in the Morea. It succeeded in severely mauling the Venetian army and retaking the territory in 1464. Mehmed then led another army to Bosnia and drove the Hungarians back, and began making raids into Hungary. But once again, he failed to dislodge the Hungarians from Belgrade.

Nonetheless, the Ottoman victories effectively crippled the crusade, which soon ground to a halt leaving the pope dying in sorrow at its failure at Ancona on August 15, 1464. With the threat posed by the crusade laid to rest, Mehmed turned his attention to Albania once again, but his campaign there was inconclusive. Indeed, he only succeeded in reestablishing the previous Ottoman position there after the death of Iskander Beg in 1468, and it was to take another decade before all of Albania came under Ottoman control.

With the situation in Europe stabilized, at least for the moment, Mehmed was again free to lead a major expedition into Anatolia, presumably to pick up where he had left off in 1461. The initial target of the campaign was the principality of Dulgadir, which was under Mamluk occupation. Mehmed used the occasion to call upon his nominal vassal, the Qaramanid prince Pir Ahmad, to provide forces for the campaign. When the latter declined the sultan's invitation to join him, Mehmed attacked and seized the western part of the Qaramanid territory. Pir Ahmad fled to the Taurus, where he organized the local tribes into a resistance movement against the Ottomans. Then, in 1470, when Mehmed was once again distracted and drawn back to Europe by the reappearance of the Venetian fleet in the eastern Aegean, Pir Ahmad easily regained control of most of his territory. Indeed, with the help of the Venetians, who provided supplies, and the Aq-Qoyunlu, who kept the Ottoman eastern frontier in Anatolia in a state of constant turmoil, Pir Ahmad began to make deep penetration raids into Ottoman territory in central Anatolia.

In the summer of 1470, Mehmed retaliated against Venice by seizing Negroponte (Egriboz) on Euboea, which had been in Venetian hands for 264 years and was its principal naval base in the Aegean. Having dealt effectively with the immediate threat posed by the Venetians, Mehmed devoted his full attention to the problem of Qaraman, which he attacked in force and finally conquered in 1471, putting an end to the Qaramanid dynasty.

With the Ottomans now ensconced along the entire western frontier of the Aq-Qoyunlu, Uzun Hasan felt he could temporize no longer. His ongoing competition for regional supremacy with the Qara-Qoyunlu had come to an end on November 11, 1467, when he decisively defeated Jihan Shah while the latter attempted the conquest of Diyarbekir. Considering himself the legitimate successor to both the Il-Khanids and the Timurids, Uzun Hasan claimed large portions of Anatolia as his rightful territory. As a loyal vassal of the Timurids, he expected this development to be welcomed by the Timurid ruler Abu Said. The latter, however, hoped to benefit from the conflict between the competing hordes by recovering western Persia for himself.

When Uzun Hasan took control of Azerbaijan after the death of Jihan Shah, the latter's son Hasan Ali requested Abu Said's assistance in regaining it for the Qara-Qoyunlu. The Timurid leader was only too pleased to accede to this request and readily declared war on the Aq-Qoyunlu. Abu Said entered Azerbaijan with his army and marched on Uzun Hasan's headquarters at Qarabagh in the lower Aras and Kura steppe. However, Uzun Hasan managed to slip away, and with winter approaching Abu Said decided to march on Qarabagh anyway and to wait for spring there. This turned out to be a disastrous decision, since he found his way to the Aras River blocked by Uzun Hasan at Mahmudabad. Caught in the hill country without adequate supplies, Abu Said tried to retreat to Khorasan but was soon trapped and captured by Uzun Hasan's forces at the end of January 1469 and was put to death a few days later.

Given the internal problems that afflicted the Timurid Empire in the east, Abu Said's death brought a decisive end to Timurid efforts to regain control of western Persia. The defeat of both the Qara-Qoyunlu and the Timurids effectively made Uzun Hasan the undisputed ruler of most of the territory between the Caucasus and the Persian Gulf, including almost all of southern Persia. This promised, under the leadership of Uzun Hasan, the emergence of the Aq-Qoyunlu as a major new imperial force in the Middle East.

However, this dream of an Aq-Qoyunlu empire was seriously threatened by the Ottoman advance, since Uzun Hasan's ambitions now clashed directly with those of the equally ambitious but more powerful Mehmed. Uzun Hasan became determined to seize the initiative from Mehmed by entering into an alliance with Venice. In 1470, he dispatched an embassy to Venice as well as to the pope announcing his victories over the Timurids and the Qara-Qoyunlu, and assuring them that "the sole obstacle and enemy remaining is Mehmed Beg, the Ottoman; humbling his power and rooting out his dominion is a simple matter."[4]

The Venetians, who were engaged in peace negotiations with Mehmed at the time, were proceeding cautiously and did not respond to Uzun Hasan's overture until April 1472, when they offered him continued support in his efforts against the Ottomans. Venice hoped to organize a serious threat to the Ottomans by upgrading the armaments used by the Aq-Qoyunlu and then mounting coordinated simultaneous assaults on the Ottoman eastern and western flanks in Asia and Europe. Under the treaty with Venice, Uzun Hasan was to receive title to all of Anatolia, but was to be prohibited from building any fortresses along the coastline or interfering with the free passage of Venetian ships. The promised Venetian arms were delivered to the Aq-Qoyunlu late in 1472 while a new European crusader fleet sailed into the Aegean. Uzun Hasan then mobilized the numerous emirs who had been dispossessed by the Ottomans, promising to restore their territories in return for their assistance in defeating Mehmed.

With his augmented forces, Uzun Hasan invaded central Anatolia, taking Sivas and Tokat and driving the Ottomans out of Qaraman. He then proceeded to march on Bursa, threatening to overrun the entire peninsula. Mehmed met these challenges with great determination and ability. He blocked attempts by the crusader fleet to enter the Turkish Strait and then led a large elite force into Anatolia in April 1473 to deal with the Aq-

Qoyunlu. In a major battle near Erzerum that took place on August 11, the Ottoman Janissary and artillery forces smashed the Aq-Qoyunlu flank. Uzun Hasan quickly realized that the disciplined professional armies of the Ottoman sultan were far different from those of the nomadic Turkish hordes over which he had been so victorious in the past. He was forced to acknowledge the inability of the Aq-Qoyunlu to defeat the Ottomans in pitched battle and had little choice but to seek an accommodation with Mehmed.

Uzun Hasan agreed to a peace treaty on August 24, 1473, that required him to abandon the territories he had conquered in eastern Anatolia. He withdrew to Azerbaijan, established his capital at Tabriz, and subsequently devoted himself to the arduous task of trying to impose order on the political chaos that he found prevailing in Persia at the time. When the Europeans realized that Uzun Hasan no longer posed a significant threat to the Ottomans, and could not be relied on to distract Mehmed from intervening in European affairs, they dropped all further support of the Aq-Qoyunlu. With the collapse of the Aq-Qoyunlu challenge to Ottoman hegemony in the region, all other effective resistance to the sultan in Anatolia came to an end. Most of the dispossessed and rebellious Turkish emirs now also sought to come to terms with the Ottomans.

With the end of any serious opposition to the Ottomans in Anatolia, Mehmed was able to give his full attention to the simmering conflicts on his European frontiers that preoccupied him for the remainder of his reign. He had to deal with three distinct challenges from the north to Ottoman hegemony in southeastern Europe. In Moldavia, Stephen had built a powerful military force and repudiated his nominal vassalage to the Ottomans. In 1471, Stephen invaded Wallachia and ousted the Ottoman puppet ruler Radu IV, thereby posing a substantial threat to the Ottoman position in Bulgaria. An entirely new and potentially the most serious challenge to Mehmed's ambitions began to emerge from the principality of Muscovy far to the northeast. Ivan III "the Great" (1462–1505) had married Zoe (Sophia) Palaeologus, daughter of the last Byzantine despot of the Morea and niece of the last Byzantine emperor, and therefore claimed to be the legal heir to the Eastern Roman Empire. To dramatize this point, he attempted to make Moscow the religious center of the Orthodox Church. At the same time, Ivan began encroaching on the fringes of the Ottoman sphere of influence by contesting Mehmed's suzerainty over Mengili Giray (1469–1475 and 1478–1515), the khan of the Crimean Tatars. The khan was becoming increasingly concerned about the scope of Ottoman ambitions in the northern Black Sea region and welcomed the support of Muscovy as an offset to further Ottoman advances in the region. A third challenge came from the Jagellonians of Lithuania and Poland, whose domains now reached as far eastward as the Black Sea along the Moldavian border. The Jagellonians entered into an alliance with the Golden Horde, which still held sway farther north, and thereby posed a threat to Ottoman interests that Mehmed could ill-afford to ignore.

Despite the inherent conflicts of interest among these parties, who competed among themselves for preeminence in the Black Sea region, they found it to be in their interests to make common cause in opposing Ottoman domination of the area. Although he suffered a significant setback at the battle of Rakovitza on January 17, 1475, at the hands of Stephen of Moldavia, supported by Jagellonian and Hungarian troops, Mehmed nonetheless succeeded in re-imposing his hegemony over the Crimea. By exploiting an internal dispute within the Tatar ruling house, he contrived to oust Mengili Giray as khan and replace him with the latter's son Erminak Giray (1475–1478). In return for Mehmed's support, Erminak Giray restored the vassalage of the Crimean Tatars to the Ottomans and assisted in the naval expedition that Mehmed launched against the European toeholds on the northern Black Sea coast. With Tatar help, the sultan succeeded in capturing all the remaining Genoese trading colonies that had been established along the littoral. Mehmed subsequently agreed to restore a grateful Mengili Giray to the position of khan of the Tatars, thereby establishing relatively firm Ottoman domination of the nominally autonomous khanate, a relationship that kept the Crimea from being absorbed into the growing Muscovite empire. As a consequence, the Crimean Tatars became the principal buffers between the Ottomans and the Russians over the course of the next two centuries.

No sooner had the wars ended in the principalities of Moldavia and Wallachia, and in the Black Sea region, than Mehmed directed his attention to settling the long-standing conflict with Venice once and for all time. Mehmed had been conducting a low-level holding campaign against the Venetians in Albania since 1474, when he laid siege to Scutari. His strategy was to force Venice into making peace by completing the conquest of Albania, thereby giving the Ottomans a firm foothold on the Adriatic coast from which they would be in a position to seize control of what had been a virtual Venetian lake.

Mehmed began his campaign in 1477 by laying siege to the port of Lepanto and the town of Kroya, the former capital of Iskander Beg. The Venetians attempted to distract Mehmed with raids along the shores of western Anatolia. However, this stopped after Mehmed sent Bosnian raiders into Italy where they ravaged the region near Venice. By the end of 1478, all of Albania was in Ottoman hands. Mehmed also took Montenegro, which placed him directly astride the coastal areas of Dalmatia that were under Venetian rule. He had also cut the lines of communication between Venetian Dalmatia and Italy, threatening to completely isolate the former. At the same time, the assistance to Venice promised by Hungary never materialized. Under the circumstances, Venice acknowledged that it could no longer reverse the Ottoman advances, and negotiations between the two powers began. The peace treaty that was signed in Istanbul on June 25, 1479, recognized Ottoman control of Albania and all the islands of the northern Aegean except for the Sporades, which remained under Venice, and Chios, which continued to be held by Genoa. In return for these concessions and its agreement to pay him an annual indemnity of 10,000 gold ducats, Mehmed allowed Venice to keep a number of ports in Dalmatia and most of its former possessions in the Morea and restored its commercial privileges in the Ottoman Empire.

Once having neutralized Venice, the dominant regional maritime power, Mehmed set his sights on the conquest of Rhodes. It was now the only major Aegean island that was not under Ottoman control, and he wanted it as a base for further expansion into the eastern Mediterranean region. He also entertained plans for the conquest of Italy, which was torn by internal wars and appeared particularly vulnerable to invasion at the time.

An Ottoman force took the Greek islands of Cephalonia and Zanta and placed Rhodes under siege on December 4, 1479, while a second invasion force landed at Otranto on the Italian peninsula on August 11, 1480. Rome went into a panic as the pope prepared to evacuate the city. A new crusade was hastily proclaimed, but only received the support of the Italian city-states, France, and Hungary. Both Italy and Rhodes were spared, however, by the death of Mehmed on May 3, 1481. Internal problems relating to the succession to the Ottoman throne caused the cancellation of the planned campaigns against them.

The new Ottoman sultan Bayezid II (1481–1512) spent the initial years of his reign restoring the country's finances, which had been depleted for the most part by the constant wars during his father's reign. He also had to deal with a revolt by his brother Jem who sought to split the empire and establish his own dynasty in Asia. Although Bayezid effectively consolidated his control of the empire by the end of 1483, the attempts by the European states to exploit his brother's rebellion by organizing yet another crusade served to restrain the sultan from undertaking any serious expansionist moves until after Jem's death in 1495. However, this is not to suggest that the preceding years by any means constituted a period of peace.

Bayezid's first foreign policy priority was to deal with Moldavia, which still posed an obstacle to a reliable direct land connection between the Ottoman Empire and its Crimean vassal. Control of Moldavia also had strategic importance in the event of a renewal of the war with Hungary. Moreover, since the Danube emptied into the Black Sea in Moldavia, control of the river's delta region would permit Bayezid to prevent raids by Christian pirates against Ottoman shipping and coastal positions in the Black Sea. Stephen had actually overtly challenged Bayezid in the early summer of 1481 when he sought to take advantage of the sultan's preoccupation with

Jem's revolt by invading Wallachia, as well as by crossing the Danube and launching raids into Bulgaria.

At the same time that the Hungarian king Mathias Corvinus (1458–1490) was engaged in the conquest of Austria, making an intervention on behalf of Stephen unlikely from that quarter, Bayezid crossed into Moldavia from Wallachia and captured Kilia on the Danube on July 14, 1484. Then, a force of Crimean Tatars took Akkerman (Cetatea-Alba) on the Dniester in Bessarabia on August 3. This gave the Ottomans control of the western shores of the Black Sea and the mouths of both the Danube and the Dniester Rivers. This effectively brought to an end the roles of Hungary and Moldavia as entrepôts for the trade of central and northern Europe, which passed down the rivers and through the Black Sea to its ultimate destination. Control of this trade and consequently of the prosperity of the countries through which it transited now passed to the Ottomans. Although Stephen quickly re-acknowledged Ottoman suzerainty in an attempt to salvage the situation, he repudiated it once again as soon as Bayezid and Mengili Giray withdrew their forces from his territory. However, Stephen was unable to regain control over the river outlets to the Black Sea, which remained firmly in Ottoman hands.

Another trouble spot for Bayezid was his southern frontier with the Mamluks. The latter had lent their support to Jem during the early phase of his revolt, giving new currency to the long-standing conflict of interests between the Ottomans and Mamluks over Anatolia, as well as over control of the holy cities of Islam. When the Mamluks attempted to secure a more friendly regime in the Anatolian buffer state of Dulgadir by removing its ruler, the latter solicited the aid of the Ottoman governor of Kayseri who responded with an invasion of Mamluk territory, triggering an Ottoman-Mamluk war that lasted from 1485 to 1491. The struggle, which was nothing more than a protracted series of skirmishes, was inconclusive although the Mamluks appeared to have had the best of it. However, they were unable to follow up on their initial victories because of internal political and financial problems. In May 1491, Bayezid accepted a Mamluk peace offer that was precipitated by the widespread famine and plague that had struck Syria. The six-year conflict ended without any significant changes in the disposition of the troubled frontier between the two empires.

On the sultan's western frontiers, relations with Venice had deteriorated once more as a consequence of continued rivalries in the Adriatic, Albania, the Morea, and the Aegean. At the same time, the relative lack of Ottoman activity against the Christians of Europe gave spur to the spread of heterodox religious movements in Anatolia that originated in the eastern part of the peninsula and neighboring Azerbaijan. Of particular concern in this regard was the growth of the Azerbaijan-based Safaviyya Order, about which more in the following chapter. These religious movements also served as vehicles for the organization of political dissent and began to make inroads among the population in the cities as well as among the Janissaries. Bayezid concluded that a new war against Christian Europe would serve to defuse the danger to central Ottoman control represented by these movements and would cause the growing number of dissidents to rally around the sultanate.

Pursuing this political strategy, Bayezid attempted to provoke a war with Venice. In 1496, he closed all Ottoman ports to Venetian grain merchants and sent forces from Albania to occupy Montenegro, which was a Venetian protectorate. The following year, a Venetian passenger ship bringing Christian pilgrims to Jerusalem was captured and all aboard were either killed or enslaved. In response, Venice increased the size of its fleet in Aegean waters, while Bayezid undertook a major naval construction program and began to raid Venetian Dalmatia. Then, when Venice entered into an alliance with France, Bayezid treated it as a *casus belli* and, on July 4, 1499, imprisoned all the Venetian residents in Istanbul.

The Ottoman fleet quickly undertook an offensive that captured Venice's major ports in the Morea and Aegean, thereby seriously weakening its position in the region. At the same time, Bosnian raiding parties devastated Croatia and Dalmatia, and reached as far as the gates of Venice itself by August 1501. Pope Alexander VI tried to organize a new crusade but his efforts were hampered significantly by aggressive Ottoman diplomacy, which kept Milan and Naples from participating in it by offering them some highly desirable commercial concessions in the Ottoman Empire. Poland and Moldavia were similarly neutralized through negotiated peace agreements. The financial pressures on Venice from its loss of markets in the east began to take their toll and the maritime state was soon ready for an accommodation with the Turks. At the same time, with new problems arising on his eastern frontiers, Bayezid too was prepared to come to terms. With Polish mediation, a new peace treaty was signed in Istanbul on December 14, 1502, that restored Venice's trading privileges as well as its ports in Albania and the Morea. On balance, however, it was a significant victory for the Ottomans. According to one assessment of the results of the war:

It marked the emergence of the Ottoman Empire as a major Mediterranean naval power. The bases won from Venice gave it strategic locations that could be used for further advances, not only in the eastern Mediterranean but also in the West. The war and the concluding peace agreements also marked the entry of the Ottomans into European diplomacy as an increasingly important factor in the balance of power. The Ottomans had also become a major economic power by virtue of their control over the international trade routes passing through the eastern Mediterranean—Venice, for one, determined never again to become involved in war with the sultan, since this would harm its economic interests.[5]

NOTES

1. Franz Babinger, *Mehmed the Conqueror and His Time*, p. 249.

2. Ibid., p. 112.
3. John Glubb, *Soldiers of Fortune: The Story of the Mamlukes*, p. 352.
4. John E. Woods, *The Aqquyunlu*, p. 127.
5. Stanford Shaw, *History of the Ottoman Empire and Modern Turkey*, vol. 1, p. 76.

17

The Rise of the Safavids

It was noted earlier that the growing influence of heterodox religious movements in eastern Anatolia, particularly the Shiite Safaviyya Order, began to be seen by the sultan as a threat to the internal stability of the empire. This concern took on more definite geopolitical dimensions at the beginning of the sixteenth century, and became a significant factor underlying Bayezid's readiness to come to terms with Venice.

The Safaviyya Order was founded at Ardabil in Azerbaijan by Shaikh Safi ad-Din (1252–1334). By contrast with other Sufi orders, it took on a dynastic character from the very beginning, thereby developing within it the potential for an easy transition into a political movement. Safavid influence in the region grew steadily, especially after Tamerlane accorded the order special treatment, effectively placing it under Timurid protection. The order began to take on increasingly significant political aspects with the accession of Junayd (1447–1460) to its leadership.

From the moment Junayd took control of the movement, he made it evident that he harbored serious political ambitions. His activities, including his unilateral pursuit of a holy war against the infidel, aroused the suspicions of Jihan Shah, leader of the Qara-Qoyunlu and ruler of Azerbaijan, who ordered him into exile. After several years of wandering in Syria and eastern Anatolia, in 1456 Junayd and his followers were given sanctuary in Diyarbekir by Uzun Hasan, leader of the orthodox Sunnite Aq-Qoyunlu, who hoped to exploit the Safaviyya Order in his ongoing struggle for regional supremacy with the Shiite Qara-Qoyunlu. In 1460, Junayd marched into Shirvan with an army of some 10,000 troops, presumably to seize the territory and establish a base from which to invade Persia. However, this expedition turned into a military disaster as Junayd was successfully attacked and killed by the shah of Shirvan on March 4, 1460, near Tabarsaran, on the banks of the river Kur.

The Safavid bid for temporal power intensified under Junayd's successor Haydar (1460–1488). He consolidated his relations with the Aq-Qoyunlu by marrying Uzun Hasan's daughter and began to prepare to contest the Qara-Qoyunlu for dominance in northwestern Persia. Following the pattern set by his father, he sought to give his men the necessary battle experience before taking on the Qara-Qoyunlu and first launched a series of expeditions against the Christians of Circassia and Daghestan. However, to do this, he had to cross Shirvan. He was permitted to cross the territory twice, in 1483 or 1486 and in 1487, without incident. In 1488, however, Haydar overplayed his hand by exploiting the opportunity presented by his unimpeded passage through Shirvan to sack the capital of the country. The shah of Shirvan, Farukhyasar, appealed for help to his son-in-law Yaqub (1478–1490), sultan of the Aq-Qoyunlu. He told him: "At the moment, Haydar owns no territory, but he has mobilized a warlike army, and his ambitions will not be contained within the confines of the district of Ardabil. Nor if he succeeds in acquiring a kingdom such as mine, will he long be satisfied with such a meager empire. On the contrary, it will merely whet his appetite."[1]

At this juncture, Yaqub decided to reverse the standing Aq-Qoyunlu policy of support for the Safavids and sent some 4,000 men to assist Shirvan. While the Safavids were considered to be useful allies in the struggle against the Qara-Qoyunlu, once the latter were defeated by Uzun Hasan in 1467 the value of the Safavids to the Aq-Qoyunlu diminished considerably. The Shiite movement was now seen as a destabilizing factor and Yaqub welcomed the opportunity to rid himself of an autonomous and well-armed heterodox power center within the Aq-Qoyunlu Empire. Thus, with Aq-Qoyunlu help, the Safavids were defeated at Tabarsaran on July 9, 1488, Haydar being killed in the battle.

Haydar was succeeded as sheikh of the Safavids by his son Ali who, as an indication of his temporal ambitions, adopted the title of *padishah*, or king, and was reported to have begun preparing to avenge his father's death. To forestall this, Ali as well as his brothers Ibrahim and Ismail were arrested on Yaqub's orders and interned in the fortress of Istakhr, in Fars. They were saved from certain death only by the intercession of their mother, who was Yaqub's sister.

Yaqub died shortly thereafter, in December 1490, and a major succession struggle broke out between as many as a half-dozen claimants to the Aq-Qoyunlu realm. One of these, Rustam (1493–1497), sought to exploit the Safavids as allies in his struggle for the throne. Accordingly, he released the three Safavid brothers he was holding prisoner in 1493, and Ali subsequently played a major role in Rustam's victory over his chief rival. However, it was not long before Rustam too became seriously concerned about

Safavid political ambitions and attempted to imprison the brothers once again. This time, they escaped and headed for their base of support in Azerbaijan, with Rustam in hot pursuit. Rustam caught up with them near Ardabil, and Ali was killed. Leadership of the Safavids then passed to Ismail, who was seven years old. With the help of his retainers, Ismail successfully evaded capture by the Aq-Qoyunlu and took refuge in Gilan. Rustum was about to invade the province in 1497 when he was himself killed as a result of the resumption of the internecine struggle that was tearing the Aq-Qoyunlu Empire apart. This gave the small band of advisers of the young Safavid sheikh the respite necessary to prepare for the seizure of power in Persia from the Aq-Qoyunlu in Ismail's name.

Ismail and his supporters emerged from Gilan in August 1499 to make an open bid for political power. Since succession to leadership of the Safaviyya Order was dynastic and the now twelve-year-old Ismail was without an heir, his only surviving brother Ibrahim having defected to the Aq-Qoyunlu, this was a very risky venture and was approached with some caution. During the winter of 1499, both the Aq-Qoyunlu and the ruler of Shirvan sought to nip the problem in the bud by seizing or killing Ismail, but they were unsuccessful.

In the spring of 1500, Ismail dispatched messengers to his supporters in Syria and eastern Anatolia calling for a rendezvous near Erzincan in the Armenian highlands. The call brought some 7,000 volunteers that, added to those who had already joined him, gave him a formidable force, but one which was hardly large enough for the enterprise Ismail had in view. However, Ismail was to become the principal beneficiary of the internecine struggles that afflicted the Aq-Qoyunlu and tended to give his relatively small force far greater weight than it would have had against a unified Aq-Qoyunlu state. At about the same time that Ismail initiated his campaign for empire, the two surviving princes of the Aq-Qoyunlu civil war, Alvand and Murad, decided to resolve the succession crisis by a partition of the empire—Murad taking the Jibal (Media), Fars, and Kerman, while Alvand kept Azerbaijan and Diyarbekir.

The Safavid offensive began late in 1500, and was directed initially at the conquest of Shirvan. It has been suggested that "Two motives may have influenced his [Ismail's] decision: the practical desire to test his army against a less formidable enemy before risking a pitched battle with the Aq Quyunlu; and a psychological motive, namely, the desire to avenge the deaths of his father and grandfather at the hands of the rulers of Shirvan."[2] In any case, Ismail crossed the Kur into Shirvan in December 1500 and decisively defeated Farukhyasar at Gulistan. He then marched on to the Caspian seacoast and took Baku. At this point, Alvand proceeded north from Tabriz and crossed the Aras to challenge the Safavid forces. The two armies clashed at Sharur, near Nakhichevan. Although the Safavids were outnumbered three to one by the Aq-Qoyunlu, they emerged from the battle with a decisive victory. Ismail (1501–1524) now had control of Azerbaijan, and he was proclaimed as shah in Tabriz in the summer of 1501. Although Alvand was still free to build another army in Diyarbekir, and Murad still had control of central and southern Persia along with a large army, as a practical matter, the Aq-Qoyunlu grip on Persia was shattered beyond restoration.

The announcement by Ismail that the "Twelver" form of Shiism practiced by the Safaviyya Order was henceforth to be the official religion of the new Safavid state had an electrifying effect on the region. It was a shrewd political move on his part, calculated to harness latent Persian nationalist sentiments to the religious leadership of the Safavids, making the latter the preeminent power center in the country. As observed by Said A. Arjomand: "The conversion of Iran to Shiism—this most important of the religiously relevant political acts of the Safavid rulers—was, for the most part, carried out for 'reasons of state' and aimed at stamping out actual or potential centers of power."[3] This not only sharply differentiated the new militant Persian Shiite state from the Sunnite Ottoman Empire. It also served as a lightning rod and rallying cry for the many fervid supporters of the Shiite form of Islam who were held in disdain by the Sunnite majority in the Muslim world.

Although the Safavids had ridden to state power on a wave of revolutionary religious fervor, perhaps their most immediate concern quickly became that of containing this revolutionary zeal and channeling it to serve the interests of the state. The difficulty of this task became compounded by the steady influx of new adherents of the religion into Azerbaijan from eastern Anatolia, further swelling an already volatile population of religious zealots. Ismail sought to deal with the growing problem by diverting some of this incendiary religious fervor to serve practical geopolitical purposes. It was primarily for this purpose that he began organizing expeditions against the Sunnite Ottomans in Anatolia.

It was this highly troublesome development on his eastern frontier that helped convince the Ottoman sultan in 1501 of the need to reach a peace agreement with Venice. He simply could not devote his full energies to expansion in Europe while the security of his flank in Asia was being eroded by what he considered to be a bunch of heterodox fanatics. To reduce the possibility that eastern Anatolia might be entirely subverted by the Safavids, Bayezid ordered a large-scale population transfer of Shiites from Anatolia to the Morea in 1502.

Notwithstanding the growing tensions along their common frontiers, it was to take another decade before a serious confrontation between the Ottomans and the Safavids took place. This was primarily because the Safavids had become preoccupied with the conquest of the rest of Persia. The first order of business for Ismail in this regard was the defeat of the Aq-Qoyunlu under Murad, who still held central and southern Persia. This occurred in 1503, when Murad was defeated decisively near Hamadan, with the remnants of his forces taking sanctuary in Mazanderan. Husain Kiya Chulavi, the ruler of this Caspian province, was also a Shiite and was therefore seen by Ismail as both a religious and a political rival. As a consequence, the ensuing battle for control of Mazanderan was particularly ferocious, but it ultimately fell to Ismail along with the neighboring Caspian province of Gurgan in 1504. That same year he also took Yazd in the center of the country. Ismail was occupied for the next three years with the conquest of Diyarbekir from the Aq-Qoyunlu and the pacification of his western frontier, which now abutted the Ottoman Empire. In 1508, Ismail completed the conquest of southwestern Persia and seized Baghdad. He then returned to the north for the pacification of Shirvan.

While Ismail was engaged in the struggle with the Aq-Qoyunlu in western Persia, the Uzbeks of Transoxiana conquered Khorasan in 1507 from the Timurids, who were still in control of eastern Persia. The Uzbeks then began raiding into Kerman, evoking protests from Ismail. His objections were dismissed derisively by the Uzbek leader Muhammad Shibani Khan. Accordingly, once he secured his western frontiers, Ismail invaded Khorasan in November 1510. A major pitched battle was fought between the Safavid and Uzbek forces on the outskirts of Merv on December 2, and the Uzbeks were defeated decisively. Muhammad Shibani Khan was killed and, perhaps as an unmistakable indication of his intentions, Ismail sent the khan's head as a gift to Bayezid, an act that the sultans long remembered with bitterness and one that overshadowed all subsequent Ottoman-Safavid relations.

Ismail's immediate goal was to reestablish Persia's northeastern frontier at the Oxus, thereby extending his hegemony to the buffer region of Transoxiana. Because of this, Ismail was quite prepared to lend his support to the displaced Timurid prince, Zahir ad-Din Babur, who offered to accept Safavid suzerainty in return for help in regaining control of Transoxiana. In October 1511, a combined Safavid-Timurid force succeeded in taking Samarkand and, shortly thereafter, Bukhara as well. Once the Safavid troops withdrew back to Persia, however, the Uzbeks returned to the attack and drove Babur out of Bukhara in May 1512. Ismail responded by dispatching a large army under the *vakil* (vice-regent), Amir Yar Ahmad Isfahani, to Transoxiana to support the Timurids. This decision soon turned into a debacle for the Safavids.

One of the fundamental problems that Ismail failed to deal with, and which now undermined his policy in Transoxiana, was the reconciliation of the two antipathetic ethnic groups that constituted the basis of the Safavid state. The fact was that Ismail rode to power primarily on the shoulders of his Turkish followers, known as the *qizilbash* because of the distinctive headdress they wore. As a result, for the first half-dozen years of his reign as shah, the office of vakil, a position of ultimate importance in the state, was occupied by the qizilbash leader Husain Beg Lala Shamlu. In 1508, however, Amir Najm, who was an ethnic Persian, replaced Husain Beg as vakil. It appears that Ismail undertook this change of incumbents as a matter of policy, in order to offset what was widely perceived as the inordinate extent of qizilbash influence in the ruling circles of the Safavid state. When Amir Najm died about 1510, Amir Yar Ahmad Isfahani, another Persian, replaced him in that office, further increasing the disaffection of many of the qizilbash officers. Matters came to a head during the subsequent siege of the fort of Ghujduvan in Transoxiana, in the late fall of 1512, by the combined Safavid-Timurid armies. As supplies began to run short, some of the senior qizilbash officers urged that the campaign be suspended for the winter and that a new offensive be mounted the following spring. The vakil, however, refused to heed their advice. Then, when a large Uzbek relief force arrived at Ghujduvan on November 12, many of the qizilbash, along with the Timurids, simply abandoned the vakil and deserted. The effect on the Safavid forces was devastating. The vakil, with more courage than good sense, fought on alone and was captured and executed by the Uzbeks, who then poured into Khorasan and captured Herat and Mashad. Ismail eventually succeeded in pushing the Uzbeks back across the Oxus the following year and entered into an uneasy truce with them that lasted for some eight years. As a result of the limited benefits secured by this costly campaign, Ismail apparently concluded that it was prudent to place limits on the extension of the Persian Empire, and he effectively renounced all further territorial ambitions in Transoxiana and Central Asia.

With matters more or less settled on his eastern frontiers, Ismail turned his attention westward once again. Thus, after a decade of relative quiet on the Ottoman-Safavid frontier, the Safavids precipitated a major confrontation between the two states. Even though Ismail had been preoccupied with the conquest of Persia and the extension of his eastern frontiers, Safavid efforts to subvert the loyalty to the sultan of the Shiite Turks of eastern Anatolia had continued unabated. In the spring of 1511, the Safavid ruler Shah Kulu, who described himself as the caliph (successor) of Ismail, successfully exploited the resentment of the Anatolian Shiites against the Ottoman regime. He triggered a major revolt at Antalya that also received the support of many of the Ottoman troops that were sent to suppress it. The Ottoman efforts to restore control were seriously hindered by the bitter rivalry over the prospective succession to the Ottoman throne between two of Bayezid's sons, Ahmad and Korkut, who were the governors of Amasya and Antalya respectively. Taking advantage of this situation, Shah Kulu was able to march north from Qaraman and lay waste much of central Anatolia, defeating an Ottoman army near Alasehir in June 1511 and opening the road for an assault on Bursa. Bayezid, ill and withdrawn, belatedly dispatched an army of some 8,000 Janissaries under the grand vizier Hadim Ali Pasha that succeeded in defeating the rebels near Kayseri in August, killing Shah Kulu in the process. Nonetheless, emboldened by their relative successes in challenging the Ottomans, a major Safavid expedition under Nur Ali Khalifa penetrated deeply into eastern Anatolia in 1512, plundered the town of Tuqat, and inflicted a number of defeats on the local Ottoman forces. But perhaps of even greater significance as a factor in triggering the war between the Ottomans and Safavids was the attempt by the latter to intervene in the Ottoman succession crisis that reached a critical point that same year.

As already noted, one of the reasons that Bayezid did not respond to the Safavid threat more forcefully was the growing internal struggle over the succession that plagued the last years of his reign. The competition was reduced to two sons, Ahmad and Selim, by 1512. Ahmad, the eldest, was the popular choice and was Bayezid's personal choice as well. However, he favored a continuation of Bayezid's policies of peace and consolidation and was strongly opposed by the Janissaries and the frontier beys of Serbia and Bosnia, who favored the far more aggressive but widely disliked Selim. The Janissaries ultimately forced Bayezid to abdicate in favor of Selim on April 25, 1512, on the grounds that only he could save the empire from the Safavid threat. But it was evident to Ismail that if Selim became sultan, the Safavids would be confronted by an implacable foe in the west. Ismail therefore lent his initial support to Ahmad, whose foreign policy orientation would clearly favor Safavid interests.

The following year, Ahmad declared himself sultan of Anatolia, but disdained any Safavid help because of his abhorrence of Shiism. Instead, he sought help from the Mamluks. In any case, he was defeated by Selim at Yenisehir on April 15, 1513, and eliminated as a rival for the Ottoman throne. After this, Ismail offered his support to Ahmad's surviving son Murad in the hope of using the latter to mobilize indigenous opposition to Selim. Nothing came of this scheme, however, since Murad had little support among the Ottomans and was soon forced to seek asylum with Ismail.

No sooner did Selim "the Grim" (1512–1520) seat himself firmly on the throne than he began to prepare for the invasion and conquest of Persia. To assure that his flanks in Europe would remain secure while he was occupied in Asia, he renewed the agreements with both Hungary and Venice, offering new trade concessions and privileges as inducements for maintaining the peace. His concern about the security of his southern frontier was easily resolved by the fact that the Mamluks were equally worried about the threat from the Safavids to their position in Syria and their control of the holy cities in the Hejaz. As a result, they were quite amenable to joining in an alliance with the Ottomans against the Safavids in 1513. By the spring of 1514, Selim was finally in a position to launch his campaign, not only against the Safavids but also for the expansion of the Ottoman Empire to cover the entire Middle East.

NOTES

1. Roger Savory, *Iran under the Safavids*, p. 18.
2. Ibid., p. 25.
3. Said A. Arjomand, *The Shadow of God and the Hidden Imam*, p. 109.

18

Ottoman Expansionism under Selim

Selim's highest foreign policy priority was the defeat of the Safavids and the elimination of the heterodox religious challenge on his vulnerable eastern flank. He set out across Anatolia with a substantial army of some 140,000 men in April 1514. However, as soon as he began to penetrate into the eastern frontier region he encountered a severe supply problem. His original intention was to keep his army supplied from Dulgadir, an Ottoman vassal state. The latter, however, refused to participate in the resupply operation, apparently concerned that if Selim succeeded in defeating the Safavids its own prospects for continued autonomy would soon vanish. Accordingly, Dulgadir would not act against its own self-interest by helping the Ottomans eliminate a countervailing regional power. Selim was therefore forced to have the most critically needed supplies brought by sea from Istanbul to Trebizond, and delivered from there to his forces in the field. But this only reduced the problem; it did not really solve it. The sultan soon found that the constant shortages of supplies, exacerbated by an unceasing barrage of Safavid propaganda, was having an unsettling effect on his troops. He therefore decided to alleviate the supply problem by reducing his forces by half, exploiting the opportunity to remove known malcontents among his troops before engaging the Safavids in battle.

The Safavids acknowledged the general superiority of the Ottoman troops, led by a large Janissary force, to their own and decided not to engage them in battle in open territory, where they were likely to be overwhelmed by the Turkish cavalry. Instead, they withdrew to the foothills of Armenia as the Ottomans advanced, applying a scorched earth policy to the country as they retreated across the provinces of Erzincan and Erzurum, thereby denying the Ottomans access to sorely needed supplies. Despite the difficulties, Selim drove onward toward Tabriz, finally engaging the Safavid forces in a major battle in the valley of Chaldiran on August 23, 1514. Although the Safavids initially gained the upper hand, it was the Ottomans who emerged with the ultimate victory, primarily as a result of their technological superiority; the Ottoman army was the first in the region to adopt the use of firearms on a large scale. Firepower, especially from artillery, proved to be the decisive factor. The Venetian ambassador to the Aq-Qoyunlu provides a contemporary account of what took place:

The monarch [Selim], seeing the slaughter, began to retreat, and to turn about, and was about to fly, when Sinan, coming to the rescue at the time of need, caused the artillery to be brought up and fired on both the janissaries and the Persians. The Persian horses hearing the thunder of those infernal machines, scattered and divided themselves over the plain, not obeying their riders' bit or spur anymore, from the terror they were in. . . . It is certainly said, that if it had not been for the artillery, which terrified in the manner related the Persian horses which had never before heard such a din, all his [Selim's] forces would have been routed and put to the edge of the sword.[1]

Given the one-sided and disastrous consequences of the Ottoman employment of firearms in this critical battle, it is puzzling why the Safavids did not employ firearms as well. However, it appears that the Safavids, at least at the time of Ismail, looked upon the use of firearms with disdain, as a cowardly and unworthy act. Although they had long employed cannon in siege warfare, their negative attitude toward modern hand weapons precluded their effective use in conjunction with cavalry, their favored military instrument. A modern analyst has written: "Had the Ottomans not employed firearms on such a large scale in the battle of Chaldiran and in the battles which followed it, it is reasonably certain that their victory—even if they had been able to win—would have been far less decisive. In other words, the Ottomans would have acquired far less Safawid territory in that event and a much stronger Safawid army would have been left intact to prepare for a war of revenge."[2]

The battle at Chaldiran had a major demoralizing effect on the Safavids; it was Ismail's first defeat. According to the Iranian historian Nasr Allah Falsafi, Ismail went into mourning after the battle, wore only black afterward, and never again led the Persian forces into action in person. "Since in his experience he had always been victorious, and his enemies defeated and conquered, he considered no adversary his equal, and thought himself invincible; the defeat at Chaldiran had a profound effect on Ismail's character and behaviour; his egotism and arrogance were changed to despair and dejection."[3]

Although both sides suffered heavy losses, the Ottoman army remained a viable force and Selim moved on and occupied Tabriz. The Safavids, however, were saved from decisive defeat by the calendar. With winter approaching, and unable to resupply his forces before it set in, Selim had little choice but to terminate the campaign until the following spring. He withdrew from Tabriz to Qarabagh in the Caucasus to wait out the winter before returning to complete the conquest of Persia. However, no sooner did Selim withdraw from Tabriz than it was reoccupied by the Safavids, creating the probability of his needing to fight a second time for the same piece of real estate, a rather unappealing prospect for him. This consideration, coupled with the increasingly serious supply problems, which remained unsolved and were further exacerbated by the severe weather that also caused the death of thousands of his troops, led Selim to decide to defer renewal of the campaign to some future date and to withdraw back into Anatolia.

He arrived at Amasya in late November 1514, his army substantially diminished by the heavy losses it sustained, having achieved very little other than to assure Ottoman control of Erzincan. After considering the problems he encountered throughout the campaign, perhaps most notably the refusal of Dulgadir to act as a loyal vassal, Selim evidently concluded that, before resuming his drive against the Safavids, it would be necessary to assure his complete mastery over eastern Anatolia. He would have to deal decisively with the variety of rebellious anti-Ottoman sectarians that were to be found there.

Unexpectedly, Selim also decided to accord a higher priority in his timetable of conquest to the elimination of the Mamluks. He became determined to undertake their defeat before resuming his assault on Persia. For one thing, the Mamluk presence in Syria posed an ultimately unacceptable threat to his flank, even though they professed friendship and common cause with the Ottomans against the Safavids. But perhaps the most important consideration for Selim was the fact that the Mamluks were particularly vulnerable at the time as a result of other developments in the region, and Selim was anxious to take advantage of what might have proved to be only a temporary weakness.

The Mamluks had come under increasing political and economic pressure from Portugal, whose growing naval presence in heretofore Mamluk-dominated waters posed a direct threat to their security. In 1498, a Portuguese fleet under Vasco da Gama rounded the Cape of Good Hope, reaching Calicut in May of that year. The Portuguese purpose was to find a means of diverting the oriental trade away from Venice and Genoa, which together monopolized the commerce that had long passed overland from the Indian Ocean to the Mediterranean through Mamluk territory.

Portugal established its foothold in the Indian Ocean littoral with Affonso d'Albuquerque's construction of a port at Cochin on India's western coast in 1502. From there the Portuguese started to compete successfully with the merchants from Egypt and Syria who were entrenched farther north at Calicut. They soon began to force the trade between India and Europe to use the all-water route around Africa that was under Portuguese control instead of the traditional overland routes that were not. This had very serious impact on the revenues normally earned by the Mamluks from the transit of such trade across their territory.

The situation became further aggravated by the Portuguese capture of Socotra Island in the Gulf of Aden in 1507, followed by that of Hormuz at the entrance to the Persian Gulf in the following year. From these positions, the Portuguese were able to impose a quarantine of the Red Sea and Persian Gulf ports that fed the overland caravan routes, effectively diverting most maritime traffic to the oceanic route. This had severe economic repercussions in the major port cities of Suez and Alexandria, which served as entrepôts for the Red Sea trade, and for Basra, Aleppo, and Tripoli, which served as the transit points for the Persian Gulf trade. As a consequence, both Egypt and Syria were struck by financial crises as the Mamluks faced bankruptcy.

Matters became somewhat confused during the next several years as the Safavids under Shah Ismail, who had just extended their realm to the Persian Gulf, were not at all pleased to see the Portuguese in a dominant position there. Thus, when Ismail demanded payment of the annual tribute owed to him by the ruler of Hormuz, Saif ad-Din, the latter appealed to the Portuguese for instructions as to how to respond. Albuquerque replied that "the Kingdom of Ormuz belonged to the King of Portugal, gained by his fleet and his men, and that he might know of a certainty that if any tribute should be paid to any other King, except the King Dom Manoel, his lord, he would take the government of the Kingdom and give it to some one who would not be afraid of Xeque (Shah) Ismael."[4] Nonetheless, Ismail proposed to facilitate the resupply of the Portuguese fleet in exchange for Portugal's support against the Ottomans.

The sultan responded to Ismail's initiative, in January 1511, by sending aid to the Mamluks in the form of arms and technical assistance for the rebuilding of their Red Sea fleet. He hoped to use the Mamluks to offset the growing European presence in the southern maritime frontier of the region. The Mamluks viewed this as a mixed blessing because they correctly surmised that Selim's purpose was to help preserve their empire only until he was prepared to make a grab for it himself. Accordingly, despite their avowed antipathy to the sectarian regime in Persia, the Mamluks sought to maintain a reasonable semblance of neutrality in the Ottoman-Safavid conflict. Selim thus soon came to believe that the time was becoming ripe to deal with the Mamluks decisively, that is, as soon as he succeeded in consolidating Ottoman control over eastern Anatolia.

In the spring of 1515, Selim undertook a major campaign in eastern Anatolia, the first fruit of which was the conquest of the strategically important fort of Kemah, which controlled the line of communication between Sivas and Erzerum. This raised eyebrows not only in Tabriz but in Cairo and Dulgadir as well. The Ottoman move was perceived as a strategic threat to all three states, impelling them to join forces in an anti-Ottoman alliance, even though none of them were prepared to risk an open challenge to the Ottoman advance. Selim next directed his attention to the weakest of his enemies, Dulgadir. By exploiting a quarrel between the ruler of Dulgadir, Ali Daulat, and his nephew, to whom the sultan had given his support, Selim was able to decisively defeat the army of Dulgadir at Turna Dagh in Albistan on June 12, 1515. The absorption of Dulgadir into the empire gave the Ottomans effective control of Cilicia and its Mediterranean ports, and placed them in a good position to move against the Mamluks in Syria.

To alter the regional balance of power further in his favor before beginning his drive southward, Selim also sought to gain control of Kurdistan, the region between Lake Urmia and the northern Euphrates. With eastern Anatolia and Kurdistan in Ottoman hands, Selim would be in control of the principal strategic passes leading from Anatolia into Syria, Persia, and the Caucasus, as well as in a position to dominate the overland international trade routes linking Persia and the Orient to the West. Not only would the latter serve as new sources of revenue for the Ottoman treasury, but also they would place the sultan in a position to choke off the lucrative Persian silk trade with Europe and to cut off the Mamluks from their primary sources of manpower in the Caucasus. Selim, however, was reluctant to attempt the direct conquest of Kurdistan, which would have demanded a greater commitment of troops and resources than he could afford to invest in the project at the time. He therefore sought to rely on diplomacy to achieve his aims.

The Kurdish chiefs had earlier accepted Safavid suzerainty. However, since Ismail's defeat at Chaldiran, the significance of this formality became questionable since the Sunnite Kurds increasingly asserted their independence once they perceived Safavid power as beginning to decline. By offering financial and military support to the Kurdish chiefs, Selim was able to obtain their shift of allegiance from the Safavids to the Ottomans. Although the Ottomans had discontinued vassalage elsewhere in the region in favor of direct annexation, at least for the moment Selim was satisfied merely to extend his suzerainty over the Kurdish districts. The most important immediate consideration for him was the ability to contain the Safavids while he was engaged with the Mamluks to the south.

In anticipation of an impending invasion by the Ottomans, the Mamluk sultan Qansuh al-Ghori (1501–1516) dispatched an army to Aleppo in October 1515. In the meanwhile, the governor of Aleppo, Hayir Bey, as well as other Mamluk leaders, had already been in contact with the Ottomans to whom they indicated a readiness to cooperate against the Mamluk sultan in exchange for promises of high position under a successor regime. On July 28, 1516, Selim finally invaded Mamluk territory near Malatya in southern Anatolia, where local resistance quickly disintegrated. He then continued his march southward and soon confronted the Mamluk army at

Marj Dabiq, near Aleppo, on August 24. Although the Mamluks initially seemed to be holding their own against the superior Ottoman forces, their front soon collapsed as Hayir Bey, who commanded the Mamluk left flank, suddenly withdrew from the battlefield, probably as a consequence of his collusion with the Ottomans. Aleppo fell four days later, followed by Hama on September 19 and Damascus on September 27, in each instance without offering any effective resistance.

It appears that Selim was anxious to return to the north after the conquest of Syria. He seems to have been reluctant to be absent for any extended periods. Presumably, this was the result of a reasonable concern that his protracted absence from the Ottoman heartland might encourage renewed instability on his European and Persian frontiers. Accordingly, he was prepared to reach an accommodation with the new Mamluk sultan, Toman Bey (1516–1517), that would leave the latter as governor of the Mamluk territories south of Gaza under Ottoman suzerainty. Syria and Palestine as far south as Gaza was to become a province under direct Ottoman administration. These terms were conveyed to Toman Bey in mid-November 1516 with the warning: "If you do not submit, I will come to Egypt and kill all the Turks [Mamluks], and rip up the belly of every pregnant woman."[5] Toman Bey was prepared to accept the Ottoman terms, but his emirs were not, and so the war continued.

The Ottomans subsequently took Gaza on December 22, 1516, and continued their drive toward Egypt. Between January 11–16, 1517, the Ottoman army crossed the Sinai desert with all of its canon and heavy equipment, a remarkable feat for the time, and prepared for an invasion of Egypt. Heavily outnumbered by the Selim's forces, Toman Bey assembled all the forces he could muster at Raidaniyya, which commanded the road from Sinai to Cairo, to attempt to block the Ottoman advance. But it proved of little avail. The Ottomans easily outflanked and then overwhelmed the Mamluk positions on January 22. They inflicted a decisive defeat on the Mamluks, who lost most of their remaining forces, some 25,000 troops, in the battle. Selim entered Cairo on January 26 after three days of heavy fighting in the city. Although Toman Bey began a guerrilla war in the Nile delta and in Upper Egypt, which lasted until his capture and execution on April 13, 1517, the Mamluk Empire had essentially been brought to an end.

Once it was clear that Egypt was firmly in Ottoman hands, Selim soon received assurances of loyalty from the chiefs of the major Bedouin tribes of the Arabian Peninsula and, on July 3, from the sharif of Mecca. This gave the Ottomans effective control of the holy cities of Islam without the need to take them by force, and prepared the ground for the subsequent claim of the sultan to the dormant caliphate.

When Selim died on September 2, 1520, he left to his successor an empire, with its capital at Istanbul, which included virtually all of the Middle East except for Persia, Khorasan, and part of Iraq, which remained under

Safavid control. He also had begun construction of a new and powerful fleet, which he had intended to use to facilitate Ottoman expansion into the western Mediterranean against both the Spanish Hapsburgs and the French, as well as to break through the Portuguese blockade of the Red Sea and Persian Gulf ports.

NOTES

1. Caterino Zeno, "Travels in Persia," in *Travels of Venetians in Persia*, p. 61.
2. D. Ayalon, *Gunpowder and Firearms in the Mamluk Kingdom*, p. 109.
3. Roger Savory, *Iran under the Safavids*, p. 45.
4. Albuquerque's *Commentaries*, cited in Arnold T. Wilson, *The Persian Gulf*, p. 117.
5. John B. Glubb, *Soldiers of Fortune: The Story of the Mamlukes*, p. 432.

19

The Era of Suleiman the Magnificent

Suleiman (1520–1566), Selim's heir and successor, was able to pick up where his father left off without encountering the typical delays caused by the need to consolidate his domestic position first. His accession to the Ottoman throne was uncontested. Nonetheless, he quickly deferred any plans for the conquest of Persia, which, with Ismail still reeling from the disaster at Chaldiran, did not constitute any immediate threat to the eastern frontiers of the empire. He turned instead toward Europe, where political developments in Hungary had already commanded Selim's attention and now became Suleiman's primary foreign policy concern.

Hungary, under the rule of Louis II (1516–1526) who was also king of Bohemia, was undergoing internal political convulsions that made it a tempting target for external intervention. The feudal nobility was challenging the king for effective control of the country. Louis' sister Anna was married to Archduke Ferdinand I of Austria (1521–1564), the brother and successor of the Hapsburg emperor Charles V (1519–1558), and there was significant dissent in the country over the extent of Hapsburg influence. Finally, John Zapolya, prince of Transylvania, organized a national movement that was opposed both to Louis and the feudal nobility. It appeared that Hungary was a likely candidate for Hapsburg expansionism, and Suleiman was determined to bring it under Ottoman control instead.

To prepare the ground for a thrust northward, Suleiman first launched a campaign to eliminate the last of the Christian enclaves in Serbia and Bosnia. Belgrade finally fell to the Ottomans on August 8, 1520, providing them with a wedge into the Danube defense line of Christian Europe. Nonetheless, the Ottoman invasion of Hungary was delayed for several years because of the sultan's need to deal with a number of other pressing problems. First among these was the final disposition of Rhodes, which continued to exist as a Christian bastion within the Ottoman sphere of control in the Aegean and eastern Mediterranean. The heavily fortified island served as a base for pirates that plundered the commercial fleets bringing gold and grain from the new Ottoman acquisitions in the region, as well as the ships carrying pilgrims en route to and from the holy cities in Arabia. Rhodes also represented a strategic threat to the security of the Ottoman lines of sea communications in the Aegean, and had to be dealt with before Suleiman could renew his expansionist drive in Europe.

Rhodes was placed under siege by a large expeditionary force in the summer of 1522, and it was finally forced to capitulate on December 20 of that year, after months of heavy fighting. The terms of surrender were quite generous; in fact, from an Ottoman perspective, they were ultimately to prove to have been rather counterproductive. All those who wished to leave the island were permitted to do so, and the Knights were also allowed to take their weapons and other property with them. The latter were transported on papal ships to Malta, where they established a new bastion against Ottoman expansion. Thus, while Suleiman assured the security of the Ottoman lines of communications in the eastern Mediterranean, he unintentionally increased the threat to Ottoman interests in the central Mediterranean region.

Suleiman was prevented for some time from following up on his conquest of Rhodes with a new campaign in Europe because of a number of problems that had arisen in the newly acquired Mamluk territories. Revolts had broken out in Syria and Egypt, and Suleiman evidently accorded these a higher priority, probably because these territories were already Muslim and a successful revolt could have had negative consequences for the cohesiveness of the empire. The successful suppression of these rebellions kept him preoccupied for several years.

Finally, in the spring of 1526, Suleiman launched his invasion of Hungary. The internal situation in the country had not improved any in the intervening years, and Louis II was therefore prevented from organizing an adequate defense of the country. A decisive battle between the Ottoman and Hungarian forces took place on the plain of Mohacs, south of Buda, on August 29, 1526. The poorly organized Hungarians were no match for their antagonists. Most of the Hungarian army was destroyed and Louis was killed while attempting to flee. Buda and Pest fell ten days later, and Suleiman was in effective control of Hungary. However, he was prevented from occupying and annexing the country at the time because of several revolts that had erupted in Anatolia while he was engaged in the Hungarian campaign. Safavid propaganda and the increasing turbulence along the Ottoman-Safavid frontier helped trigger these outbreaks.

Ismail died on May 23, 1524, and was succeeded as shah of Persia by Tahmasp (1524–1576), a ten-year-old. However, no sooner did the latter mount the throne than the country was shaken by an internal power struggle that led to the outbreak of a civil war in the spring of 1526 that threatened to spill over into Ottoman territory. Since Suleiman did not have the resources to occupy a territory as large and volatile as Hungary and simultaneously deal with serious problems elsewhere in Europe and Asia, he was prepared to reach an accommodation with regard to the status of Hungary. Accordingly, on September 24, 1526, he accepted the offer of John Zapolya of Transylvania to rule Hungary as an Ottoman vassal. Having concluded this arrangement, Suleiman withdrew his army from Hungary, leaving behind only a few small garrisons to guard the southern approaches to Ottoman territory.

While Suleiman was engaged in quelling the major revolt in Anatolia led by Kalender Chelebi, who was finally defeated and killed on June 22, 1527, the Hapsburgs were preparing to overturn the settlement that the Ottomans had imposed on Hungary. The Hungarian nobles who leaned toward the Hapsburgs encouraged Archduke Ferdinand of Austria, who had become king of Bohemia upon the death of Louis II who had no heir, to occupy the northern and western parts of their country. John Zapolya, who had effectively repudiated Ottoman suzerainty by becoming king of Hungary on September 16, 1527, sought help from Sigismund I (1506–1548) of Poland. While the latter was prevented from responding quickly because of a division of opinion on the question among his nobles, Ferdinand defeated Zapolya at Tokay on September 26, 1527, and occupied most of Hungary. Even though the existing Ottoman garrisons prevented him from taking control of the southern part of the country, Ferdinand proclaimed himself king of Hungary on December 17.

At this point, Zapolya turned to Suleiman once again, and by an agreement of February 28, 1528, Zapolya reaffirmed his acknowledgment of Ottoman suzerainty. In return, Suleiman agreed to drive the Hapsburgs out of the country. The sultan was still not in a position to undertake the direct occupation of Hungary and was quite prepared to settle for having an autonomous vassal state serve as a buffer between the Ottoman and Hapsburg empires. Suleiman's second invasion of Hungary began in the summer of 1528. It took a year of campaigning before he was able to seize Buda once again on September 3, 1529. He then crossed the frontier into Austria and laid siege to Vienna on September 27. His apparent purpose was either to capture Ferdinand's capital, or at least to seriously disrupt the Hapsburg defense system. He clearly wanted to prevent the Hapsburgs from consolidating their position in Hungary, looking forward to a time when the Ottomans would be able to maintain effective direct control of the country. However, Suleiman's plans began to go awry when he found himself unable to break into Vienna before the winter set in. Bogged down outside the Hapsburg capital, the Ottoman army was beset by severe supply and communications problems that made it difficult for Suleiman to keep his troops in the field until the campaign could be resumed in the spring. It was simply too risky to have the bulk of his army tied down in Austria, with the main supply base as far away as Istanbul, and thereby rendering it unavailable for redeployment to respond to other needs that might arise in Europe or Asia. Suleiman decided to break off the siege of Vienna for the winter and return to Istanbul, from where he could deploy his forces in whatever direction circumstances dictated.

It appears that Suleiman was ready to acknowledge that he had reached the effective limit of Ottoman expansion into central Europe, and that he was prepared to be satisfied with the perpetuation of the situation there as it now stood. But such a stabilization of relations was prevented by Ferdinand's refusal to drop his claim to the Hungarian throne and his seizure of Buda in December 1530. Suleiman evidently felt a need to respond in kind, and he launched a major campaign against the Hapsburgs in the summer of 1532. From the size of the army that Suleiman committed to the project, estimated by some to have been as large as 300,000 men, it seems clear that the sultan was determined to smash the Hapsburg army and establish unquestioned Ottoman supremacy in central Europe. However, the Hapsburgs succeeded in thwarting such an outcome by avoiding pitched battles with the powerful Ottoman forces. As Suleiman vainly scoured the Hungarian countryside in search of the Hapsburg army, his timetable became completely upset as winter set in before he had accomplished any of the aims of the campaign.

Once again, the effective practical limits of Ottoman expansion had been demonstrated, and Suleiman, always realistic and pragmatic, was now prepared to reach an accommodation with the Hapsburgs over Hungary. Under the terms of the agreement of June 1533, mediated by Poland, Ferdinand agreed to recognize Suleiman's suzerainty over Hungary and to pay him an annual tribute. Furthermore, the Hapsburgs were to relinquish virtually all the territory they held in Hungary, except for the border regions occupied by them since the original Ottoman conquest. Although Suleiman had failed to achieve the annexation of Hungary, the peace settlement left the sultan with a friendly buffer state between the Ottoman and Hapsburg empires and enabled him to redirect his attention to unfinished business in Asia.

Although the Ottomans were now the masters of the eastern Mediterranean and most of the Middle East, they were unable to reap the full benefits of their dominant position. Safavid control of Persia and Iraq enabled the shah to interfere with the overland trade routes between Europe and East Asia, at the same time that the Portuguese were still diverting traffic from Ottoman ports to the southern sea route around Africa. In effect, the Ottoman Empire was being subjected to a virtual and intolerable economic blockade. In addition, Safavid religious militancy generated pressures on Suleiman, in his role as preeminent leader of the orthodox Sunnite Muslim world, to take action against the spread of Shiite beliefs and practices, which were widely considered to be heretical.

Safavid military activism along the Ottoman frontier also resulted in the defection of the khan of Bitlis, south of Lake Van, and the defeat of the Ottoman troops who had attempted to seize the town. To make matters worse, the governor of Baghdad, who had just recently pledged his allegiance to Suleiman, had been murdered and the city was returned to Safavid control.

Ibrahim Pasha, the Ottoman grand vizier, had been advocating a campaign against Persia for years but could not convince Suleiman to take action while the Safavid Empire was still in a state of disarray as a result of the civil conflict that erupted over the succession to the Persian throne. After the last two incidents, however, Suleiman became determined to march against the Safavids. Within three months after the 1533 peace agreement with the Hapsburgs, advance elements of Suleiman's army, under the command of Ibrahim Pasha, were on the march in Asia.

Coincidentally, the year 1533 also marked the end of the civil war in Persia and the reassertion of royal authority by Tahmasp, who ended a decade of rule by his qizilbash regents and advisers. During that time, Persia had been challenged in the east repeatedly by the Uzbeks, who invaded Khorasan from Central Asia five times in the preceding ten years. Now, with the country unified under Tahmasp's centralized control for the first time in a decade, the shah marched into Herat in the fall of 1533 in preparation for an invasion of Transoxiana, where he hoped to complete the decisive defeat of the Uzbeks. As he was preparing for this expedition, Tahmasp received the alarming news that the Ottomans were attacking his positions far to the west. He quickly abandoned his plans for the conquest of Transoxiana to deal with the mortal threat to the Safavid state posed by the sultan's armies. However, as a practical matter, Tahmasp was not yet in a position to mobilize an effective defense against the Ottoman onslaught.

Ibrahim Pasha quickly seized control of the region between Erzerum and Lake Van in October 1533 in preparation for an invasion of Azerbaijan. Suleiman left Istanbul in June 1534 and marched into central Persia as far as Sultaniye. Contrary to Suleiman's expectations, Tahmasp chose to sacrifice territory in order to avoid the risks of a decisive battle. After a brief defense of the city, Tahmasp evacuated his capital at Tabriz, which Ibrahim took on July 13, 1534, and withdrew into the Persian interior while his forces continued to harass the Ottomans with devastating effect. Tahmasp could ill afford to gamble with what forces he had in an effort to defeat the Ottomans while he was under attack in the east once again by the Uzbeks.

Under the leadership of Ubaid Allah Khan, who had earlier seized Herat, the Uzbeks now intensified their attacks as the Safavid armies were shifted to Azerbaijan to deal with the Ottoman advance into the heart of the country. Tahmasp adopted the stratagem of drawing the Ottoman armies ever deeper into Persia, stretching thin their lines of communications while he carried out a scorched earth policy that denied them the ability to live off the land. This left Suleiman, who joined forces with Ibrahim in the fall of 1534, with the prospect of having to conduct a winter campaign without adequate supplies, something he clearly preferred to avoid if there were any alternative. As it turned out, the sultan decided to withdraw from Persia across the Zagros and to march southward into Iraq, where he anticipated spending an easier winter in the field. Suleiman easily took Baghdad, where a popular revolt against the Safavid occupation had broken out at his approach to the city, and then swept through the rest of Iraq, meeting with only minor opposition before winter set in, effectively bringing the campaigning season to an end.

When military operations were renewed in the spring of 1535, the results were disappointing for the Ottomans. They clashed inconclusively with the Safavids a number of times in the rough terrain between Kurdistan and the Armenian highlands. Unable to lure Tahmasp into a pitched battle, and unwilling to engage in a long-term positional campaign of attrition, Suleiman had to be satisfied with having added most of Iraq and Kurdistan to the Ottoman Empire, and he had to forego his goal of destroying the Safavid armies and conquering Persia. He withdrew from Tabriz at the end of August 1535 to direct his attention once again to the expansion of the empire in the west. As a consequence, the shah managed to retain a hold on parts of eastern Iraq, Azerbaijan, and the southern Caucasus, which remained the effective frontiers between the Ottoman and Persian empires into modern times.

Suleiman spent the next decade conducting a series of inconclusive campaigns in central Europe and the central Mediterranean that reconfirmed the idea that the Ottoman Empire, for all practical purposes, had reached its outer limits. Indeed, it would take all of Suleiman's efforts and resources to retain control of the territories that had been incorporated into the empire.

Relations between Suleiman and the Hapsburg emperor Ferdinand had become strained as a result of a series of cross-border raids that had taken place in Bosnia and Croatia. Suleiman's Hungarian vassal, John Zapolya, became concerned that the deteriorating situation might lead to an Ottoman intervention in Hungary that would jeopardize his position. Zapolya therefore entered into an agreement with Ferdinand in February 1538 that was calculated to prevent this from happening. Unmarried and childless, and thus without an heir to his throne, Zapolya agreed to will all of Hungary to Ferdinand in return for his commitment to assist Zapolya in the event of an Ottoman attack.

This unanticipated development clearly ran counter to the interests of Sigismund of Poland, who had his own ambitions in Hungary. Accordingly, he quickly arranged for the marriage of his daughter Isabella to the Hungarian king, a union that soon produced an heir, Sigismund Janos. Now concerned about preserving the throne of Hungary for his son, Zapolya repudiated the agreement that he had made with Ferdinand in 1538. He turned to both Suleiman and Sigismund for assurances that they would oppose any attempt by the Hapsburgs to implement the agreement, which the latter continued to consider as valid and binding.

Upon the death of Zapolya on August 22, 1540, Ferdinand declared the Hungarian heir to be illegitimate and invaded the country, occupying Pest. To assuage Ottoman concerns about this development, he proposed that Suleiman retain nominal suzerainty over Hungary but that Ferdinand should rule the country as an Ottoman vassal. It was a novel proposal, but Suleiman would have no part of it. The sultan simply would not countenance any expansion of Hapsburg power on his frontiers and, to make this point crystal clear, he invaded Hungary the following year and drove the Austrians out. This time Suleiman decided to annex the country rather than run the risk of the turmoil that was likely to accompany the accession of the infant Zapolya heir to the throne. The Hapsburgs did not take their discomfiture in Hungary lightly and continued the attempt to reassert their influence in the country. This led to a renewal of hostilities with the Ottomans in 1542 and 1543, and the subsequent Turkish conquest of most of the remaining Hapsburg enclaves in Hungary as well as in Slavonia. Although Suleiman was now positioned for another assault on Vienna, he had no wish to risk a repetition of his earlier experience in Austria and chose to resist the temptation of further expansion; he was satisfied merely to consolidate his grip on Hungary. An Ottoman-Hapsburg truce was concluded on November 10, 1545. It confirmed the situation as it was at the time and also incorporated mutual pledges of non-belligerence by the parties to the agreement. The truce was subsequently transformed into a permanent peace agreement on June 13, 1547.

With his frontiers in Europe stabilized, and after having spent several years working on the internal development and restructuring of the Ottoman state, Suleiman was free once again to attempt to deal with the lingering Safavid threat once and for all time. The moment seemed especially propitious since quarrels had broken out within the ruling family and Tahmasp's brother, Alqas Mirza, had taken refuge in Ottoman territory in 1547. Suleiman hoped to exploit these internal problems to seize the Caucasus and Azerbaijan, opening the way to the heart of Persia. However, Tahmasp once again adopted the strategy he had employed so successfully in 1534, and withdrew into the interior, putting Azerbaijan to the torch in the process. Thus, although the Ottomans were able to occupy the province without difficulty, it gave them little comfort. Again faced by a harsh winter in Azerbaijan without adequate supplies, Suleiman withdrew to Aleppo in November 1548. The following June he once again marched into Safavid territory but was still unable to lure Tahmasp into a decisive battle. After the pretender Alqas Mirza fell into the shah's hands, Suleiman gave up all hope of supplanting Tahmasp. He returned to Istanbul at the end of 1549 with little to show for his efforts beyond a few Georgian forts and Van, which he fortified as a bulwark against any future Safavid attempt at expansion into Anatolia.

Although Suleiman's primary attention was again drawn to Europe, where the conflict with the Hapsburgs erupted once more in 1548 over Transylvania followed by the Mediterranean War, which lasted from 1551 to 1562, consolidation of the Ottoman position in the Middle East continued unabated. In 1538 an Ottoman fleet from Suez succeeded in capturing Aden, from which Suleiman hoped to contest the Portuguese blockade of his southern ports. Aden also became the key to the penetration and conquest of the Yemen, with Sana falling to the Ottomans in 1547. That same year Basra and southern Iraq, which had acknowledged Ottoman suzerainty since 1539 but continued to be ruled by local Bedouin chiefs, came under direct Ottoman administration. A new Persian Gulf fleet was constructed that, in conjunction with the Red Sea fleet, posed a challenge to continued Portuguese hegemony in the coastal region. However, the expansion of Ottoman power in the region drove the local Arab chiefs along the gulf to seek the support of the Portuguese who had established strong positions at Hormuz and Muscat, enabling them to control passage into the Persian Gulf. Their confrontation with the Portuguese ended badly for the Ottomans, whose attempt to wrest control of the gulf from Portugal floundered after they experienced a major maritime defeat off Hormuz on August 25, 1554. Farther west, however, Ottoman control of the Red Sea enabled them to break the Portuguese blockade and partially restore Egypt's position as an entrepôt for the oriental trade destined for the Mediterranean region and western Europe.

The Ottoman-Safavid frontier had remained relatively quiet for several years, but the equilibrium was shattered in 1553 by the provocations of Iskandar Pasha, governor of Van and afterward of Erzerum, who mounted raids against Khvuy and Erivan, precipitating another Ottoman-Safavid war. This time, Tahmasp did not wait for the expected Ottoman attack and took the initiative himself. He trapped and soundly defeated Iskandar Pasha outside Erzerum. This brought Suleiman east to Nakhichevan to confront Tahmasp the following summer, only to find that the shah had withdrawn to the mountains of Luristan after having put the region to the torch once again. For the third frustrating time Suleiman found himself unable to engage Tahmasp in a decisive battle, as well as unable to keep his army in the field because of the lack of provisions. Faced simultaneously with an internal revolt in Macedonia that soon spread to Thrace, and which later developed into a virtual civil war between prospective heirs to the Ottoman throne, Suleiman finally agreed to conclude peace with the Safavids. He signed a peace treaty at Amasya on May 29, 1555 (reconfirmed in 1562), that was to have a somewhat erratic record of compliance.

After Suleiman's return from his expedition against the Safavids the external situation of the Ottoman Empire remained generally stabilized for a decade. In 1566, however, new frontier problems with the Hapsburgs arose in central Europe and Suleiman emerged from relative retirement to personally lead the Ottoman armies once again. However, the aging sultan fell ill while on the march and died on September 7, 1566. The campaign was successfully concluded, nonetheless, under the leadership of his capable grand vizier Sokullu Mehmed, who succeeded in capturing the last of the important Hapsburg strongholds in northern Hungary.

During Suleiman's long reign, the frontiers of the Ottoman Empire were extended to include Rhodes and the most important Aegean islands, Hungary and Transylvania, Algiers and Tripoli, Iraq and Yemen, part of Georgia, and eastern Anatolia from Van to Ardahan. The sultan also transformed the Ottoman state into a major naval power, successfully challenging Portugal in the western Indian Ocean and the Hapsburgs in the Mediterranean. Under Suleiman's leadership, the Ottoman Empire reached its zenith.

20

The End of Islamic Ascendancy

None of Suleiman's successors proved worthy of the legacy bequeathed by the sultan appropriately named "the Magnificent." The first of these, Selim II "the Sot" (1566–1574), mounted the throne without challenge since he had succeeded in eliminating his brother Bayezid four years earlier with the assistance of the Safavids. Bayezid, who was seeking Persian assistance in his long struggle with Selim in anticipation of the forthcoming succession to the Ottoman throne, was killed in Persia on July 23, 1562, with the collusion of Tahmasp. Since the shah had little to gain from any direct intervention in the conflict, which had developed into a veritable civil war that kept the Ottomans preoccupied and therefore served his interests, it seems quite evident that his cooperation commanded a significant price from Selim. Thus, it appears that Selim, in addition to his reconfirmation of the Treaty of Amasya, also promised to turn over Kars and some other territories to Tahmasp. This was in addition to a one-time payment to the shah of some 400,000 pieces of gold, a commitment that was fulfilled soon after Selim became sultan. The very manner by which Selim reached the throne earned him many domestic enemies, and he proceeded to deal with this problem through the lavish use of bribery. He thereby established a pattern of expectations that seriously eroded the internal discipline of the regime, and undermined its capacity to maintain the territorial integrity of the far-flung empire against the several forces that worked to tear it apart.

The first serious challenge to Selim's dominion came in the Yemen, where Ottoman rule had never been fully established in the interior of the country. That region had come under the control of the indigenous Zeydis, who were "Fivers," that is, proponents of a form of Shiism that involved the fifth imam, Zeyd ibn Ali. Suleiman had divided the Yemen into two provinces for the purpose of improving the administration of the territory, a move that had the unanticipated consequence of also dividing the Ottoman forces there and making it more difficult for them to meet a serious challenge to Turkish control of the country. On August 16, 1567, shortly after Selim came into power, the Zeydis succeeded in wresting Sana from the Ottomans and then swept down along the coast to conquer Aden, posing a threat to Ottoman control of the Red Sea. It was only after Selim ordered the reunification of the Yemeni provinces in April 1568 under the Circassian governor of Aleppo, Ozdemiroglu Osman Pasha, that he succeeded in driving the Zeydis back into their mountain strongholds, which remained outside the Ottoman sphere of control.

Then, with the situation on the Hapsburg frontier relatively stable for the moment, Sokullu Mehmed, who remained in the regime as Selim's grand vizier, pressed the sultan to take steps to deal with the emerging threat from the northeast. Under Ivan IV "the Terrible" (1533–1584), the Russians had begun a major expansion eastward and southward along a front stretching from the Ural Mountains to the Black Sea. They subdued most of the remaining independent Tatar khanates in the region, and were using the Cossacks to conduct a guerrilla campaign against both the Ottomans and their Crimean Tatar vassals, as they drove toward the Black Sea, the Caucasus, and the Caspian Sea. Ivan's forces had taken Kazan in 1552 and Astrakhan at the mouth of the Volga four years later. Sokullu Mehmed wanted to counter the growing Russian threat by conquering Astrakhan and using it as the hub of a fortified forward defense system to block any further Russian advance.

The Ottoman grand vizier, showing a rare flair for strategic thinking, also wanted to build a canal between the Don and Volga Rivers, which would effectively link the Black and Caspian Seas. By these means, not only would the Russian threat be thwarted but the Ottoman forces also would be placed in a position to drive the Persians out of the Caucasus and Azerbaijan. In addition, the canal would provide for easier communications between the Crimean Tatars and the Uzbeks on Persia's eastern flank in Transoxiana, and it would facilitate coordination of simultaneous assaults on the Safavids. Finally, it might permit the restoration of the old northern caravan routes to Central Asia, perhaps allowing some of the oriental overland trade to bypass Persia entirely.

It was, by any measure, a bold strategic plan and Selim embraced it. He put it into effect by mounting a major expedition northward in the summer of 1570. The initiative failed, however, both because the Ottoman commanders failed to assure adequate supplies for the difficult campaign and because of the eventual defection of the Crimean Tatars from the enterprise. It seems that Russian propaganda succeeded in convincing them that Selim's success would only further tighten the Ottoman grip on their territories, a not unreasonable argument. Nonetheless, the same Crimean Tatars effectively blocked the Russian advance in the southeast toward the Black Sea. By 1572, the Tatars succeeded in forcing the Russians out of Kabarda, north of the Caucasus. The Russians had penetrated the region as far as the Terek River and had tried to secure their position there by the marriage of Ivan to one of the daughters of the Kabardian chief, Temriuk. In the southwest the Russian advance was stymied by the strengthening of Ottoman influence in Moldavia, Wallachia, and Poland.

Selim also sought to make use of the powerful naval capability bequeathed to him by Suleiman and undertook a number of expansionist initiatives based on the use of the fleet. He seized Chios from Genoa in the Aegean and sent an expedition to Southeast Asia to assist the Muslims of Sumatra in their struggle against the Portuguese. Of greater significance, he also undertook the conquest of Cyprus from Venice, ostensibly because it was being used as a haven for Christian pirates who were raiding Ottoman shipping in the eastern Mediterranean. The island was invaded in May 1570, and was conquered within a year. In the meantime, Venice appealed for assistance to the other European powers and Pope Pius V proclaimed the organization of a Holy League to challenge the Ottomans. However, the pope received only the support of Genoa and Spain. Austria was unwilling to upset the peace it had just recently (1568) renewed with the Ottomans, and France would not jeopardize the lucrative financial agreements it had recently concluded with the Sublime Porte, as the chief executive and administrative center of the empire came to be known.

As early as 1536 the French entered into a trade agreement with the Ottomans, subsequently known as the Capitulations, that was modeled on earlier similar agreements between the Porte and the Genoese and Venetians. What was distinctive about the Capitulations agreement was that it gave French merchants and residents in Ottoman domains virtually complete immunity from Ottoman law in civil and criminal cases where no Ottoman subjects were directly involved. Instead, they came under the legal jurisdiction of the official French representative in Istanbul. This was a simple extension of the contemporary conception of sovereignty as extraterritorial, as relating to people rather than territory. That is, as the concept was reflected in the Capitulations, the king of the French had sovereign rights over Frenchmen outside the territorial boundaries of France. A new Capitulations agreement between France and the Ottoman state was signed on October 18, 1569, that provided additional benefits of considerable significance to the former. Specifically, the pact allowed for the free passage of French ships into Ottoman waters and ports and required other European vessels that wished to have the same privilege to fly the French flag. This effectively gave the French consular representatives at Istanbul the status of leaders of the European community within the Ottoman Empire. Under the circumstances, it is not surprising that France refused to join the pope's crusade on behalf of Venice.

Nonetheless, the Holy League was able to send a fleet to the eastern Mediterranean with the grandiose mission of liberating not only Cyprus, but also all Christian lands that had been conquered by the Ottomans. Under the leadership of Don Juan of Austria, the fleet arrived in the Aegean at the beginning of October 1571, just as the Ottoman fleet had returned from Cyprus to spend the winter at Lepanto on the Greek coast. With most of its complement already sent home for the winter, the Ottoman fleet was hardly prepared for a major naval engagement. Despite its poor state of readiness, it left the safety of the harbor to engage the Europeans and suffered a serious defeat on October 7. The battle of Lepanto marked the first time that the Ottomans had experienced defeat since the fifteenth century, and the event was celebrated in Europe as the beginning of the end of the Ottoman Empire.

The celebration, however, proved somewhat premature since the battle was by no means decisive. While the European powers were musing over the imminent re-conquest of Cyprus, to be followed by that of the Holy Land, Selim was busy rebuilding his fleet, making it even more powerful than it had been previously. With little prospect of an Ottoman collapse, and with Venice desperately in need of peace, the Holy League soon withdrew from the eastern Mediterranean. As a result, on March 7, 1573, Venice reluctantly signed a peace agreement with the Porte that acknowledged the permanent loss of Cyprus. Moreover, the treaty required an increase in the level of the annual Venetian tribute payments in exchange for continued trading privileges in the Ottoman Empire.

Upon the death of Selim in October 1574, and the succession to the throne of Murad III (1574–1595) the character of the Ottoman regime took a dramatic turn for the worse. The new sultan was inclined to engage in debauchery, and the power of the sultanate became the object of sharp contention between two parties, one connected to the sultan's mother and daughter, the latter being the wife of Sokullu Mehmed, who continued to serve Murad as grand vizier. The second party was tied to the sultan's wife. Nonetheless, at least for a time, Sokullu Mehmed was able to continue to carry out his well-tested policy of maintaining the existing balance of power with the empire's principal enemies.

Following the era of Suleiman the Magnificent, the Ottoman Empire began to slip into seemingly irreversible decline, even though it was still to take some years before this became fully evident. Coincident with Ottoman decline came the end of the millennium-long political ascendancy of the Islamic world that was so tightly linked to it.

Bibliography

The following is a list of references and secondary sources consulted in the preparation of this book. Because this is primarily a work of synthesis from a geopolitical perspective, I have drawn on the scholarly expertise of numerous authors for the bits of information pieced together here to form a geopolitical mosaic.

Ali, Maulana M. *Early Caliphate*. Lahore, Pak.: Ahmadiyya Anjuman Isha'at Islam, 1947.

———. *Religion of Islam: A Comprehensive Discussion of the Sources, Principles and Practices of Islam*. Lahore, Pak.: Ahmadiyya Anjuman Isha'at Islam, 1983.

Ali, Syed Ameer. *A Short History of the Saracens*. London: Macmillan, 1961.

Allen, William E. D. *Problems of Turkish Power in the Sixteenth Century*. London: Central Asian Research Centre, 1963.

Allsen, Thomas T. *Mongol Imperialism: The Policies of the Grand Qan Mongke in China, Russia, and the Islamic Lands*. Berkeley: University of California Press, 1987.

Amedroz, H. F and D. S. Margoliouth, eds. *The Eclipse of the Abbasid Caliphate: Original Chronicles of the Fourth Islamic Century*. 7 vols. London: Basil Blackwell, 1921.

Amitai-Preuss, Reuven. *Mongols and Mamluks: The Mamluk-Ilkhanid War, 1260–1281*. Cambridge: Cambridge University Press, 1995.

Angold, Michael. *The Byzantine Empire, 1025–1204*. London: Longman, 1984.

Arab Historians of the Crusades. Slected and translated by Francesco Gabrielli. Berkeley: University of California Press, 1969.

Arjomand, Said A. *The Shadow of God and the Hidden Imam*. Chicago: University of Chicago Press, 1984.

Arnold, Thomas W. *The Caliphate*. New York: Barnes & Noble, 1966.

Atiya, Aziz S. *The Crusade in the Later Middle Ages*. 2nd ed. New York: Kraus Reprint, 1965.

Ayalon, D. *Gunpowder and Firearms in the Mamluk Kingdom.* London: Valentine, Mitchell, 1956.

Babinger, Franz. *Mehmed the Conqueror and His Time.* Princeton: Princeton University Press, 1978.

al-Baladhuri. *Kitab Futuh al-Buldan.* Translated by Philip K. Hitti, *The Origins of the Islamic State.* New York: Columbia University Press, 1916. Reprinted Beirut: Khayats, 1966.

Belyaev, E. A. Arabs, *Islam and the Arab Caliphate in the Early Middle Ages.* New York: Praeger, 1969.

Benvenisti, Meron. *The Crusaders in the Holy Land.* Jerusalem: Israel Universities Press, 1970.

Blankenship, Khalid Yahya. *The End of the Jihad State: The Reign of Hisham Ibn Abd al-Malik and the Collapse of the Umayyads.* Albany, N.Y.: State University of New York Press, 1994.

Bosworth, Clifford E. *The Ghaznavids: Their Empire in Afghanistan and Eastern Iran 994–1040.* Edinburgh: Edinburgh University Press, 1963.

———. *The Islamic Dynasties.* Edinburgh: Edinburgh University Press, 1967.

Boyle, J. A., ed. *The Cambridge History of Iran.* Vol. 5. Cambridge: Cambridge University Press, 1968.

Bridge, Anthony. *Suleiman the Magnificent: Scourge of Heaven.* New York: Franklin Watts, 1983.

Brockelmann, Carl. *History of the Islamic Peoples.* New York: Capricorn Books, 1960.

Brockman, Eric. *The Two Sieges of Rhodes: The Knights of St. John at War 1480–1522.* New York: Barnes & Noble, 1995.

Bury, John B. *History of the Later Roman Empire.* Vol. 2. New York: Dover Publications, 1958.

Butler, Alfred J. *The Arab Conquest of Egypt.* 2nd ed. London: Oxford University Press, 1978.

Cahen, Claude. *Pre-Ottoman Turkey: A General Survey of the Material and Spiritual Culture and History c. 1071–1330.* London: Sidgwick & Jackson, 1968.

Cash, W. Wilson. *The Expansion of Islam: An Arab Religion in a Non-Arab World.* London: Church Missionary Society, 1928.

Chahin, M. *The Kingdom of Armenia.* London: Croom Helm, 1987.

Choniates, Niketas. *O City of Byzantium, Annals of Niketas Choniates.* Detroit: Wayne State University Press, 1984.

Cohen, Amnon and Gabriel Baer, eds. *Egypt and Palestine: A Millennium of Association (868–1948).* New York: St. Martin's Press, 1984.

Comnena, Anna. *The Alexiad of Anna Comnena.* London: Routledge and Kegan Paul, 1928.

Creasy, Edward S. *History of the Ottoman Turks: From the Beginning of Their Empire to the Present Time.* London: 1878. Reprinted Beirut: Khayats, 1961.

Dames, M. Longworth. "The Portuguese and Turks in the Sixteenth Century." *Journal of the Royal Asiatic Society* 1 (1921): 1–28.

Davis, William S. *A Short History of the Near East.* New York: Macmillan, 1943.

Dawson, C., ed. *Mission to Asia.* New York: Harper and Row, 1966.

Djevad Bey, Ahmed. *Etat militaire Ottoman depuis la fondation de l'empire jusqu'a nos jours.* Paris: E. Leroux, 1882.

Donner, Fred McGraw. *The Early Islamic Conquests*. Princeton, N.J.: Princeton University Press, 1981.

Doukas. *Decline and Fall of Byzantium to the Ottoman Turks*. An annotated translation of "Historia Turco-Byzantina" by Harry J. Magoulias. Detroit: Wayne State University Press, 1975.

Dunlop, D. M. *The History of the Jewish Khazars*. New York: Schocken Books, 1967.

Ehrenkreutz, Andrew S. *Saladin*. Albany, N.Y.: State University of New York Press, 1972.

Enan, Muhammad A. *Decisive Moments in the History of Islam*. Lahore, Pak.: Shuhammad Ashraf, 1943.

Eversley, Lord. *The Turkish Empire: From 1288 to 1914*. New York: Howard Fertig, 1969.

Finlay, George. *A History of Greece, from Its Conquest by the Romans to the Present Time, B.C. 146 to 1864*. Vol. 3. Oxford: Clarendon Press, 1877.

Fischer-Galati, Stephen A. *Ottoman Imperialism and German Protestantism 1521–1555*. Cambridge, Mass.: Harvard University Press, 1959.

Foord, Edward. *The Byzantine Empire*. London: Adam and Charles Black, 1911.

Franzius, Enno. *History of the Byzantine Empire: Mother of Nations*. New York: Funk & Wagnalls, 1967.

Freeman, Edward A. *The History and Conquests of the Saracens*. 3rd ed. London: Macmillan, 1877.

Fregosi, Paul. *Jihad in the West: Muslim Conquests from the 7th to the 21st Centuries*. Amherst, N.Y.: Prometheus Books, 1998.

Friendly, Alfred. *The Dreadful Day: The Battle of Manzikert, 1071*. London: Hutchinson, 1981.

Gabrieli, Francesco. *Muhammad and the Conquests of Islam*. New York: McGraw-Hill, 1968.

Gardner, Alice. *The Lascarids of Nicaea: The Story of an Empire in Exile*. London: Methuen, 1912. Reprinted Amsterdam: Adolf M. Hakkert, 1964.

Ghirshman, R. *Iran: From the Earliest Times to the Islamic Conquest*. Baltimore: Penguin Books, 1954.

Gibb, Hamilton A. R. *Saladin: Studies in Islamic History*. Beirut: Arab Institute for Research and Publishing, 1974.

Gibbon, Edward. *The History of the Decline and Fall of the Roman Empire*. Vols. 5–6. New York: Harper & Brothers, 1879.

——— . *The Rise and Fall of the Saracen Empire*. London: Frederick Warne, n.d.

Gibbons, Herbert Adams. *The Foundations of the Ottoman Empire: A History of the Osmanlis up to the Death of Bayezid I 1300–1403*. London: Frank Cass, 1968.

Glubb, John B. *The Empire of the Arabs*. London: Hodder and Stoughton, 1963.

——— . *The Great Arab Conquests*. Englewood Cliffs, N.J.: Prentice-Hall, 1964.

——— . *The Course of Empire: The Arabs and Their Successors*. Englewood Cliffs, N.J.: Prentice-Hall, 1966.

——— . *The Lost Centuries: From the Muslim Empires to the Renaissance of Europe 1145–1453*. Englewood Cliffs, N.J.: Prentice-Hall, 1967.

——— . *A Short History of the Arab Peoples*. New York: Dorset Press, 1969.

——— . *Soldiers of Fortune: The Story of the Mamlukes*. New York: Dorset Press, 1973.

Grousset, Rene. *The Empire of the Steppes: A History of Central Asia*. New Brunswick: Rutgers University Press, 1970.

————. *Histoire de l'Armenie: des origines a 1071*. Paris: Payot, 1973.

Grunebaum, G. E. von. *Classical Islam: A History 600 A.D.-1258 A.D.* Chicago: Aldine Publishing, 1970.

Har-El, Shai. *Struggle for Domination in the Middle East: The Ottoman-Mamluk War 1485–91*. Leiden, Neth.: E. J. Brill, 1995.

Head, Constance. *Imperial Twilight: The Palaiologos Dynasty and the Decline of Byzantium*. Chicago: Nelson-Hall, 1977.

Higgins, Martin J. *The Persian War of the Emperor Maurice (582–602)*. Washington: Catholic University of America Press, 1939.

Hindley, Geoffrey. *Saladin*. New York: Harper and Row, 1976.

Hinds, Martin. *Studies in Early Islamic History*. Princeton, N.J.: Darwin Press, 1996.

A History of the Crusades: The First Hundred Years. Edited by Marshall W. Baldwin. Philadelphia: University of Pennsylvania Press, 1955.

A History of the Crusades: The Later Crusades 1189–1311. Edited by Robert L. Wolf and Harry W. Hazard. Philadelphia: University of Pennsylvania Press, 1962.

Hitti, Philip K. *The Origins of the Islamic State*. Vol. 1. New York: Columbia University, 1916.

————. *History of Syria*. New York: Macmillan, 1951.

————. *The Near East in History*. Princeton: D. Van Nostrand, 1961.

————. *History of the Arabs*. 10th edition. New York: St. Martin's Press, 1970.

Holt, P. M., ed. *The Eastern Mediterranean Lands in the Period of the Crusades*. Warminster, England: Aris & Phillips, 1977.

————. *The Age of the Crusades: The Near East from the Eleventh Century to 1517*. New York: Longman, 1986.

Holt, P. M., Ann K. S. Lambton, and Bernard Lewis, eds. *The Cambridge History of Islam*. Vol. I. Cambridge: Cambridge University Press, 1970.

Hourani, Albert. *A History of the Arab Peoples*. Cambridge: Harvard University Press, 1991.

Humphreys, R. Stephen. *From Saladin to the Mongols: The Ayyubids of Damascus, 1193–1260*. Albany, N.Y.: State University of New York Press, 1977.

Inalcik, Halil. *The Ottoman Empire: The Classical Age 1300–1600*. New York: Praeger Publishers, 1973.

Irwin, Robert. *The Middle East in the Middle Ages: The Early Mamluk Sultanate 1250–1382*. London and Sydney: Croom Helm, 1986.

Itzkowitz, Norman. *Ottoman Empire and Islamic Tradition*. New York: Alfred A. Knopf, 1972.

Jandora, John W. *The March from Medina: A Revisionist Study of the Arab Conquests*. Clifton, N.J.: Kingston Press, 1990.

Jenkins, Hester D. *Ibrahim Pasha: Grand Vezir of Suleiman the Magnificent* (Dissertation). New York: Columbia University, 1911.

Juan de Persia. *Don Juan of Persia: A Shiah Catholic, 1560–1604*. New York: Harper, 1926.

Juvaini, Ala ad-Din Ata-Malik. *The History of the World-Conqueror*. 2 vols. Manchester: Manchester University Press, 1958.

Kaegi, Walter E. *Byzantium and the Early Islamic Conquests*. Cambridge: Cambridge University Press, 1992.

Kafesoglu, Ibrahim. *A History of the Seljuks: Ibrahim Kafesoglu's Interpretation and the Resulting Controversy*. Translated and edited by Gary Leiser. Carbondale and Edwardsville: Southern Illinois University Press, 1988.

Kann, Robert A. *A History of the Hapsburg Empire 1526–1918*. Berkeley: University of California Press, 1974.

Kennedy, Hugh. *The Early Abbasid Caliphate: A Political History*. London: Croom Helm, 1981.

——— . *The Prophet and the Age of the Caliphs: The Islamic Near East from the Sixth to the Eleventh Century*. London: Longman, 1986.

Khadduri, Majid. *The Islamic Law of Nations: Shaybani's Siyar*. Baltimore, Md.: Johns Hopkins University Press, 1966.

Khowaiter, Abdul-Aziz. *Baibars the First: His Endeavours and Achievements*. London: Green Mountain Press, 1978.

Kinnamos, John. *Deeds of John and Manuel Comnenus*. New York: Columbia University Press, 1976.

Koprulu, M. Fuad. *The Origins of the Ottoman Empire*. Albany, N.Y.: State University of New York Press, 1992.

Lamouche, Leon. *Histoire de la Turquie*. Paris: Payot, 1953.

Lane-Poole, Stanley. *The Mohammadan Dynasties*. Westminster: Archibald Constable, 1894.

——— . *Turkey*. New York: G. P. Putnam's Sons, 1899.

——— . *Medieval India under Mohammedan Rule 712–1764*. New York: G. P. Putnam's Sons, 1903.

——— . *Saladin and the Fall of the Kingdom of Jerusalem*. Beirut: Khayats, 1964.

Lang, David M. *Armenia: Cradle of Civilization*. London: George Allen & Unwin, 1970.

Langdon, John S. *Byzantium's Last Imperial Offensive in Asia Minor*. New Rochelle, N.Y.: Aristide D. Caratzas, 1992.

Lewis, Archibald R. *Naval Power and Trade in the Mediterranean, A.D. 500–1100*. Princeton: Princeton University Press, 1951.

Lewis, Bernard. *The Arabs in History*. New York: Harper and Brothers, 1960.

——— . *The Political Language of Islam*. Chicago: University of Chicago Press, 1988.

Maalouf, Amin. *The Crusades through Arab Eyes*. New York: Schocken Books, 1985.

Al-Makrizi. *A History of the Ayyubid Sultans of Egypt*. Boston: Twayne Publishers, 1980.

Malik, S. K. *Khalid bin Walid: The General of Islam*. Lahore, Pak.: Islamic Book Centre, 1968.

Manz, Beatrice Forbes. *The Rise and Rule of Tamerlane*. Cambridge: Cambridge University Press, 1989.

Mason, Herbert. *Two Statesmen of Medieval Islam*. The Hague, Neth.: Mouton, 1972.

Mayer, Hans Eberhard. *The Crusades*. London: Oxford University Press, 1972.

Merriman, Roger B. *Suleiman the Magnificent 1520–1566*. Cambridge, Mass.: Harvard University Press, 1944.

Mijatovich, Chedomil. *Constantine: The Last Emperor of the Greeks or the Conquest of Constantinople by the Turks*. London: Sampson Low, Marston, 1892.

Morgan, David. *Medieval Persia 1040–1797*. London: Longman, 1988.

Muir, William. *The Caliphate: Its Rise, Decline and Fall*. London: 1898. Reprinted Beirut: Khayats, 1963.

————. *Annals of the Early Caliphate*. London: 1883. Reprinted Amsterdam: Oriental Press, 1968.

Munro, Dana C. *The Kingdom of the Crusaders*. New York: D. Appleton-Century, 1935.

Naima, Mustafa. *Annals of the Turkish Empire from 1591 to 1659*. Translated by Charles Fraser. New York: Arno Press, 1973.

Nicholson, Robert L. *Joscelyn III and the Fall of the Crusader States*. Leiden, Neth.: E. J. Brill, 1973.

Nicol, Donald M. *The Last Centuries of Byzantium*. New York: St. Martin's Press, 1972.

Noldeke, Theodore. *Sketches from Eastern History*. 1892. Reprinted Beirut: Khayats, 1963.

Ockley, Simon. *The History of the Saracens*. London: Frederick Warne, n.d.

Oldenbourg, Zoe. *The Crusades*. New York: Pantheon Books, 1966.

Olson, Robert W. "The Sixteenth Century 'Price Revolution' and Its Effect on the Ottoman Empire and on Ottoman-Safavid Relations." *Acta Orientalia*. 37 (1976): 45–55.

Oman, Charles W. *The Byzantine Empire*. New York: G. P. Putnam's Sons, 1898.

Ostrogorsky, George. *History of the Byzantine State*. New Brunswick: Rutgers University Press, 1957.

Pachi, Z. P. "The Shifting of International Trade Routes in the 15th–17th Centuries." *Acta Historica* 14 (1968): 287–321

Pasdermadjian, H. *Histoire de L'Armenie: Despuis les Origines jusqu'au Traite de Lausanne*. Paris: Librarie Orientale H. Samulian, 1949.

Pernoud, Regine, ed. *The Crusades*. New York: Putnam, 1963.

Philippides, Marios, translator and annotator. *Byzantium, Europe, and the Early Ottoman Sultans 1373–1513: An Anonymous Greek Chronicle of the Seventeenth Century*. New Rochelle, N.Y.: Aristide D. Caratzas, 1990.

Pitcher, Donald E. *An Historical Geography of the Ottoman Empire: From Earliest Times to the End of the Sixteenth Century*. Leiden, Neth.: E J. Brill, 1972.

Prawer, Joshua. *The Crusaders' Kingdom: European Colonialism in the Middle Ages*. New York: Praeger Publishers, 1972.

Price, M. Philips. *A History of Turkey: From Empire to Republic*. London: George Allen & Unwin, 1961.

Al-Qalanisi. *The Damascus Chronicle of the Crusades*. Extracted and Translated by H.A.R. Gibb. London: Luzac, 1932.

Ragg, Laura M. *Crises in Venetian History*. London: Methuen, 1928.

Ramazani, Rouhollah K. *The Foreign Policy of Iran, 1500–1941*. Charlottesville: University of Virginia Press, 1938.

Rice, Tamara T. *The Seljuks in Asia Minor*. New York: Frederick A. Praeger, 1961.

Richard, Jean. *The Latin Kingdom of Jerusalem*. 2 vols. Amsterdam: North-Holland Publishing, 1979.

Rouillard, Clarence D. *The Turk in French History, Thought and Literature (1520–1660)*. Paris: Boivin, n.d. (c. 1938).

Runciman, Steven. *A History of the Crusades*. 3 vols. Cambridge: Cambridge University Press, 1962.

————. *The Fall of Constantinople 1453*. Cambridge: Cambridge University Press, 1965.

Sadeque, Syedah F. *Baybars I of Egypt*. Dacca: Oxford University Press, 1956.

Salibi, Kamal S. *Syria under Islam: Empire on Trial 634–1097*. Delmar, N.Y.: Caravan Books, 1977.

Salmon, W. H. *An Account of the Ottoman Conquest of Egypt*. A translation from the third part of the *Chronicle of Muhammad ibn Iyas*. London: Royal Asiatic Society, 1921.

Sanaullah, Mawlawifadil. *The Decline of the Saljuqid Empire*. Calcutta: University of Calcutta, 1938.

Saunders, J. J. *A History of Medieval Islam*, London: Routledge and Kegan Paul, 1965.

————. *The History of the Mongol Conquests*. London: Routledge and Kegan Paul, 1971.

Savory, Roger. *Iran under the Safavids*. Cambridge: Cambridge University Press, 1980.

The Secret History of the Mongols. Translated by Francis W. Cleaves. Cambridge, Mass.: Harvard University Press, 1982.

Shaban, M. A. *The Abbasid Revolution*. Cambridge: Cambridge University Press, 1970.

————. *Islamic History: A New Interpretation A.D. 600–750 (A.H. 132)*. Cambridge: Cambridge University Press, 1971.

————. *Islamic History: A New Interpretation A.D. 750–1055 (A.H. 132–448)*. Cambridge: Cambridge University Press, 1976.

Shaw, Stanford. *History of the Ottoman Empire and Modern Turkey*. Vol. 1. Cambridge: Cambridge University Press, 1976.

Shoufani, Elias. *Al-Riddah and the Muslim Conquest of Arabia*. Toronto, Can.: University of Toronto Press, 1973.

Spuler, Berthold. *The Mongols in History*. New York: Praeger Publishers, 1971.

————. *History of the Mongols: Based on Eastern and Western Accounts of the Thirteenth and Fourteenth Centuries*. Berkeley: University of California Press, 1972.

Stark, Freya. *Rome on the Euphrates: The Story of a Frontier*. New York: Harcourt, Brace and World, 1966.

Sykes, Percy. *A History of Persia*. 3rd ed. 2 vols. London: Macmillan, 1930.

————. *A History of Afghanistan*. 2 vols. London: Macmillan, 1940.

al-Tabari. *The Reign of al-Mu'tasim*. Translated and Annotated by Elma Martin. New Haven: American Oriental Society, 1951.

————. *Chronique de Abou-Djafar-Muhammad-Ben-Djarir-Ben-Yezid Tabari*. 4 vols. Paris: Editions Besson et Chanterle, 1958.

Theophanes. *The Chronicle of Theophanes*. Translation and notes by Harry Turtledove. Philadelphia: University of Pennsylvania Press, 1982.

Travels of Venetians in Persia. London: Hakluyt Society, 1873.

Tursun Beg. *The History of Mehmed the Conqueror*. Text published in facsimile with English translation by Halil Inalcik and Rhoads Murphey. Minneapolis: Bibliotheca Islamica, 1978.

Vasiliev, A. A. *History of the Byzantine Empire*. 2 vols. Madison: University of Wisconsin Press, 1958.

Vryonis, Speros. *The Decline of Medieval Hellenism in Asia Minor and the Process of Islamization from the Eleventh through the Fifteenth Century*. Berkeley: University of California Press, 1971.

Wellhausen, J. *The Arab Kingdom and Its Fall*. 1927. Reprinted Beirut: Khayats, 1963.

Wilson, Arnold T. *The Persian Gulf*. London: George Allen and Unwin, 1928.

Woods, John E. *The Aqquyunlu: Clan, Confederation, Empire*. Minneapolis: Bibliotheca Islamica, 1976.

Index

About the Author

MARTIN SICKER is a private consultant and lecturer who has served as a senior executive in the U.S. government and has taught political science at American University and George Washington University. Dr. Sicker has written extensively in the fields of political science and international affairs, with a special focus on the Middle East. He is the author of twelve previous books, including a companion volume in his multi-volume history of the Middle East, *The Pre-Islamic Middle East* (Praeger, 2000).

ISBN 0-275-96892-8

HARDCOVER BAR CODE